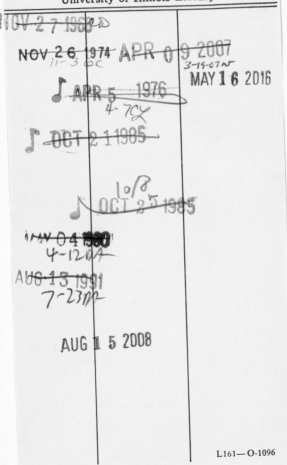

Paul Robeson: The American Othello

PAUL ROBESON

THE AMERICAN OTHELLO

EDWIN P. HOYT

THE WORLD PUBLISHING COMPANY
Cleveland and New York

Published by The World Publishing Company
2231 West 110th Street, Cleveland, Ohio 44102

Published simultaneously in Canada by
Nelson, Foster & Scott Ltd.

Library of Congress Catalog Card Number: 67–25579

FIRST EDITION

Copyright © 1967 by Edwin P. Hoyt

Ballad for Americans text by John Latouche, music by Earl
Robinson. Copyright 1940 Robbins Music Corporation,
New York, N.Y. Used by permission.

For Alice Grey
An old friend of mine

ACKNOWLEDGMENTS

The author is much indebted to a number of persons and institutions for assistance in compiling the research on which this book was based. Some of them are: Harvard University's Houghton Library and several reference librarians there for helping with the use of the Alexander Woollcott correspondence with Essie Robeson; Yale University's Sterling Library and the Johnson Collection for use of several important books about Paul Robeson, and much other material in magazine and newspaper files; the New York Public Library at Fifth Avenue and 42nd Street, the Schomburg Collection of Negro Americana at the Harlem branch library; the files of the New York *Times* and the files of the *Amsterdam News*.

The author's interest in this book began a long time ago, and conversations that elicited research material were held with a large number of persons over a great number of years. Howard Fast was helpful, quite out of context, during a period when the author was doing research for an article on the American Communist party for the late *Collier's* magazine.

The author is particularly indebted to James Hicks, editor of the *Amsterdam News*, to attorney Hope Stevens, one of the leading citizens of Harlem and a long-time friend to Paul Robeson, to Dame Rebecca West for steering him clear of some pitfalls that appeared early in the writing, to Robert Markel for interesting information about the Robesons at one period, to Louis Michaud, Harlem's bookseller and philosopher, and to many other citizens of Harlem, New York City, and other cities and towns in the United States. Authorities at the Hamilton College library were helpful, and most helpful of all in some respects were the librarians and administrators of Rutgers University, who put much material from their files at the author's disposal and eased several taxing administrative problems about research.

The author is also indebted to Olga G. Hoyt for research and editing, including translations from the German relative to Paul Robeson's life, and to Mrs. Milo Chase for typing the manuscript.

Bomoseen, Vermont
November 1, 1966

CONTENTS

Chapter 1

NOT WISELY,
BUT TOO WELL

One night, early in the autumn of 1943, stage producer and actress Margaret Webster brought to the Shubert Theater in New York a unique production of William Shakespeare's *Othello*—unique because it starred a Negro in the role of the blackamoor. The Negro was Paul Robeson, singer, actor, lawyer, and defender of his race. He had once been an all-American athlete. He had ambled through life, picking up honors and troubles as he went; more than any other Negro in the world he had been honored by a white society in Europe and even in America where the Negro was still cast in a subservient role. He was a brilliant man—some called him genius—and he had aptitudes for learning, particularly in languages, that were shared by few citizens of his nation. He enjoyed the sympathies of thousands of friends and well-wishers who were only acquainted with him; and also the sympathies of millions of common folk of every color and every view. A handful of skeptics claimed on this October day that The Theater Guild's production of *Othello* would fail, not because Paul Robeson was playing the leading role, but because *Othello* had never succeeded in twentieth-century America. The skeptics had already been proved wrong in a lesser attempt: *Othello*, with Robeson playing the title role, had been performed at the Cambridge summer theater in Brattle Hall in the summer of 1942 and had been immensely successful. The play had been tried in Princeton, New Jersey, that same summer, again before an audience that applauded and cheered as the final curtain fell, and could only be satisfied with a half-dozen curtain calls. This production of *Othello* had been cut and polished in the following months. In the summer of 1943, Miss Webster's production had played in New Haven and then in Boston. *Othello* had been a success wherever it had gone.

Just before the play came to New York City's Shubert Alley, Paul Robeson had been given the keys to Boston city, so highly was he regarded as an artist and as a human being. When the play opened that October night in New York, and when Paul Robeson's heavy-timbred, mellifluous voice began to speak the lines of the Moor, the audience hushed and hundreds knew they were witnessing a historic performance. Never before in America had a Negro played the role of *Othello* in a cast of whites, and as the audience now saw the Moor, he was a black man, but primarily a man. As they saw Paul Robeson in the role for the first time many of them realized how deep and ingenious had been William Shakespeare's writing, for the Moor, like Robeson, was different from the others—the whites —and the play, with all its overtones of racial conflict in sixteenth-century Venice, took on a new life four centuries later.

Margaret Webster's *Othello* was a stunning success. It ran for 296 performances in New York City, which had sometimes been a graveyard for Shakespeare. The reviewers were almost unanimous in praise of Robeson's *Othello*. Oh, there were cavils—about the cutting of some lines from the "substantive" text of the play, for example. There was complaint that Robeson's delivery of his lines was too deliberate in the early scenes, that he showed anger through gesture more than words in later scenes (as the Moor's jealousy was aroused). Yet Howard Barnes in the New York *Herald Tribune** gave an opinion as to the source of success of this revival of a play which had so often failed. It was, Barnes said,

* October 31, 1943 issue.

. . . Robeson's color as much as his fine acting skill which brings a rather tricky melodrama into sharp and memorable focus. Lines which meant nothing when a white man played the part of the Moorish soldier of fortune who became a great Venetian general, married the fair-skinned Desdemona and then let himself be led into a homicidal frenzy, loom impressively in the Shubert offering, giving a motivation for murder which has been obscure to most of us in the past.

So it was. Audience after audience sensed that in this four-hundred-year old melodrama lay the wellsprings of the emotional and racial conflict which was even in 1943 and 1944 burgeoning in America. This understanding was sensed, it was not spoken openly, it may not even have been fully realized by the audiences that flocked to the Shubert. But as those audiences filed out of the theater night after night their members were bemused and thoughtful, knowing that they had witnessed an important event in the world of the theater. Some were reasonably sure that they had seen a glimpse into the soul of man.

Paul Robeson achieved the pinnacle of popularity in the United States in the early 1940s. Born an American, bred an American, educated an American, he had found that it was easier for a Negro to live abroad. He had gone to England to live late in the 1920s. Then he was still virtually unknown in his native land. His name was familiar to the *cognoscenti* of the theater and the literary world; he had been written about in the *New Republic, Theater Arts,* smaller magazines and even the *Literary Digest* but he was not a public property in the larger sense. In the 1920s and 1930s Paul rose to fame in England and on the Continent, following a first triumph in *Show Boat* at the Drury Lane Theater in London. In that musical Robeson came on stage, sang "Ol' Man River," and London was his. His first *Othello,* amateur and inept by the standards of the later one, was played at the Savoy Theater in 1930. There were more plays, and a motion picture in 1933. Then came more successful motion pictures produced in England; these were interspersed with and followed by concert tours of the British Isles and the Continent. Occasionally Paul returned to the United States for concerts and to make recordings, but his home was in Europe. For a time he considered taking British citizenship. But after war broke out in Europe in 1939 Paul Robeson returned home. In America he found himself a celebrity. *Time* wrote him up. So did *Collier's*, and *The American*. He continued to be popular with the *cognoscenti* and his name appeared often in the special journals of the stage and the world of the intelligentsia, but he had also become the creature of the public. He was immensely popular with the whites because he represented "the highest type" of Negro. His success represented what white Americans wanted to believe was the opportunity offered to Negroes in America. But this belief of the whites was ill-founded. Paul had made success in Europe on his own, but few Americans stopped to think about that or examine the reasons for it.

Only a handful of determined bigots in 1940 would talk against Robeson. Most talk was the other way—if all Negroes were like Robeson, went the cliché of the moment, there would be no race trouble in the United States. Paul had, as *The American* said, "established himself firmly as America's most distinguished living Negro."

In 1939 and 1940 it was becoming important to white Americans to feel that they still maintained the atmosphere of freedom they claimed and believed to exist in the United States. The treatment of the Negro in America, at least in the twentieth century, and at least by "right-minded" whites, was a result of ignorance, fear, and misinformation. Southern states had established "separate but equal" educational facilities. Americans elsewhere gulled themselves into believing the facilities *were* separate but equal; they would not dream of investigating, perhaps because they feared the truth. The average white American detested, as did Shakespeare's Brabantio, the marital intermingling of whites and blacks. Above all else this was the underlying cause of most white Americans' fear of Negro equality. The whites knew that black Americans wanted full equality, and that full equality must in the final analysis do away with racial lines. The more intelligent among these white

Americans could see how equality worked in the American territories of Hawaii and Alaska; most of them could accept the intermingling of white Americans, Chinese, Japanese, Hawaiians, and Eskimos, but on the mainland below the 54th parallel they drew a further color line against the intermarriage of blacks and whites. As to misinformation, whites convinced themselves that they were slowly leading the American Negro into enlightenment, and that at some vague undefined time (certainly not in the immediate future) the blacks would be ready for "full citizenship." What full citizenship meant was anyone's guess; the guess conformed to the prejudices of the guesser.

This was America in a racial sense in 1939, and America was most displeased with the drubbing it was taking from other countries because of American racism, not just the racial policies of the deep South, but the discrimination practiced in the most enlightened communities in the land. Harlem, the Negro ghetto of New York, was the most prominent example. By 1939, Americans were beginning to divest themselves of the fantasy that the Negroes lived in Harlem because they liked it. The fantasy was torn apart, chiefly by the Communists of the world, for the Communists preached absolute racial equality.

(No one has ever tried to reduce the abnormal fear of Americans of Communism to its essentials and apportion these elements. The fear of absolute racial equality by white Americans has never been isolated in this hatred of the Communist system, but it exists and it is a real part of the over-all fear. One scarcely needs to point out that the Soviets have never practiced absolute equality; their resurgent anti-Semitism speaks for itself. One need not go into the demerits of Communism to discuss its effects on white Americans in the 1940s; the point is that the Communists above all others were embarrassing Americans by calling attention to the plight of American Negroes.)

What Americans needed—late in the 1930s—was a Negro hero to whom they could point with pride. Joe Louis, the boxer, was a Negro hero, but Joe was the ill-educated, slow-speaking, slow-thinking product of an early boyhood spent in the deep South. Joe Louis would not do, no matter how great his physical prowess. Needed was an American Negro of intellectual and social stature, a male who could boast the charm and sophistication of Josephine Baker, who chose to live in Paris. No longer could Americans satisfy themselves with a Bojangles Bill Robinson, mayor of Harlem, big, good-natured Negro of the ill-educated, uncultured school. The figure must be heroic and dignified.

Paul Robeson returned to the United States at the psychological moment to fulfill this need. He had moved so long and so profitably among whites that he had almost completely overcome the sense of inferiority that is drummed into every Negro American from that day in childhood when he first sees a white face and wonders why there is a difference.

Paul had been all over the world. He was much taken by Russia, and the Soviet warmth of feeling toward Negroes. His natural friendliness to such people as those he met in the Soviet Union—who lionized him—was strengthened by the political philosophy of his wife, Eslanda Goode Robeson. She was an intellectual Communist by 1939, whatever she might profess in terms of affiliations. She believed deeply in the Soviet Union and its works, and her attitudes had then and would later have influence to a great degree on Paul Robeson's actions.

At the moment, in 1939, Paul Robeson was not seriously concerned with racial affairs. Rebecca West put it this way many years later: "I don't think he was deeply moved by the sufferings of his race in any specific way—I don't mean that in a derogatory sense, he was a generous soul who would have hated any injustice—but he had a curious languor and that forbade him using his imagination too vigorously."

Paul had shown his basic concern for humanity in many ways. He had gone to Spain to sing for the Spanish Loyalists, and he had been deeply moved by the young men of the International Brigades who were giving their lives freely for principles they felt to be important. One need not go into the politics of the matter; the Spanish Loyalists, rank and file, fought for what they thought was freedom, without serious consideration of the political chess game in which they were pawns.

Paul Robeson came back to America to live in 1939, genial and unafraid. "I feel closer to my country than ever," he told interviewer Julia Dorn shortly after his arrival. "There is no longer a feeling of lonesome isolation. Instead—peace. I return without fearing prejudice that once bothered me. It does not hurt or anger me now, for I know that people practice cruel bigotry in their ignorance, not maliciously."

So it was that the country was prepared to accept a successful, intelligent Paul Robeson and he was prepared to accept his country in 1939. He came back to America, and his success was immediate and tremendous. He did not move into the ghetto of Harlem, but into an apartment on New York's east side. He then moved to a manor house in Connecticut where he lived as a country squire when he was not appearing in a play or traveling across the nation on concert tour.

Here was his position in the 1940s, and it was growing year by year.

1940: *Collier's* called him "the favorite male Negro singer" of the concert goers, and "America's #1 Negro entertainer." The play in which he appeared that year, *John Henry,* ran only five performances, but this failure did not hurt Robeson a bit. He was making dozens of records for the most important recording companies. He received a Doctorate of Humane Letters from Hamilton College.

There was talk in America that Paul held left-wing political views, but in 1940 this talk did not disturb many Americans nor did it seem to be too important.

Paul refused to appear in a benefit sponsored by Herbert Hoover for Finnish civilian relief, after the Russians attacked Finland, and his reasoning was this: "I feel that England's influence is pronounced in the Scandinavian countries and that this influence is not democratic but reactionary. It possibly may have inspired the Finnish hostilities, which simply means that Russia is fighting a defensive war."

This statement was one of the first indications of radicalism that Paul was to show the American public. To understand it one must realize that Paul and Essie Robeson had been so impressed with the position of the Negro in the Soviet Union that they had sent their son Paul, Jr., to be educated there rather than in the West. Paul said that he had done this so that his son would not grow up with the feeling of being "different." It was hard for Paul Robeson to believe that the self-interest of the U.S.S.R. would call for an aggressive war against a small country. Further, Paul was not the only person, by far, to believe that the British government of the late 1930s and even during the "phony war" was far to the right. Paul's friend, Rebecca West, no soft heart or fellow traveler, wrote Alexander Woollcott just after the Munich Pact which sacrificed Czechoslovakia to the Nazis that she had an awful feeling that her government had just sold the British people down the river.

No matter how it might be read a quarter century later, Paul's outspoken attitude in the Finnish matter was a minor bit of the Robeson story in 1940. Many humanitarians took similar positions, although the Finnish war, coming atop the Soviet-Nazi pact, caused serious splits among liberals. The fact of importance, however, was that these were matters for deep debate among people of good will.

In 1941, Paul spoke and sang at a mass meeting designed to protest the imprisonment of Communist leader Earl Browder. Again, he was among many Americans in 1941, after the Nazi attack on Russia, who turned toward Soviet Russia and were neither particularly radical nor embittered in their political beliefs.

In 1942, Paul became more vociferous about the matter of Negro freedom than ever before. In Kansas City one day he discovered that he was singing before a segregated audience. Long before, Paul had vowed that he would never sing before a segregated audience, and in this case, surprised as he had been to find segregation in Kansas City, he might have walked out. He did not. He stopped his concert, told the audience that he opposed segregation, and that he was singing under protest against such action, and then continued. Certainly Paul's protest was well-mannered and decent. Some bigots walked out of the concert after his protest, but he gained stature with the performance.

That year, 1942, Earl Schenck Miers, a Rutgers man and an admirer of Paul's, published a novel, *Big Ben,* which was based on the life of Paul Robeson. Miers had this to say:

> It is part of Robeson's tragedy as a Negro that there are incidents in those [college] years at Rutgers which are not recalled for the simple reason that they were never understood. But Robeson knew why he could not sing with the glee club. He knew that his presence on the campus would be resented by some, and there was at least one moment when violence sprang from that resentment; he knew, too, that there was a line over which he could not pass and he never tried to. He studied to be a lawyer but for his own good reasons that ambition was abandoned. Yet, despite those moments that could make any man feel low-down and mean, Robeson looks back upon his four years at Rutgers and reckons them among the happiest of his life. He values highly the friendships which were formed there, he believes great wisdom came from the classes he attended . . .*

Like so many other white Americans, Miers thought he understood the motivations of this big, successful Negro. He was wrong.

In 1943, Paul Robeson achieved a peak of fame and affection in America. His good humor was apparent to all, he was forever astounded by the degree of affection that was lavished on him by Americans, and they responded to him with enormous enthusiasm.

In 1944, Paul devoted his efforts—or many of them—to the common cause of war. He broadcast to help the war bond drives. He sang for various agencies of relief. He was honored by various organizations, unions and others, including the American Academy of Arts and Letters. He was active in Negro affairs, particularly those of the Council on African Affairs, in which he had become the leading figure. He was refused permission for use of a theater in Baltimore for a recital, but this was more or less to be expected in America

---

* *The Nation,* May 27, 1950.

below the Mason-Dixon line. He was earning well over
$100,000 a year. In every sense of the word Paul Robeson was
successful. There was some rumor this year about Robeson's
relationships with Uta Hagen, the white actress who played
Desdemona to his Othello. Miss Hagen's marriage to Jose
Ferrer, who played Iago, came to disaster that year. Some of
the magazines wrote luridly of a confrontation in a Detroit
hotel room, but Paul's general popularity was unaffected.

Paul Robeson was accepted in 1944 in white America as a
great American figure.

In 1949, four years after the end of the Second World War,
when Paul Robeson went to sing at a concert arranged for him
at Peekskill, New York, the affair ended in violence, not once,
but twice. Many people were injured in actual rioting. A year
later—1950—Paul Robeson's passport was voided by the
United States Department of State after he refused to yield it
to State Department officers. Obviously, in those years, something had happened.

Why did the white community of Peekskill disapprove so
stringently of Paul Robeson in 1949? Four years earlier thousands of Peekskill residents had come out gladly to applaud
him and cheer him. Why had hatred replaced the honest
affection of four years before?

In those four years, Robeson, led and now persuaded by his
wife, had become a militant fighter for Negro rights. Unlike
Thurgood Marshall, Ralph Bunche, or Jackie Robinson, Paul
chose to fight along the grounds of politics. A dozen years of
his life had been spent in Europe, and he had made many
voyages to the Soviet Union. His belief in 1945 was that the
United Nations who had fought the war would now join
together in peace to bring freedom to all the colonial peoples
of the world, including the American Negroes who struggled
for full rights within their own nation.

Almost before the war ended in 1945, it became apparent
that the policies of the United States and the Soviet Union
would be disparate in the years to come, that the war alliance
was no more than that, and that the basic distrust between
Communist and capitalist worlds, submerged in the face of the

common danger, was now reappearing on both sides. The Paul Robeson who had left the United States in 1928—by his own statement to "escape" the troubles of being a Negro in America —had come back in 1939 to find an America that had changed somewhat, but he had changed more.

Beginning in 1945, after a tour of Europe, Paul had decided to devote himself to the Negro cause. A year later he had gone as a member of a delegation to visit President Truman and protest about lynchings in the South, and had come away shaken, believing no longer in Truman's stand on civil rights. In January 1947, he announced that he would abandon the stage for two years in order to fight against racial bias in America. Three months later he announced that he would abandon the formal concert field to sing in groups of workers and liberals who fought for civil rights for all Americans. During the two years just before Peekskill, Paul Robeson had, by extension, become an ardent advocate of Sovietism. He found the spokesmen of the U.S.S.R. stating views that appealed to him as a spokesman and fighter for Negro freedom, and with his strong ties to the Russians he found it easy to criticize his own country's policies and unnecessary to criticize the policies of the nation that most Americans looked upon as inimical to the United States. He became a thorough Soviet apologist. Once, in 1949, on tour in Europe, he refused to sing in a Copenhagen concert when he learned that the series was sponsored by *Politiken*, the most prominent newspaper in the city, because that newspaper supported the Atlantic Alliance, which had been formed to protect western Europe against Soviet aggression. Paul's position was that the Soviet Union would never commit aggression, and that the Atlantic Alliance was not defensive but aggressive. His whole life had become political in nature; as an artist, he was trapped by politics.

So here was part of the answer. In 1949, Paul was entrapped by his sponsorship of Soviet policy. In April of that year he was so unwise as to say that American Negroes would never fight for their own country against the Soviet Union. Paul Robeson then ran afoul of his own race, or at least of a certain faction of leaders of that race: the National Association for the

Advancement of Colored People, Congressman Adam Clayton
Powell of Harlem, A. Philip Randolph of the Sleeping Car
Porters Union, Jackie Robinson and other athletes. One could
not say that Paul brought about a deep split in the Negro
community, but he had made the one statement that was
guaranteed to alienate him from white society. He had said
flatly that white America and black America were two different nations. White America was not then prepared for the
statement; it was greeted with general disbelief and suspicion
of the motivations of Paul Robeson.

The story of the first and second Peekskill riots is a sad,
brutal story in the annals of America. Thousands of people
coming back from a concert were forced to run a gauntlet of
hatred that lasted for miles and miles—little groups of rock
throwers lined the roads and committed mayhem at will. Here
is one description of part of a wild ride out of that concert
grounds that night. It comes from Howard Fast, novelist, one-
time Communist, and ardent advocate of civil liberties, who
was on hand at Peekskill:

> One reacts slowly, and I only comprehended what was
> happening when the first rocks crashed against the car. The
> first hit the door frame, between the front and rear windows;
> the second hit the frame of the windshield; two more heavy
> rocks crashed into the body of the car. The cops held their
> bellies and howled with mirth.
>
> Fortunately I had a block or two of empty road in front
> of me, and I was able to step on the gas and shoot ahead.
> Forty or fifty yards, and there was the second group, and this
> time, full of rage, I turned my car into them and roared over
> the shoulder at forty miles an hour. The group scattered and
> the cops tumbled away for shelter. The third group, however,
> caught us like sitting ducks, and once again the flood of
> boulders crashed against the car . . . And so it went, from
> group to group, through that nightmare gauntlet. . . .
>
> Two miles or so from the concert grounds, a car had pulled
> into a gas station. This car, like so many others, left a trail of
> blood behind it. Five adults and one child emerged, and they
> were all covered with blood from head to foot. The child was
> weeping softly and they stood like people dazed, and a few

feet away a group of young hoodlums hurled rocks at the passing cars. I pulled over to the gas station to stop and see if we could help the wounded people, but a cop stationed there ran at us screaming oaths and beating the car with his club. When he started to draw his revolver, we drove on. Another car stopped and R———— [not Robeson], turning around, saw the policeman beat the windshield of the car in with his club while he drew his revolver with his other hand. It was behavior which bordered on the paranoid, and though I have many times in the past seen police go into their frenzied dance of hatred against workers or progressives, I never saw anything to equal this display. . . .*

That last statement from Howard Fast is indicative of the fury to which Paul Robeson had driven his white countrymen only four years after he was given standing ovations whenever he sang. What happened to this kindly, generous man who had moved through most of his life in what Rebecca West termed "a curious dream" is a tragedy every bit as poignant and deeply moving as the tragedy of the Moor of Venice. How, why, and where did the tragedy develop? To understand, one must go back to the very beginnings of Paul Robeson, black boy born into the midst of a white America.

* Howard Fast, *Peekskill, U.S.A.* (New York: Civil Rights Congress, 1951), pp. 87–88.

Chapter 2

BLACK SLAVE, BLACK PREACHER

Paul Robeson, American, was born of a father who had been a slave, a piece of property on a plantation near Raleigh, North Carolina. The name Robeson does not belong to the family of slaves; it is a borrowed name, taken from the family of masters. The Negro slaves who were forcibly brought to America came into an alien culture with names that the slave-owners could not pronounce, and so they were given Christian names.

Paul's paternal grandfather was named Benjamin. That was all there was to it, Benjamin, slave of the Robesons. In time Benjamin was bred to Sabra, another slave of the Robesons, and from this union came William Drew.

William Drew escaped the hateful life of slavery by fleeing north in 1860. A year later began the War between the States, a conflict that was to determine his fate. William, a boy of sixteen, joined the Union army to fight against his former masters. The war ended, he learned to read and write and sought an education. He eventually went to a Negro college called Lincoln University, but he was a long time in getting there. The war ended in 1865; it was a decade before William Drew Robeson went to college. The fact that it was a Negro college and not just an ordinary college is significant in the history of Paul Robeson's father, and thus of Paul Robeson.

Why should it have been a Negro college?

Simply because Negroes, while no longer considered private property, were still not free in America. They had some freedom but they were not free. There is a great deal of difference between the two concepts. In effect the Civil War and the Emancipation Proclamation and the final results of Reconstruction took the Negro up from slavery to a second-class citizenship which was specially created for him. There the Negro stood, virtually without change between 1876 and the middle of the twentieth century; anyone who would understand the tragedy of Paul Robeson must understand that fact. The Negro actually slipped in position between 1865 and 1876; he was granted freedom, first by Emancipation and then by Constitutional guarantee, and then that freedom was taken away from him in the tacit, unholy compromise made by Republicans to southern Democrats in order to retain the Presidency in the election of 1876. Rutherford B. Hayes became President of the United States, but the white Democrats resumed the old, upper-class-white control of the southern states, and almost immediately thereafter the Negro became a valueless and then spurious token in the currency of American politics.

While a student at Lincoln University, William Drew Robeson met Maria Louisa Bustill, a Philadelphia schoolteacher who was then in her twenties. Robeson had no genealogy, except for vague beliefs that his black forebears had been Bantus, and the even vaguer belief that he was descended from royal Bantu stock. Maria Louisa Bustill claimed an ancestry that her family said was traceable back to 1608; it was given in individual stories as of 1732 with the birth of Cyrus Bustill. Maria Louisa was a brown-skinned, straight-haired woman. Was she a Negro? Well, she was called a Negro in nineteenth-century America because of the color of her skin, but the family shamelessly talked of intermarriage between Delaware Indians, English Quakers, and free Negroes of the Quaker colony of Pennsylvania to produce this line.

Note here again the basic difference in approach to racism between the Bustills of Philadelphia and white Americans. A white American might in the middle of the twentieth century

claim an American Indian streak of blood and be regarded
only as a mild oddity. He could even be admitted to private
clubs, for in the vanishing of the American Indian the question
of intermarriage had become moot. But let a white American
admit to a touch of the tarbrush and his life changed. It need
not even be the tarbrush, but a touch of any but Indian red
color. This was a truth with which every colored person lived
every day in America.

The Bustills, brown as they were, claimed a part in the
history of America. A Bustill was a founder of the Free African
Society in 1787. Bustills were teachers and seamen and one of
them, Joseph Casey Bustill, claimed to have given aid to a
thousand Negroes along the Underground Railroad. Another
Bustill was a painter, and it was said that Abraham Lincoln
once posed for him. Robert Bustill was another painter, and he
studied at the Academy of Fine Arts in Philadelphia and at the
National Gallery of Fine Arts in London.

Maria Louisa Bustill married William Drew Robeson in the
summer of 1878, and soon they went to Princeton, New Jersey,
where the Reverend Mr. Robeson was in charge of the Witherspoon Presbyterian Church, a Negro institution. Of the children born to them in the next twenty years, five survived. They
were William Drew, Jr., who became a doctor and went to live
in Washington, D.C.; Reeve, who eventually settled in Detroit;
Benjamin, who became a pastor; Marion, the sole girl, who
became a teacher; and Paul, the last of the children, born on
April 9, 1898.

Maria Louisa Robeson taught her family with the gentling
influences of a Quaker background, although she was now a
professing Presbyterian, and often wrote her husband's ser-
mons. She was a warm person as well as a gentle one, and in
the early years of Paul's childhood she brought a security to
the family which was unusual among American Negro house-
holds. As a minister, the Reverend Mr. Robeson held the
highest position that a Negro could then achieve in American
society, and this post brought a certain respect to him and a
certain tolerance by whites.

The family suffered a serious blow in January 1904, when Maria Louisa Robeson was burned to death in a household accident. She had been troubled with cataracts and increasing blindness, and this affliction led to an accident with the parlor stove. Her clothes caught fire. Brother Ben tried to help his mother, and neighbors beat out the flames in her voluminous skirts. A doctor came to the household, but too little was known then about severe burns, and Maria died within a few hours.

Were this not enough trouble for the Robeson family, Rev. Robeson then lost his post at the Witherspoon Presbyterian Church. The family had no income. "Poverty was my beginning," Paul Robeson said. He slept in a bed with three other children and for his dinners ate the discarded greens of vegetables and cornbread. The Reverend Mr. Robeson moved to Westfield, New Jersey, where he found a job in a tiny corner grocery store. The older children had gone, but until the younger ones could join their father they were farmed out to live with relatives.

It must have been a relief, in a way, to be out of Princeton, for Princeton was a southern town in many ways. Some of its most substantial citizens had emigrated there from the deep South, bringing their plantation past with them, and many southern white students were attracted to Princeton University. After the factional dispute that had brought his unwilling ouster as Presbyterian pastor, Rev. Robeson had somehow found a horse and wagon, and for a few months earned a precarious living as an ashman and coachman, catering to the college students.

In this period came an illustration of another basic difference between a Negro American family and a family of whites, quite aside from poverty. The oldest Robeson children had escaped the disaster of their father's ouster from the church. William, Jr., was in college and the career he planned was launched. The second son, Reeve, fell into trouble with the law. He was a roughneck, and he was extremely sensitive in racial matters. "Many was the time," Paul wrote later, "that

Reed [as the family called him], resenting some remark by a southern gentleman-student, would leap down from his coachman's seat, drag out the offender and punish him with his fists. He always carried for protection a bag of small, jagged rocks— a weapon he used with reckless abandon whenever the occasion called for action."

Rev. Robeson lamented his second son's wayward behavior but no lecture had much effect. Paul admired his elder brother in spite of the frequent brushes with law and order, because the law and order was *white man's law and order*, and the Negro, excluded from the white man's society, had but little respect for white man's law. This truism must be understood by white readers in any judgment of Paul Robeson or any other Negro American. If in later years Paul's conduct was to ignore the moral codes of the whites in personal and political affairs, it must be remembered that from his earliest boyhood he lived in the Negro underworld of America. The authorities could not countenance a hackman who carried a blackjack and beat up the Princeton college students, and eventually Reeve was sorrowfully sent away from Princeton by his father to avoid certain white punishment for his breaches of the law. But Paul, living by the underworld code of the Negro, never thought the less of his brother for lawlessness; he admired him the more instead.

"Restless, rebellious, scoffing at conventions, defiant of the white man's law—I've known many Negroes like Reed," Paul wrote. " 'Don't ever take low,' was the lesson Reed taught me. 'Stand up to them and hit back harder than they hit you!' When the many have learned that lesson, everything will be different and then the fiery ones like Reed will be able to live out their lives in peace and no one will have cause to frown on them."

Those words were written late in the 1950s by a Paul Robeson who was thoroughly alienated from the American society of whites. They are an indication of the elder Robeson, not the younger. By all accounts Paul was a singularly protected and happy child, particularly among Negroes. After his father left Princeton, Paul was cared for by relatives and friends, passing

from hand to hand. Yet he felt no fear or alienation in this
moving around, for external security among the Negroes of
Princeton was at best a precarious commodity. The peculiar
structure of a Negro society tacked haphazardly onto a white
one is suggested by the position occupied in Princeton and
Westfield by Rev. Robeson. Paul and his brothers and sisters in
Princeton attended Negro schools, for Princeton's schools were
segregated. The minister became ashman and grocery clerk,
yet he sent son William to Lincoln University; son Benjamin to
what was then Biddle University in North Carolina, and
daughter Marion to Scotia Seminary, a school for Negro girls
in North Carolina.

Even after his father left Princeton, Paul remained on until
his ninth year. He recalled Princeton with fond memory: days
of playing sandlot baseball and sandlot football. The society in
which he moved there was almost purely Negro, although he
did remember a few white faces, mostly children of his own
age who lived in the neighborhood. In 1907, Paul went to
Westfield to join his father, and they moved into an attic above
the grocery store where Rev. Robeson clerked. Their kitchen
and bathroom was a dark lean-to that stood at the rear of the
store. Soon, Rev. Robeson decided to return to his calling, but
not as a Presbyterian. The struggle in Princeton had soured
him on Presbyterianism, and he turned now to the African
Methodist Episcopal Zion Church. He organized a tiny coterie
of supporters and they began, with their own labor, to lay the
foundation for the Downing Street A. M. E. Zion Church. Paul
went to school, this time to an unsegregated school, because
there were not enough Negroes in Westfield for the whites to
declare that there was a problem. Not so in Somerville, the
next town to which the Robesons moved. Here again Paul
entered a segregated elementary school. He was taught there
by a Negro educator named James L. Jamison for one year.

The Reverend Mr. Robeson had come to Somerville to spend
the remainder of his life as pastor of the St. Thomas A. M. E.
Zion Church, so after the one year in the segregated grammar
school, Paul went on to Somerville High School, which was not
segregated. He had graduated from grammar school at the

head of his class; the brightness of mind and the excellent coordination of body that made him a fine athlete opened many doors for Paul in Somerville. Life in the high school for a Negro boy was most satisfactory, because there were only two Negro children in the school.

Still, "I was always remembering that I must not do this or that, or I must not hit a boy back because I was colored," Paul said later. He made many white friends, among them Douglas Brown, who later became a dean at Princeton University. He joined the glee club and learned that he had musical ability. He joined the drama club and practiced elocution. His music teacher encouraged him to use his voice and his English teacher, who also coached the drama club, put him into the title role of *Othello* for the first time.

Paul's hardest teacher was his father, who insisted that instead of concentrating on the manual arts, as many Negroes were wont to do because opportunity for them was so limited, Paul must become a classical scholar. So Paul took courses in Latin, Greek, philosophy, history, and literature. He took chemistry and physics, too. No matter the subject, his father insisted that Paul measure himself against the highest standards. If Paul's grades were less than the highest possible, explanations were called for.

The white teachers appeared to have taken special interest in this bright Negro youngster. They trained his mind and opened it to new experiences. They encouraged him to come to social affairs.

At these latter, Paul was uncomfortable—one of two blacks amid a sea of white faces. In high school Paul perfected the protective coloration pattern of the intelligent Negro in white America. Later he said, "Even while demonstrating that he is really an equal (and, strangely, the proof must be *superior* performance!) the Negro must never appear to be challenging white superiority." Above all, Paul said the Negro must never give the whites any cause to fear him, for then the whites would set out to oppress him.

Paul indicated that his best teacher in this respect was the high-school principal who, Paul said, did not like him, and who opposed every honor that others wished to give the young Negro. Paul played on the football team, but against the principal's wishes. He became soloist of the glee club, but again the principal objected.

In high school Paul learned that he, like his brother Reeve, possessed a violent temper. One day he told his father that he would beat up the high-school principal if the man laid a hand on him, although the elder Robeson had given the teachers permission to discipline the sometimes refractory boy. Paul also learned to control and sublimate this temper most of the time, by withdrawing inside a protective shell. This tendency, which stayed with Paul Robeson for many, many years, gave him a dreamy, absent quality on which many of his friends remarked. This quality also left the white world of America unprepared for the severity of temper and strength of feeling that Paul Robeson was to display, even to the point of intemperate and foolish remarks, in the later years of his life.

In the biographies of Robeson that have been written by those who would apologize for him, there are several different versions of his early life. When he lived in England he seldom spoke of the years before college, and when he did speak he left the impression that he had moved through the white community with the same effortlessness that he adopted in Europe. Only in his own book, *Here I Stand*, published in 1958, did Paul indicate the elements of struggle he faced. Probably by then the tales were exaggerated, for by 1958 Paul Robeson had become a political personality. All memories, all his personality, had now to be recast to fit the mold of militant Negro. Had he been so militant, even with an artist's power of dissimulation, some of this feeling would have been evident to his teachers and fellow pupils, and he would not have been the popular fellow that he was in high-school years. The witnesses to Paul's childhood and adolescence are relatively few, and their views have become confused and blurred by the later political years, but the indication is that Paul suffered relatively little as a Negro because he was brilliant, active, and athletic. His very excellence protected him from the blows that might have fallen on him had he been less so. Certainly he must have received the scars of his Negrohood, but these could only have been relatively shallow ones.

When Paul was fourteen years old he began to learn something of the outside world. That summer Paul's brother Ben took him along to Narragansett, Rhode Island, where Ben had a job as a waiter at a restaurant on the pier. Paul became a kitchen pot boy, peeling potatoes, scrubbing pots, mopping the floors, and doing all that the other kitchen help told him to do from early morning until late evening. The work was hard, but the experience was satisfying enough to send him back in future summers.

In Paul's senior year in high school, it was decided that he would go on to college. He expected to go to Lincoln University, but during his final year at high school he learned of a competitive examination to be given for a four-year scholarship to Rutgers College. Rutgers was then a private institution. A few Negroes had attended in years past, but at that time there were none among the student body. Still, the examination was open to all, white or black, and Paul took it, against considerable odds. Other students had been planning for this examination for two years. An elimination had been held the year before, covering the first three years of high school work, but Paul had not taken the examination. If he wished to compete at this date he must complete an examination on four years of work while the others taking it needed to cover only their senior year. He decided to face these odds, and he won the competition.

His graduation from high school is another milestone in which there are serious discrepancies among the biographers of Paul Robeson. Eslanda Goode Robeson, who wrote the first biography of her husband in the 1920s, said he was the most popular child in town, "mainstay of the football team, center on the basketball team, catcher for the baseball team." She said he fraternized with the "finest type" of child at the school, played with the "sons and daughters of the most cultured white people" in the town and was loved by all. In 1946, Negro writer Shirley Graham became Paul's second biographer, and she, in a study that included much fabricated dialogue, indicated also that Paul was the darling of his class, a leader in every field and beloved by all. Dr. Ackerman, the principal of the high school, she said was particularly proud of him and friendly to him. Twelve years later, in his autobiographical *Here I Stand*, Paul Robeson painted Dr. Ackerman as his enemy, an implacable white supremacist who hunted Paul down and persecuted him at every turn. Gone were the references to Paul's myriad white friends of childhood. Politics changes memory, there can be no doubt about it.

Paul graduated from high school in the spring of 1915, honor student and star debater of the school. He entered a statewide oratorical contest that summer, but lost out to another Negro boy and a white girl who placed first and second respectively. The speech (chosen for him by someone in his family) was an oration by the famous Abolitionist Wendell Phillips on Toussaint L'Ouverture, the Haitian patriot who fought against the French. The speech aroused the specters of black power; as originally delivered by Phillips it was an attempt to show the nobility as well as the ferocity of the Haitian revolutionary leader who burned the cities of his island, destroyed the harvests, tore up the highways, poisoned the wells, and murdered the whites who had been the masters of the island. Half a century later, Paul Robeson could perhaps be placed among the extremists who advocated black power, but in 1915 he was just a high-school boy sent off by his father and elder brothers to make a speech that sounded fiery, but which meant nothing at all to him.

Chapter 3

IN IVIED HALLS

Whether Paul Robeson was the kinky-haired favorite of all the whites who knew him in his younger days, as his wife Essie once would have it, or a "mean nigger" by Princeton's gentle standards, as Earl Schenck Miers put it, when he went to Rutgers College in the autumn of 1915, he found himself in more congenial surroundings than in the past.

Shortly after his matriculation, when he embarked on an extension of his classical education, Paul indicated some interest in playing football. Coach Foster Sanford soon learned that there was a big Negro boy back in New Brunswick, who wanted to come to Eatontown where the Rutgers team was preparing for its big game with Princeton. In 1915 football was more game and less scientific business, and there were no niceties about eligibility. Any boy who could play football, no matter what his age or class in college, was welcome to the team. Any but Paul Robeson, freshman Negro, it seemed.

Coach Sanford had then a squad of some thirty players. When they heard that he proposed to invite the Negro boy to play with them, half the squad rebelled and a spokesman declared that, if Robeson came to Eatontown, they were going home. Half the squad leave? That would give Coach Sanford just fifteen men to put on the field, and some of these were the worst kind of scrubs. The coach yielded, as gracefully as he could to the white supremacy of his students. Robeson remained on the Rutgers campus attending to his studies. The

Rutgers squad practiced hard. Then came the game with Princeton. The score was Princeton 10 Rutgers 0. Coach Sanford told his boys that if they wanted to go home it was all right with him. He was going to give the Negro a try.

And he did.

The white members of the Rutgers football team did their best to see that Paul did not make the squad. He was roughed up every day. His nose was broken in a scrimmage. His shoulder was dislocated. In a later period of the century such injuries would sideline an athlete, but not in 1915. Paul continued to try out. One day he suffered the final indignity and injury on the field. After a play, one of his white teammates stamped on Paul's bare hand with his cleated football shoe, smashing several fingers. The Robeson temper was aroused and on the next play he made for that man, picked him up, and threw him to the ground. His teammates learned that the big, rangy Negro could be aroused to violence and they began to treat him with more respect. In later years those teammates laughed off the roughing up as "ordinary hazing," but it is obvious that it was more than that, and Robeson knew it. More than a quarter of a century later, when Earl Schenck Miers related the incident to Paul Robeson, a broad smile changed into a tight-lipped grimace.

"Yeah, I remember it," Paul said.

Paul played on the Rutgers football teams for four years. As he grew and matured he became an excellent football player, particularly good as end because of his speed and size, but also capable of playing many other positions. He was never a ball carrier but he was excellent as a pass receiver and defense man. In Paul's junior year, 1917, Louis Lee Arms of the New York *Tribune* said this about the game between Rutgers and the Newport Naval Reserves:

> A tall, tapering Negro in a faded crimson sweater, moleskins and a pair of maroon socks ranged hither and yon on a wind-whipped Flatbush field yesterday afternoon. He rode on the wings of the frigid breezes; a grim, silent, and compelling figure . . . The Negro was Paul Robeson of Rutgers

College, and he is a minister's son. He is also nineteen years
of age and weighs two hundred pounds. Of his football
capacity you are duly referred to Cupid Black of Newport
and Yale. He can tell you. It was Robeson, a veritable Othello
of battle, who led the dashing little Rutgers eleven to a
14–0 victory over the widely heralded Newport Naval Reserves . . .*

A few days later Charles A. Taylor of the *Tribune* wrote a
similar report, this time about the Rutgers 28–0 victory over
Fordham:

A dark cloud upset the hopes of the Fordham eleven
yesterday afternoon. Its name was Robeson . . . the maroon
football warriors were completely smothered by it and its
accompanying galaxy of Rutgers stars . . . Robeson, the
giant Negro, appeared in the line-up as left end, but he . . .
played in turn practically every position in the Rutgers
team. . . .

By the end of that season George Daley of the New York
World ranked Paul as one of the finest of American football
players of all time, "with such men as Tack Hardwick and
Eddie Mahan of Harvard, Charley Barrett of Cornell, Jim
Thorpe of the Carlisle Indians, Elmer Oliphant of West Point,
and Ted Coy of Yale. . . ."

Twice, in 1917 and 1918, Paul was selected by Walter Camp
for the all-American team, and toward the end of his football
career Paul became the team's acknowledged hero—or almost.
It was never quite that way, as was indicated in a game
scheduled in 1918 between Rutgers and Washington and Lee
University, a southern white college. Officials and students of
Washington and Lee objected to playing against a Negro, and
Rutgers withdrew Paul Robeson from the lineup of the team
for that game.

As an athlete, Paul was as successful as his college and his
teammates and the American social system would let him be.
He became catcher on the baseball team, center on the basketball team, and he threw the discus in track. He was a four-

* New York Sunday *Tribune,* November 25, 1917.

letter man, and as a star athlete he earned the nickname "Robey" and a certain admiration from the other students, all white. He became a member of the Student Council. He was elected to Phi Beta Kappa in his junior year. He was elected to the senior honor society. He joined the debating society and became captain of the Rutgers debating team. In the summers he went back to Narragansett Pier to work as busboy and then as waiter, earning money to see him through the following academic year.

With its few dark moments, college was a pleasant experience for Paul Robeson. He did not join the glee club at Rutgers, for the simple reason that the glee club's singing was always followed by a college dance, and Paul would not be welcome at a social gathering of his white fellow students. He was careful. There was a color line even for the star student and athlete, and he did not overstep it. He might be the college's leading public speaker, winning the spring extemporaneous speaking contest four years in a row—but he could not talk himself out of the second-class position in which he found himself in white America. He was restrained in his approach to this problem. For his senior thesis Paul chose a subject close to his heart: the Fourteenth Amendment to the United States Constitution, sometimes known as the Due Process amendment, which was passed to guarantee the rights of Negroes. Paul chose this subject, but he did not attack it directly, rather he chose to discuss the effect of the law on *property*, and the growing tendency to "invade the liberty of the individual." He wrote:

> So long as the Constitution of the United States continues to be observed as the political creed, as the embodiment of the conscience of the nation, we are safe. . . . State constitutions are being continually changed to meet the expediency, the prejudice, the passions of the hour. It is the law which touches every fibre of the whole fabric of life which surrounds and guards the rights of every individual, which keeps society in place; which in the words of Blackstone, "is universal in its use and extent, accommodated to each individual, yet comprehending the whole community." This Amendment is a vital

part of American Constitutional Law and we hardly know its sphere but its provisions must be duly observed and conscientiously interpreted so that through it, the "sleeping giant of our Constitution" the American people shall develop a higher sense of constitutional morality.*

Paul was valedictorian of his class at Rutgers in 1919, then he graduated and moved on. He began his law studies at Columbia University Law School in February 1920—not earlier, because he had to work to raise money for further education. In the summers, he worked as waiter at Narragansett. In the winters, he held other jobs. But always he had to work to pay his fees.

His father had died in the spring of 1918, destroying what home Paul had left after his mother's death. As he entered Columbia he moved to Harlem to live in the Negro ghetto. He worked in the post office, he coached basketball teams (and played on the Columbia Law School team), and he sang with choirs and choral groups. He took time out to play professional football with a team from Akron, Ohio, and also with a Milwaukee team. He received as much as $1,000 a game for this work, and there seemed to be an excellent future for him in professional athletics, but Paul shared a public revulsion against professional football players that existed in the 1920s and he would not consider this method of earning his living. The teachings of the Reverend Mr. William Drew Robeson were still with him, and he was determined to seek a more honorable method of making his way.

One day in Chicago, he was approached by two men who told him they were sure they could train him to be successful enough as a prize fighter to fight Jack Dempsey for the world's heavyweight title. They dangled the promise of a million dollars before Paul Robeson, and, like any other young man, he was tempted. The question became a matter for discussion in the press. Some writers said yes. Others, either remembering the excesses of Jack Johnson or seriously concerned for Paul's

---

* Paul Robeson, Senior Thesis (New Brunswick, N.J.: Rutgers University, 1918).

welfare, said no. The argument that reached him, finally, was the claim that if he turned professional prize fighter he would disgrace Phi Beta Kappa and Rutgers. In those days Paul had the fondest memories of his college and his fraternal associations. He decided against the ring.

Although Paul continued to be successful in his various activities, each year it became more apparent to him that the stigma of race created special problems. He was invited as an honored guest to sit at the speakers' table at the Columbia University senior class dinner at the Hotel Astor in February 1921. The matter was brought to the attention of the press, for no other reason than that Paul was a Negro.

L. R. Condon, president of the senior class, felt impelled to answer the questions that were being asked. "There is no reason why Robeson should not be here," he said. "At present he is taking a senior course in law at Columbia, although he is a Rutgers graduate. There has been no dissent about him being here, and he was invited by the whole class."

The question to a Negro was why any question should be asked at all, but questions were asked and would be asked any time Paul stepped out of the role assigned to Negroes. By 1920 there was some acceptance of Negroes in athletics, although Jack Johnson's marriage to a white woman had created an atmosphere most inimical to Negro acceptance. The fear was only enhanced by Johnson's skill as the best prize fighter of the land in his day. And fear was the basic reaction of the white community to any Negro advances; this was the reason, unaccountable to Paul Robeson in his youth, for the attitude of the whites. He found it difficult to understand why he must excel in order to be considered equal, and then only in the narrow field of his excellence. The reason was more simple than he suspected: the whites would object until excellence overcame all objection.

In many of his jobs, Paul Robeson encountered the usual prejudice against Negroes. At Narragansett, one family on which he was called to wait at table took particular dislike to him, considering him an "uppity nigger" because he was a Phi Beta Kappa, a Rutgers graduate, and all-American football

player, and because he had a proud look in his eye. The father
said as much. The Robeson temper was aroused, and, to
prevent an incident, he left the dining room and would not
return to waiting on table until the family had left the resort.
This story has been cited as an example of the horrors of race
prejudice, but there was more to it than that: the prejudiced
ones remained at the resort for some time, and Paul refused to
work while they were there. The headwaiter tolerated this
independence and did not fire him, and so the incident became
something of an example of the ambivalence of the American
white attitude toward Negro progress.

In 1920, Paul made what might be considered his debut in
the world of the theater. The Young Women's Christian Association of Harlem decided to put on a theatrical performance
that year, and chose for the vehicle a play called *Simon the
Cyrenian*, in which the central figure is a Negro who carries
the cross of Christ to Golgotha. Paul was chosen to take the
lead in the play. He was successful enough in the role to
attract the attention of several of the founders of the experimental Provincetown playhouse, whose principal gift to theatrical history was Eugene O'Neill. At the end of the single
performance, Paul accepted the congratulations of the profes-
sionals with the curious aplomb for which he later became
noted. Perhaps because of his father's many abjurations, Paul
accepted success as simply his lot in life. He made nothing
particular of it; the attitude was that there was nothing to be
said about this success; perhaps, he said, there might have
been something to say if there had been failure.

Paul spent his free time in Harlem in these days "hanging
around" on the corner of 135th Street and Seventh Avenue,
talking. He was a hero in Harlem before he ever came there
because of his triumphs at Rutgers, and his activities at
Columbia, and on the professional football field. In Harlem he
met a Jewish-Negress named Eslanda Cardozo Goode, who
claimed relationship on her mother's side to the family of
Supreme Court Justice Benjamin Cardozo. The Cardozos'
background was equal to that of the Bustills on Paul's mother's
side of the family. One of Essie's Negro ancestors had been

freed by his white master during the days of slavery—the master being his father—and sent to college at Glasgow University. This Cardozo had founded the Avery Institute of South Carolina, one of the early Negro schools. He had also held the post of Secretary of State of South Carolina during the days of Reconstruction.

Essie, even in the earliest days of her association with Paul, burned with ambition, resentment, and energy—all dedicated to the change of her condition and that of her family and people. In her veins ran the blood of two downtrodden races, and to her it was all the more infuriating and ironic that she should be regarded as a second-class citizen because she admitted to being a Negro, when her skin was fair enough, and her hair could be made straight enough to pass as white. Sometimes she did "pass," but early in life she found this most unsatisfactory and no solution to the moral problems of her race.

Paul's approach to the problems of Negrohood was much more relaxed than Essie's. He was more grateful for his own position and less resentful against the position of the Negroes than she. He did not pay too much attention to her radical views on race relations, but he was attracted to her because of her energy. She decided, she said later, that she would marry him and she did. They met at a Harlem party in the spring of 1921 and they were married in Rye, New York, that same summer.

The newlyweds lived in Harlem in an apartment. Paul went to law school, coached football and sometimes played professionally, sang, and spent hours talking over the problems of the world. Essie, after graduation from teacher's college, was honored with a job as analytical chemist in the pathology department of Columbia-Presbyterian Hospital. Honored is the word. She was the first Negro to hold such a post at Columbia and she received it after much consideration, and then only on the strongest recommendation of her professors. She was always very proud of that job, and made more of it in later years than might be strictly justified because, quite rightly, she considered it to be an incursion into the fields preempted by whites. In the 1920s, in the medical field, Negroes were not very welcome, except in menial jobs. Nursing schools did not train Negroes; to secure nursing education they were forced to establish their own schools. White medical schools did not teach Negro doctors; they had their own medical schools. White hospitals did not admit Negro patients; they had their own hospitals, far inferior in every way to those of the whites. Of course there were exceptions to all these rules, in charity wards and elsewhere, but these were the rules, and when a break like that of Essie's came the entire intelligent Negro community rejoiced. Some, like Essie, and Paul in later years, stopped sometimes to say that it was much rejoicing for little progress.

In 1922, as he continued his legal studies, Paul was chosen by Mary Hoyt Wyborg to play a leading role in *Taboo,* her own play that dealt with the South and with Africa, with whites and blacks. He played this role opposite the English actress Margaret Wycherly. The New York performance was greeted with tepid reviews, with the exception of that of the then-leading critic of New York, Alexander Woollcott. Woollcott declared that *Taboo* was less than second-rate, and had very little good to say for Paul's performance. Woollcott was impressed by Paul, personally, however, when he met the young Negro during one of his prowls backstage at the Sam Harris Theater. The critic invited Paul to visit him at his apartment on the west side, part of a community affair that Woollcott shared with Harold Ross of *The New Yorker.* Robeson visited Woollcott and they became friends, for Paul had a most engaging manner. Here is part of Woollcott's recollection of that early Robeson:

> . . . of the countless people I have known in my wanderings over the world, he is one of the few of whom I would say that they have greatness. I do not mean greatness as a football player or as an actor or as a singer. I am not, I think, confusing his personal quality with his heroic stature. I do not even have in mind what is, I suppose, the indisputable fact, that he is the finest musical instrument wrought by nature in our time. I mean greatness as a person.

In his case I despair of ever putting into convincing words my notion of this quality in him. I can say only that by what he does, thinks and is, by his unassailable dignity, and his serene, uncorruptible simplicity, Paul Robeson strikes me as having been made out of the original stuff of the world. In this sense he is coeval with Adam and the redwood trees of California. He is a fresh act, a fresh gesture, a fresh effort of creation. I am proud of belonging to his race. For, of course, we both are members of the one sometimes fulsomely described as human . . .*

There was more. Woollcott, in his most fluid, disarmingly simple manner, described the young man he saw:

Even while he was studying law at Columbia and setting up his bride in a Harlem flat, he would slip out of town for the autumn weekends to finance his studies and his new household with a few bouts of professional football. There had been a rather nasty ruckus on the field in Milwaukee one afternoon in the preceding fall. Paul's team was playing against the team from Marion, where Mr. Harding came from. It was a team of Indians, and one of them was a real bad boy. He had, Paul was warned, a mean trick of sticking his fingers into the eyes of the player opposite.

In the middle of one play that afternoon, Paul saw those fingers headed for his own eyes. He also saw red, and promptly knocked the brave unconscious. At that, the opposing eleven fell on him as one Indian. Out of the corner of his eye, Paul could see his own one hundred percent Anglo-Saxon teammates discreetly leaving the scene. It looked as if he might have to beat up all those Indians single-handed. Before intervention became effective, he had entered upon this chore with such genuine pleasure and such concentrated destructiveness that the story of his quality as a fighter spread over the country before nightfall. . . .†

[This was the affair that led to the offers of a future in pugilism.]

---

* Alexander Woollcott, *While Rome Burns* (New York: The Viking Press), p. 123.
† *Ibid.*

Woollcott learned much about the young Negro in that one visit to his apartment, and why Robeson would not become a fighter.

He was uncertain what he wanted to be, but he was quite sure it wasn't a prize fighter. No, nor a lawyer, either. He would finish the law course because he had started it, but a Negro lawyer's chances are slim, and anyway, he felt he was meant to be something quite different. An actor, perhaps . . . I was skeptical, because the number of available Negro roles was even smaller then than now.

Well, then, he might do something with his voice. He told me shyly that he had just discovered (which is more than the Rutgers Glee Club ever did) that he had a pretty good voice. He would come around some evening, he said, and roar a few spirituals at me. With which promise, he pulled his vast bulk together and roamed off through the gas-house district.

Perhaps I am only being wise after the event, but I think I felt at the time that I had just crossed the path of someone touched by destiny. He was a young man on his way. He did not know where he was going, but I never in my life saw anyone so quietly sure, by some inner knowledge, that he was going somewhere. . . .*

In that summer of 1922, in spite of Woollcott's dire warnings against a career in the theater, Paul went to London to appear briefly in the English production of *Taboo*, opposite the famous Mrs. Patrick Campbell. They played briefly in London, then took the play on the road into the provinces.

Paul was moderately successful in the role, no more than that, and he returned in the autumn of 1922 to Columbia to resume his law studies. He graduated from Columbia Law School in 1923. What would he do then?

"Perhaps a political job to tide me over until I can build up a practice," he told Essie, but he did nothing to secure one and when offers were tentatively made to him, on sober reflection he refused them. His reluctance to take up the law was showing.

* *Ibid.*

Paul was lazy, Essie Robeson wrote in her biography of her husband. He wasted month after month, waiting for something to come along. Gradually his classmates found posts, but not Paul.

As always seemed to be Paul's fate, something did turn up. He was invited by a society lawyer in downtown New York to join his firm. The invitation came because this lawyer was a trustee of Rutgers, and he knew Paul and his reputation. It was an exciting offer for a young Negro, because this firm handled the most important cases. Paul could go into the law firm, and then make his own way.

Paul accepted this offer and went to the law office to obtain experience. He was called in to write briefs on several cases, but it soon became apparent that his presence in the firm was regarded without favor by most of the other young lawyers and even by some of the partners. The senior partner who had offered Paul the post suggested that young Robeson might want to open a Harlem branch of the office and take charge of it, with the full support and financial backing of the parent firm. Paul did not wish to do so.

At this point, Paul Robeson became certain that the practice of law was not for him. He had no desire to become a Harlem lawyer, handling cases of non-support, divorces, and other minor legal matters. There was too little challenge for a Negro lawyer in Harlem. There were some Negro millionaires, some Negro banks, and some big Negro businesses, but most of these found it expedient to employ white attorneys in their relations with the outside world, and so the opportunity in the law for an American Negro was limited and frustrating.

Paul went back to the Harlem apartment to laze around the streets while Essie worked, and to wait. Wait for what? He never quite knew what he waited for, but he was willing, always, to wait.

Chapter 4

THE YOUNG ACTOR

Paul Robeson's real chance in the theater came about because of the untiring activities of a number of young men and women who were determined to bring realism to the American theater. These people were the founders and per-petuators of the Provincetown Playhouse, the playhouse which had its inception on a wharf in the Massachusetts port city of its name, but had been successfully transported to New York City and was amazing and sometimes frightening the theater-goers of Manhattan in the early 1920s.

Paul was doing nothing in 1923, except singing occasionally at the Cotton Club. He performed there for a time with Florence Mills. Then, one day, he was offered a job by the Provincetown players, to appear in the leading Negro role in Eugene O'Neill's new play *All God's Chillun Got Wings*. Without plan, without thought of anything more than the $75 a week the role paid, Paul Robeson accepted the part. It meant no more to him than a previous role in an all-Negro revue called *Shuffle Along*, in which he had received the same salary.

Early in 1924, Paul began making his way downtown every day from Harlem, to the grubby but friendly little alleys of Greenwich Village, and to the little theater on MacDougal Street which belonged to the Provincetown Players. Here he met the working geniuses of the playhouse and their helpers: O'Neill, stage manager Harold McGhee, director Robert Ed-mond Jones, playwright Susan Glaspell, poet Edna St. Vincent

Millay, novelist Theodore Dreiser. By February, the Players were certain enough of their decision that they could announce to the press that Paul would play the role. Further, he would alternate in this play and in *The Emperor Jones*. This winter, as rehearsals began, for the first time the New York *Times* drama section wrote up the new actor.

James Light directed these plays. Eugene O'Neill stood by anxiously day after day, trying to draw from Paul exactly the performance he wanted. Paul was not a very accomplished actor, he was a presence, a six-foot-three-inch presence, bulky at more than two hundred pounds, representing the savage yet somehow dignified black man who bore the weight of the white world on his shoulders.

Before spring had come, the script of *All God's Chillun Got Wings* was published in H. L. Mencken's *American Mercury*. When a number of newspapers discovered that this play dealt with intermarriage between a Negro man and a white woman, a storm was aroused. Several New York newspapers and many throughout the country began to complain loudly that O'Neill's play was un-American in concept and disastrous to the American morale in effect. (Here again was the old basic fear of white America.)

As spring came along, director James Light and author O'Neill began to shape the plays the way they wanted them. *All God's Chillun Got Wings,* in particular, depended on shock value; it was O'Neill's protest against American racism. The play opens with children, white and black, playing in the street of a city. Jim Harris is the Negro boy. Ella Downey, the white girl, is "his girl." Nine years pass. Ella succumbs to race prejudice and the other white children of the street playground become hoodlums and Negro-haters. One of them, Mickey, has now become Ella's boyfriend, but Jim Harris, the Negro, still loves her. Five more years pass. Mickey has become a prize fighter and bum and has given Ella a child but has deserted her. The child is dead. Ella has no future except to become a prostitute; rather than this, but only because the decision is that stark, she agrees to marry Jim, but she cannot bear to live in America as a white wife to a black man. They go to France.

Two years later they return, and the Negro family of Jim Harris tries to make Ella happy, but she is so ashamed of being married to a black man that slowly she becomes insane, hating Jim because of his color all this while. In the end the insane Ella sits at Jim's feet, and kisses his hand.

When the script was published in the *American Mercury* serious objection to the play began to arise within the white community. The objectors found the play's theme degrading and the action unpleasant. O'Neill was treated to a lashing of criticism, the cause being his presentation of the degradation of a white woman before a Negro. Before the opening in the middle of May, the arguments were fully aired in the press. Even some moderates suggested that O'Neill really ought not to treat with subjects that violated the community's social code—the code being opposed to miscegenation.

Neither O'Neill nor the others of the Provincetown Playhouse would listen, so in an atmosphere of strife and rancor the play opened on the night of May 15.

For weeks before the opening, the campaign of harassment had become more intense every day. The Ku Klux Klan threatened Paul, Mary Blair, the white female lead, and O'Neill. The Provincetown Playhouse directors took to censoring the mail to protect the principals from a steady stream of abuse. A Klan leader in Georgia warned O'Neill that his son would be killed if the play went on. Not all the Klan threats came from the South, either. These were the days of the ascendance of the "new Ku Klux Klan," which had powerful roots in New Jersey and in New York State.

A few hours before the opening of the play, New York Mayor "Red Mike" Hylan changed the direction of traffic on Greenwich Village's MacDougal Street in an obvious attempt to cause confusion and stop the audience from coming to the play. At about the same time, a clerk in the mayor's office telephoned the Provincetown Playhouse to report that the child actors who played in the first scene could not go on. For no apparent reason their licenses to appear had been refused.

On the night of the opening, author O'Neill secured the voluntary services of some steel-worker friends, who came to the theater and guarded the dressing rooms, the lobby, and the street outside.

The curtain went up, and the play began. Director Light came on stage and explained that he must read the scene that shows that color does not affect the relationship between children, and that human beings must learn race prejudice. He then read the scene, because his child actors could not play it.

The principals came on then, and the play began, and went straight through to its finish, where the insane Ella is sitting on the floor with Negro Jim's hand in hers.

The Ku Klux Klan did not appear.

The play was a limited success. As time went on, Negroes as well as whites began to dislike this play for basically the same reasons: racist reasons. Paul's role was that of a sentimental, good-natured fellow who was too humble and too grateful to suit the modern Negroes; and it did not please them that Ella had to become a woman of the streets before she would marry the Negro, and that she did so only to save herself. All this offended the racism of the Negroes, who would agree later with the whites that the play ought not to have been presented (proving once again that extremism knows no color).

At the time, however, Paul was pleased to appear in this production, and Negroes were delighted that the Negro was for once being treated as a serious human being in the theater in two plays. As with *All God's Chillun Got Wings, The Emperor Jones* was adapted for Paul's peculiar abilities, and the presence that served him instead of normal acting experience. Director Light added a Negro spiritual to the Brutus Jones part, because he had heard Paul sing. The idea of Light and O'Neill was to make fullest use of the raw material to bring the theatrical effects they wanted across to the theatergoers.

O'Neill was immensely pleased with Paul's performances. He said that Paul's Brutus Jones gave him "the most complete satisfaction an author can get—that of seeing his creation born into flesh and blood." He said that Paul's Jim Harris gave "complete fidelity to my intent under trying circumstances."

Critic Laurence Stallings, in the New York *World*,* spoke of the quality of Paul's acting, in the same general terms that Woollcott used. "Ability in application to Robeson's work as the Negro in *All God's Chillun* is a wretched word," he said. "The man brings genius to the piece."

George Jean Nathan said much the same in his critique in the *American Mercury*,† but went further:

> The Negro is a born actor, where the white man achieves acting. Robeson, with relatively little experience and with no training to speak of, is one of the most thoroughly eloquent, impressive, and convincing actors that I have looked at and listened to in almost twenty years of professional theater-going. He gains his effects with means that not only seem natural, but that are natural. He does things beautifully, with his voice, his features, his hands, his whole somewhat ungainly body, yet I doubt that he knows how he does them. . . .

The fact that seemed to be missed by the critics—no criticism of Paul—was that playwright O'Neill and director Light had tailored these roles to Paul's character. Indeed, more than that, Paul represented every Negro who had ever been born into the world, for range of emotion and his qualities of voice and gesture were those of the millions of his color. Part of Paul Robeson's genius lay in the fact that he was the Negro typical of what white America thought of as the "noble" Negro. He commanded respect with his intellectual and athletic attainments. These were nearly always mentioned by reviewers, these prizes that had been won in competition with whites in a white game played on a white field; they were a type of justification for this Negro's having risen so far. "Look," said the reviewers as they mentioned these accomplishments, "we have a right to take this Negro seriously because he is a winner."

During the spring and summer of 1924, Paul Robeson began to move in a new world, and quite naturally, as with every-

* June 21, 1924 issue.
† July 1924 issue.

thing that had come to him, he adopted his new profession, and his new way of life. Among all Americans, the people of the theater and the world of the intellect had the least racial prejudice. Most of them had none; they were far too much interested in the essence of mankind than in its trappings, and to them a man's skin color was simply a distinguishing characteristic.

Paul liked the freedom of the new life. In Greenwich Village no eyebrows lifted when Robeson strolled into a restaurant with Mary Blair on one side and Eugene O'Neill on the other. Life was a round of parties and long dining sessions in the Village restaurants, interspersed with weeks of hard work as a play was put together.

During the summer of 1924 and the spring of 1925, Paul "hung around" with the Provincetown Playhouse crowd, although not all that time was there much for him to do. He realized, and it was very true, that the number of roles he might play in the theater was so limited that he could not make a career of being an actor alone. Yet, typically, he waited.

In the spring of 1925, another young Negro, Lawrence Brown, returned to the United States. After a long exile in Europe, Brown had achieved a considerable reputation as a musical arranger and compiler of Negro spirituals. Brown had met Paul Robeson in 1922, when Paul was in London briefly, playing in the British production of *Taboo*. They met again now in March 1925, at the corner of 135th Street and Seventh Avenue, Paul's hangout, when Brown came by on an aimless walk. Brown stopped and they talked. Paul invited him to dinner and to spend the evening with him at James Light's apartment in Greenwich Village, and Brown agreed to come along. That night at Light's apartment Brown played and Paul sang two of Brown's arrangements of Negro spirituals, and Light and the others were so enthusiastic they persuaded the pair to give a concert, devoted entirely to Negro spirituals and songs. Someone knew that the Greenwich Village Theater would be available on the night of April 19, a Sunday. Somehow among this footloose crowd of empty-pockets a deposit of $100 was found to reserve the theater, and the arrangements for the concert began. Prime mover of the crowd was Heywood Broun, drama critic who had recently moved over to become a columnist for the New York *World*. Broun was an immense man with huge enthusiasm for causes, and in this first American concert of native Afro-American music he saw a cause that delighted him. He plumped the concert in his column, and became publicity man for the enterprise, interceding with other newspapermen in New York.

On the night of the concert, thanks to Broun and his assistant press agents, the Greenwich Village Theater was sold out, and scalpers were selling tickets on the street in front of the house for $25 a seat. It was a dress-suit audience, too, which meant one largely from uptown.

The program consisted of sixteen Negro songs, mostly spirituals such as "Go Down Moses," "Swing Low, Sweet Chariot," but including more rousing songs: "Joshua Fit the Battle of Jericho," and the work song, "Water Boy." At the end of the program the audience demanded more and there was a seemingly endless series of encores, until performers and listeners went home, happy and exhausted.

The reviews were all that could be hoped for. The *World* was lavish in its praise and suggested that Robeson and Brown had exhibited a new art form. The *Times* praised Robeson's gift of voice and the spirituals: " . . . to make them tell in every line, and that not by any outward stress, but by an overwhelming inward conviction. They voiced the sorrow and hopes of a people."

Perhaps the *Times* reviewer came closer at that moment to finding the essence of Paul Robeson's various performances everywhere, from classroom to playing field to playhouse, than anyone had ever come before. Paul had come to an awaiting world as the epitome of the black man.

That summer Paul and Lawrence Brown were signed to go on tour with their concert, and Paul's financial problems seemed to be solved. For the first time in his life, he had an adequate supply of money and a *future*.

In the summer of 1925, the London theatrical world became interested in *The Emperor Jones,* and arrangements were made to bring the play to London. James Light went to direct, Harold McGhee went to be stage manager, and Paul went to play the role of Brutus Jones, murderous American Negro Pullman porter who becomes dictator of the inhabitants of a tropical island, and is finally killed by them.

The Emperor Jones was purely New-World in its concept and execution. London had never seen anything like it, and London responded according to the prejudices of its inhabitants. The colonialists complained that it was exceedingly bad form to put a Negro into a commanding position on the stage. The anti-colonialists flocked to the theater to see the giant Negro. The plain theatergoers came for an experience that was almost religious, keyed by the pounding of a drum that was beaten incessantly throughout the pursuit of Brutus Jones through the jungle, a pounding that underscored the Robeson monologue that comprised most of the play.

The critics of London lavished many thousands of words on Robeson and his performance, analyzing his acting abilities down to the smallest degree. Harold McGhee, who knew that Paul Robeson had no acting ability to speak of, roared with laughter as he read the reviews. Paul was puzzled. He knew he had very little but his innate character to express, and he could not understand half of what was written about him in its technicalities.

When the London run of *The Emperor Jones* ended, the Robesons were in no hurry to go home. They spent an extra month in London and then journeyed south to the Riviera to spend part of the winter. For the first time in either of their lives (barring Paul's brief trip to Europe in 1922) the Robesons were in countries where no general color bar existed. There were not enough Negroes in England and France then (as there were to be later in England) for the people to have developed any racial antipathies. To Essie, in particular, the change was like a breath of fresh air. For the first time she could go into a first-class hotel, or a first-class restaurant, without the feeling that if she was "passing" she was somehow breaking the rules of the game. There were no rules in England or in France. Some Englishmen might prefer to avoid the company of an American Negro, but that was a personal matter, and could not be helped. But there was no ghetto, there were no questions about riding in elevators or entering service entrances, and there were no bars against blacks at the doors.

The Robesons came back to New York in the winter of 1925–1926, because a concert tour had been scheduled for Paul and Lawrence Brown, now known as his accompanist and arranger. The financial affairs of the group had improved to the extent that Essie was able to give up her job at Columbia-Presbyterian Hospital and come along with the pair as a business and personal manager. From that point on, Essie's influence on Paul Robeson's character and actions was to become steadily stronger.

The intellectual effort in the musical partnership was all thrown on Lawrence Brown. Paul had a stirring voice, but it was an untrained instrument, and his range was very short. The impression of a full, strong voice was often given by the music selected by Lawrence Brown and by the arrangements he made of the music. That was not taking a bit away from Paul Robeson, for it was not the timbre or the range of Paul's voice that attracted his audiences or bound them as with a spell, it was the evidence of strength and sadness and hidden power—those indefinable qualities for which the critics looked then and looked later, yet found it so difficult to describe. It was Paul Robeson's particular physical genius that carried the concerts for them.

Paul was encouraged to take voice lessons. "I don't want you to make me into a professional singer," Paul told his teacher. "Just show me how to use my voice without ruining it. I'll do the singing."

So it was apparent, even as early as 1926, that Paul was aware that the gifts he had were not those of training but were natural gifts. This awareness made him relatively unresponsive to criticism, even to the most favorable criticism, and it contributed to his lazy geniality.

By 1926, important people were seeking Paul Robeson for important projects. Jerome Kern one day read a story by Edna Ferber in a magazine, a story called *Show Boat*. Kern decided it would make a fine libretto for a musical. He wangled an introduction to Miss Ferber and the two of them began the cooperative process of creating story and music. In the course of it Kern wrote "Ol 'Man River," and as soon as he had written it and Oscar Hammerstein had provided the words, he knew he had a song for Paul Robeson. Through Alexander Woollcott he reached the Robesons in Harlem and went that very day rushing up to the north end of the city, clutching his song.

It was decided. Paul was to play in *Show Boat* and sing the song. One delay was compounded by another, and *Show Boat* opened on Broadway without Robeson because he was committed to a concert tour.

So the song that Jerome Kern had sensed to be Robeson's song was sung by another. It would be some time before American audiences would hear and see Paul in the *Show Boat* role.

Chapter 5

AN AMERICAN ABROAD

When Paul and Essie and Lawrence Brown were touring the United States with the spirituals concert, they encountered innumerable embarrassments and humiliations. In New York City, unless Paul dined in private homes, he could not eat in any first-class establishment between the boundary of Greenwich Village and Harlem. He could not register at a first-class hotel. Elsewhere, conditions were even worse. Paul could not secure good seats in a Pullman. Essie said the ticket-seller would glance up, see Paul was a Negro, then claim he had only seats over the wheels. Essie would go up to the ticket-seller later and buy three seats in the center of the car, simply because she did not look colored.

The concerts were almost uniformly successful, artistically and financially, but this did not ease the growing annoyance of Paul at second-class citizenship. Essie was even more concerned, as perhaps a woman would be, with the petty annoyances and the rudenesses that were standard treatment where they were not known, and sometimes where they were. She was becoming increasingly radical and increasingly critical of the native land that promised so much and delivered so little even to an extremely talented Negro.

In the middle of 1927, Essie began staying home when Paul and Brown traveled. She was pregnant with the baby who would be called Paul, Jr., or Pauli. Paul continued to give his concerts—even increased their number. He acted in *Black Boy* and *Porgy* and won a certain amount of acclaim in both roles. He also became the center of a controversy after the Dutch Treat Club of New York failed to honor him in a manner usually granted to guests who had entertained the group. Friends in the club said he was mistreated becase he was a Negro. The publicity was good, but he did not really need it. He led an active life that kept his name often in the newspapers, although his stature as an artist was still relatively unproved. He was then, as he would be for the next few years, more grandly acclaimed on his concert tours of Europe than in his American appearances.

For this reason, in the spring of 1928, six months after the birth of his son, Paul came home one day to announce to Essie that they were going to London, where he would appear in the English production of *Show Boat,* to sing "Ol' Man River." Paul had recently returned from a European concert tour, and he was brimming with enthusiasm for Europe.

They went to London, and Paul was more successful than he had hoped to be in the *Show Boat* part at the Drury Lane Theater. One difficulty began to appear in the Robeson family life with this move, however.

Paul was lionized by the British upper class, and particularly by many of the women of that class who had little to do but seek thrilling entertainment. Essie hinted at the beginnings of marital discord in a book that she began to write about her husband.

" 'Are you unfaithful to her?' asked Martha [a friend].

"But Paul refused to commit himself.

" 'If I were to admit I am or had been, what good would it do? She'd never believe it!' "

The argument continued, and then Essie stated her position about her husband. She said that she knew of his infidelities but they made no difference. She knew he loved her and that was all that mattered.

That was a least the temporary resolution of a serious problem. As an oddity, an intelligent, talented Negro, Paul continued to be appealing to white women in Europe, and he was most susceptible to them. Also, in his concert tours and stage roles he was subjected to constant temptation. He and Essie were often apart these days; Essie remained in Hampstead, taking care of Paul, Jr., and working on her book during most of 1929. When Paul completed the role of Joe in *Show Boat*, he loafed about the house for a time. He had begun to learn Russian several years before, discovering then that he possessed an aptitude for languages. He had also begun to learn to read Chinese, although he had not learned to speak it. Now, in England, he began to study German, so that he could sing German songs. He and Lawrence Brown worked long hours over a changing repertory, and Paul spent many hours with a record player, listening to music and to language records. Paul had been approached about playing the title role in *Othello*. He said he was afraid to try but he began studying the part.

In 1929, Paul and Lawrence Brown left London for a concert tour of Central Europe. They took the boat-train from Dover to Calais, and then the Orient Express to Vienna. Essie went along on this trip, managing affairs, as she always did manage Paul's contacts with the outside world when she was with him. This tour took the Robesons to Vienna, to Budapest, and to Prague. The tour was very successful. One Viennese critic noted that part of the success came for the wrong reasons. The people, he said, went to see an American Negro and hear how a Negro sings. They came, he said, and discovered an artist.

Whatever the reasons, Paul's successes in Europe were so much greater than those at home, and his life in Europe was so much more profitable and pleasant, that, like a number of other talented Negroes, he chose to remain in Europe. The Robesons returned to London, and he began rehearsals for the Maurice Browne and Ellen Van Volkenburg production of *Othello* at the Savoy Theater.

Essie and her mother lived in the big house at Hampstead, overlooking the heath. Between rehearsals, Paul made the rounds of polite English society. He sang at a reception given by Lord Beaverbrook, the publisher of newspapers and magazines, then mingled with the high-born and the celebrities who were guests. He went to Parliament for lunch. He met Rebecca West, who was then one of England's most successful feature writers, and he met author H. G. Wells. He gave a concert at Albert Hall, and then went on concert tour of the provinces, to Birmingham, Torquay, Brighton, Margate, and Southsea.

On this tour, Paul encountered racial incidents. (There were always incidents.) On one occasion Lady Sybil Colefax gave a party for the Robesons at the Savoy Grill—but when the guests of honor arrived at the Savoy they were refused admission to their own party. So much furore was raised among Africans and West Indians in London that the Savoy management said it had investigated and could not discover how the terrible mistake had occurred—but the "mistake" became a matter for a question in Parliament. Ramsay Mac-donald, then Prime Minister, said he did not see how anything could be done officially by the government, and a hue and cry was raised, until the major London hotels stated that they would not refuse admission or service to Negroes. Such inci-dents, even when resolved positively, left their scars on Paul and Essie Robeson.

What else could be expected?

Paul had signed the contract with Maurice Browne to play the *Othello* role in 1929, but his commitments were such, and his concern about his ability to play the part was so serious, that rehearsals did not begin for a year. In the interim, Paul made another trip to America (for a concert tour), and, while it was professionally successful, again his visit to his own country was not as satisfactory as his life in Europe. The reason, it seemed, was that the strength of race prejudice in America was such that always, or almost always, there was some minor imperfection in Paul's relations with his American hosts, whether it be an incident in registering at the hotel, refusal of service at a restaurant, raised eyebrows or open scorn on the streets, or some even smaller problem.

Paul was back in London in the beginning of 1930, then off again on another tour of the Continent. It was a frantic life, but somehow he found time to study *Othello*, and six months before rehearsals he had his part letter perfect. Yet, Paul

Robeson showed a concern for artistry far beyond talent and training: he began studying the English pronunciation of the English words, sure that any sign of his broad American accent would mark his performance on the English stage as something less than excellent in English eyes. He went back to Middle English to practice pronunciations.

When he did *Othello* they would expect an American accent, but he intended to do the role in pure honest English to bring out the music of the text. Essie Robeson indicated that he worked very hard to perfect his use of the language, just as he studied the words and intonations of the spirituals and of every other song he sang. It was part of his professionalism.

Paul had many qualms about his first professional *Othello*. He told New York *Herald Tribune* reporter Irma Kraft that he did not expect to be able to interpret the play properly. He was, after all, facing great odds. Shakespeare and his works belonged to the English people, and they were most knowledgeable and most jealous about interpretations.

Paul encountered trouble even before opening night. A major controversy arose in England when it was learned that Robeson would play the *Othello* role, not on the usual racial grounds, but because certain Shakespearian enthusiasts claimed that the Moor was a black Arab and not of Negroid stock, while others claimed that the Moor to whom Shakespeare referred was Negroid. The argument was almost purely anthropological, but that did not prevent it from becoming heated. The point was: could a Negro properly dispose of the role in the manner in which Shakespeare would have wished?

Paul wondered, too. A few weeks before the opening, long after all was settled that he *would* open, he suggested to Maurice Browne that he was inadequate for the part and that the producer ought to find another actor. It was too late, even if Browne had been willing to make a change. Browne said so, as gently as he could.

Paul's major concern was still the pronunciation of English words. He was desperately conscious that from the moment that Othello came on stage, at the beginning of Act I, Scene ii, he, as Othello, might turn high tragedy into low comedy with so simple an error as a broad American A.

As to the physical performance, Paul fretted and worried about the problems of stage "business" and action, and finally decided to abandon acting as such. He realized suddenly just what was his gift to the concert stage and the theater. The realization brought him strength to do the *Othello* in his own way, for he knew as well as anyone his limitations as performer and his lack of experience on the stage.

The secret was that his success, his power, lay in *his* representation of the tragedy and pathos of a black man in a white world. Somehow Paul brought this tragedy across to audiences as no other man had ever done. Every Negro tragedy ever written seemed to have been prepared for his performance. His strength was inherent; his performance was always basically the same. By 1930, a wide world was conscious of the growing demand of Africa for recognition and dignity, and the time was ripe for a presentation of the plight of the black man.

He would concentrate, Paul said, on portraying the suffering of the Negro in the role of the Moor.

"In taking Othello I find the lines come to life at every point," Paul told a reporter for the New York *Times*. "I feel the play is modern, for the problem is the problem of my own people. It is a tragedy of racial conflict, a tragedy of honor rather than of jealousy. Shakespeare presents a noble figure, a man of singleness of purpose and simplicity, with a mind as direct as a straight line. He is important to the state but the fact that he is a Moor incites the envy of little-minded people. Desdemona loves him, he marries her, but the seed of suspicion is sown. The fact that he is an alien among white people makes his mind work more quickly. He feels dishonor more deeply. His color heightens the tragedy."

That was the way it must be for Paul. He tried to intellectualize his role, but he could not. He talked to directors, to actors, and to writers. He spent many hours with Sir Frank

Benson, who had played hundreds of Shakespearian roles, and Sir Frank tried to tell him how to bring himself into the position of the Moor, but Robeson could not become the Moor. Instead the Moor must become Robeson.

That is how it was when the play opened at the Savoy Theater on May 19, 1930, with Maurice Browne playing Iago, Peggy Ashcroft playing Desdemona, and Sybil Thorndike playing Emilia to Paul's Othello.

As the play ended, the house at the Savoy erupted in cries and cheers. There were twenty curtain calls, and even then the audience would not subside until Robeson stepped forward and made a brief speech.

The reviews were laudatory. *The Morning Post* said there had not been so good a production of *Othello* in London for forty years. The New York *Times* and other American newspapers covered the production as a matter of American interest. The *Christian Science Monitor* reviewed it as though it was on the American stage. The *Monitor's* review was a shade more critical than most, too, bringing up the old argument:

> Paul Robeson seems afraid of posing himself; otherwise his rendering is superb. He is, of course, splendidly equipped; of fine and imposing presence, with a magnificent voice and, moreover, a Negro. But here one begins to doubt. Was Othello a Negro? He is described as a Moor, a type of colored man whom Robeson does not resemble very closely . . .*

This puzzlement did not bother many critics or audiences— least of all the London audiences. A month after the opening, these audiences were still clamoring for curtain calls. Paul moved Englishmen to shout and cheer and weep in public, no easy feat for an American. With all its imperfections, the London *Othello* was magnificent and it was granted the acclaim it deserved.

If Paul had been greeted fulsomely by the lions and lionesses of Mayfair before his *Othello*, now he became the darling of British society. Nearly every door was opened to him. All the more contrast, this, because at the same time that he

* *Christian Science Monitor* (Boston), June 18, 1930.

became an English hero, a stupid racial controversy began in America about *Othello*. Producer Jed Harris was talking about bringing Robeson back to the United States to play the title role after the London production. Harris said he thought Lillian Gish would make a marvelous Desdemona to Robeson's Othello.

When the word of Jed Harris's plan carried along the rialto, reaction came, swift and brutal; Harris was criticized for considering such a plan. The reason was the same old American fear of portraying interracial sex relationship. Americans and American newspapers had caviled at the liberal ideas stated by Eugene O'Neill in *All God's Chillun Got Wings*, and had spoken openly against the last scene in which a demented Ella kisses the hand of her black husband. Desdemona went much further in *Othello;* she and the Moor embraced a number of times. And as for the imagery, Shakespeare was never-ending in his references to sexual activity. Just after the opening of the play, Iago and Roderigo go to the house of Desdemona's father, Brabantio. "Even now, now, very now," shouts Iago, "an old black ram is tupping your white ewe." A few moments later Iago again warns: "You'll have your daughter covered with a Barbary horse," and again he refers to the "gross clasps of a lascivious Moor."

Throughout, the envious, evil Iago plays the racist role, inciting racism in others. Yet, to white Americans, the reaction was often opposite that intended by Shakespeare. The white American drew an emphasis, not on the evil of Iago's pictorial vilifications, but on the picture they conjured for him, of white girl mating with black man. The argument in America against presenting on the stage a legitimate work of art was an obscene argument, a ridiculous travesty of freedom, but it was not one bit less serious for that, nor any less vigorously pursued. In the end, Jed Harris abandoned his plans, and Paul, who heard of the controversy, was numbed and pained a little more.

The success of *Othello* changed Paul Robeson's life in several ways. First of all, he was recognized as an important actor as well as a curiosity. He had been taken seriously before, but

as an oddity, a fine representative of a downtrodden race, the
first such male to burst upon the international scene. But now
he became a man in his own right, not just a talented *Negro*.
With such a proven popular property in hand, English producers began to look for vehicles in which they could use
Paul.

The second change in Paul's life was personal; he became
heady with the wine of his popularity, and bemused with the
women who cast themselves at his feet. The proof of this
dalliance and the sad result of it came when Paul and Essie
Robeson separated in 1930. Essie continued to live in England
with little Pauli and her mother, but she and Paul lived apart,
and when the newspapers wrote of Mr. and Mrs. Robeson
appearing at one resort hotel or another, it was not Essie
Robeson who was moving about with Paul.

For her own preservation, Essie immersed herself in the
problems of Negroes in England and in Africa. She enrolled in
the London School of Economics to study anthropology and
she began in these 1930s to study languages. Rebecca West
recalled Essie in this period as a "typical C. P. convert"—not
necessarily a member of the Communist Party (for both Paul
and Essie were more interested in action than in party affiliation) but a Marxist by inclination. Paul, at this period, was
absolutely nonpolitical. His feeling for the mistreatment of the
Negro was abstract and no more than abstract, and he gave no
sign of intending to interrupt his personal career in behalf of
so nebulous a struggle as one for Negro rights.

Paul's success in London in 1930 brought him to the pages of
the British *Who's Who*. (He never achieved recognition in
Who's Who in America.) Paul's head was sculpted by Jacob
Epstein in this year, a fine recognition of an artist, for Epstein
was then the darling of London. The publicity given the
Epstein sculpture was in sharp contrast to the publicity given a
life-size bronze nude of Paul sculpted by Tony Salemme in
Greenwich Village during the Provincetown Playhouse days.
Salemme sent the bronze to Philadelphia for a fine arts exhibi-
tion, but it was refused because it was a bronze figure of a
Negro—nude. Another small shaft in the soul of Paul Robeson.

At the end of the Savoy performance of *Othello,* there was much to be done. A program was arranged at the Savoy Theater in which Paul played scenes from *The Emperor Jones* and then sang spirituals, accompanied by Lawrence Brown. This program indicated the esteem of British audiences for the performer; in later years it would have been called "An Evening With Paul Robeson."

After the Savoy performance, Paul and Brown took the show on tour of the British provinces for three months. Then came more concerts. The years 1931 and 1932 were busy ones for Paul. He was chosen to play the role of the giant stoker in the London production of Eugene O'Neill's *The Hairy Ape* at the Ambassador Theater. That same year (1932) he appeared in a revival of *Show Boat* in New York City, singing for the first time the role of Joe for an American audience. America saw Robeson from time to time—or that portion of America in which he felt he could travel saw him—but he was much Europeanized. These were the years in which Paul seriously considered taking British citizenship.

In May 1932, Essie lived in London while Paul went to New York with a "Mrs. Robeson." This was a final insult, and Essie was in touch with lawyers in New York City to bring suit there for divorce. In June, when the newspapers discovered the action, they found Paul at the Casino Theater but he would not talk about his affairs other than to say that he believed the divorce would be amicable and that Essie had been "very civilized" about it. Robeson was then very much smitten by an English woman, and he hoped to marry her. He was defiant when questioned by the press:

". . . if we do marry," he said, "I am prepared to leave the United States if there is any stir at all about it. I will not be swayed by popular opinion or prejudice from doing what I think best.

"I feel that I must maintain my dignity as an artist. I can make a living anywhere, as I speak Russian and German and am studying French.

"I have twice left this country determined not to return. I feel that the Negro is patronized too much here. If he has half a voice they call him a marvel. If he is literate, they call him a genius. Why, I had to go abroad to find out whether I could really sing or not."

With this interview, Paul revealed the changes in him in recent years. He was not yet a political figure, but he was becoming concerned about the plight of the Negro. Much more important, he had found himself as an individual. He had no fear about speaking out against wrongs and slights. He had discovered that he was treated with ordinary dignity in Europe, although because he had captured the British imagination as a man he received more than that. He did not want either slavish adulation in America, or the mistreatment accorded the ordinary Negro—yet that was to be his lot. His speaking-out in 1932 did very little, one way or another. It surprised a few persons he had known before and it angered the racists, but average white Americans simply read what Robeson had to say and preferred to consider another subject.

Essie had no intention of coming back to America at all. She was thoroughly alienated from her own people, and she considered herself to be a *Negro*, not an American. She so wrote in letters to a few friends in America, Alexander Woollcott among them. She stayed on in London, hopeful that she could become a successful playwright. She began work on a play called *Uncle Tom and His Cabin*, which dealt with the travels of a Negro jazz band to Europe, where for the first time the American Negroes discovered that black men need not live in an atmosphere of hostility and degradation in a white world.

A year later the Robeson's family problems were resolved. Paul was dropped by his white ladylove, and he returned to Essie and the family hearth.

As an artist, Paul continued to develop in what might be called his English years. He became interested in the experimental programs of Ronald Adam's Embassy Theater, and in 1933 he again played the role of Jim Harris, this time to the Ella of Flora Robson. Biographer Marie Seton came to know Robeson well in this period and she remarked that he began to show the signs of social consciousness after the collapse of his romance. In his mingling with the British upper class, Paul noted that the aristocrats addressed their white servants in the same manner that Americans addressed Negroes, and he was so disturbed (he said it upset him for a year) that he began musing on the problems of class as well as of race. One day, when Marie Seton took him to a French restaurant in Soho, a workingman's district in London, he remarked that he always enjoyed being in Soho because this poor district of the city was removed from the prejudice of the aristocrats.

Paul now began to show broader social consciousness. He had always wanted to go to Germany. He had only begun studying German, but he planned to live in Germany for a time. He met Ferdinand Kuh, an American correspondent who had been transferred to London from Berlin, and Kuh told Paul of the evils of the new Nazism. Paul began to think. Later, he was to make a concert tour of Hitler's Germany, and to be shamelessly propositioned on street corners by fey young men who claimed that they belonged to the master race. His former attraction to Germany turned to disgust.

England was his love, he said. In England he was free. He talked seriously about establishing his own theater in London. He told reporters that England was his home.

One reason he preferred England to America was the absence of race prejudice, of course. Paul met policemen and cab drivers on the street who told him how much they enjoyed his singing. He liked the absolute freedom from taints of racism in reviews of his plays. Nowhere was this better illustrated than in the London production of *All God's Chillun Got Wings*. The play, as noted, had aroused serious social controversy in the United States because of the interracial marriage and because O'Neill had, in this case, shown moral superiority in a Negro man. The English were able to accept this phenomenon as a fact of human life, where the American press had shied away from this aspect, because the play was heavy with symbolism and social commentary on America. The English, from their lofty peak, could adopt an Olympian view.

Paul's political involvements were emotional, not intellectual. This emotionalism was to become the central factor of Paul's life. Always, whatever political views he held were

dictated by emotion. Now, in 1933, when *All God's Chillun*
became successful, the play was moved from the little Embassy to the important Piccadilly Theater, which was like
moving from the Provincetown Playhouse in Greenwich Village to the Shubert Theater on Broadway.

As would happen so many times in so many years to come,
when the play was successful (and the rage of London) Paul
became the target of people with a cause. The cause was
legitimate enough: thousands of Jewish refugees from Nazism
streamed into London. Most of them had been divested of all
their earthly possessions by the Nazis, and often what little
they were supposedly allowed to take out of the country had
also been extorted from them by Hitler's border guards as the
last price of freedom. These poor people were going hungry.
Few of them spoke English, a deficiency which would have
limited their employment opportunities severely even if the
world had not been undergoing its fearful Depression of the
1930s. A committee of prominent Englishmen, many of social-
democratic leanings, was formed to help the refugees. Head of
the committee was Robeson's acquaintance, H. G. Wells. Another member of the group was James Marley, who had raised
the question in Parliament about the racial discrimination
against Robeson at the Savoy Grill. Another was writer Marie
Seton. These supporters of good cause sought a public benefit
of *All God's Chillun*. Paul was playing his role for only £10 per
week (all that the Embassy management could afford to pay
until the play became successful) because he wanted the play
to be seen. He was so apolitical that he objected, without
thought of the money, to playing the benefit for the Jewish
refugees because he would be taking sides in a political matter.
He had always avoided political controversy, he said, because
he was an artist.

Marie Seton appealed to Paul on a purely emotional and
purely racial basis. Did he think that anyone would ever let
him forget he was a Negro as long as there was any racial
prejudice in the world? she asked.

Paul then made one of the most important decisions of his
career. He agreed to play the benefit. In later years he said this

benefit marked the beginning of his political awareness. From this point in 1933—when he began working in behalf of the Jewish refugees from Nazism—can be traced the beginning political awareness that led to beliefs that would grow ever stronger, and ever more firm. Eventually politics would pit Paul Robeson against the vast majority of his own countrymen. Paul Robeson's political beliefs were, and remained, exceedingly simple: he believed in the equality of mankind. He was willing, from this day forward, to take risks and speak out for that equality. So simple, so Christian a belief had no place in the world of international politics, when that belief is accompanied by the choosing of sides, as if the world could be divided into "good guys" and "bad guys."

Paul left London in the spring of 1933 for New York, to appear in the title role in *The Emperor Jones,* a motion picture produced by John Krimsky and Gifford Cochran at the Astoria studios on Long Island, as an "art film."

The motion picture of *The Emperor Jones* was very successful. Paul was better treated by press and public in New York on this trip than before. The New York *Times* followed the filming and wrote of Paul seriously and respectfully. He was invited to appear as a guest star on Rudy Vallee's popular Fleischman Hour on the National Broadcasting Company network, and he made other guest appearances. He sang "Ol' Man River" and "Water Boy" on the radio for audiences of millions and his American reputation spread and was enhanced.

Very tired from a round of personal appearances, radio shows and filming, Paul returned to London in August. His interest in politics was increasing, although bubbles of confusion kept coming to the surface. On his return to London, when he was asked about world affairs and art, he tried to relate himself to his new, expanding theme.

He would never again sing in Italian, French, or German, said this artist who only two years earlier had been looking forward to living in Germany and France and singing in those languages. He was now looking for a Russian or a Hebrew or a

Chinese work. The reason was that as a Negro he related himself to these people.

"The trouble with the American Negro," Paul said, "is that he has an inferiority complex. He fails to realize that he comes of a great ancestry linked with the great races of the Orient . . .

"What he should do is try for 'black greatness' and not an imitation of 'white greatness.' I am more than ever convinced that the African civilization dates back to the times when Oriental culture, including that from China, began to influence the Western world. I believe that where the Afro-American made his mistake was when he began trying to mimic the West instead of developing the really great tendencies he inherited from the East. I believe the Negro can achieve his former greatness only if he learns to follow his natural tendencies, and ceases trying to master the greatness of the West. My own instincts are Asiatic."*

Anthropologically or archaeologically speaking, Paul's arguments might not be very sound, but this was less important to him than to find an emotional attachment to some "great society" to which he could cling in behalf of the Negro. His search was launched. No longer was it enough to be personally accepted in English society *as an individual*. Now he demanded to be accepted as a Negro. Marie Seton had struck him that day when she said so strongly that he could never forget that he was a Negro as long as race prejudice existed in the world.

Paul's political awareness was furthered at home by Essie, in whom the fires of Negro and Jewish awareness of persecution burned brightly. Essie was more intellectual than Paul. She was more political than he. She *stated* the arguments that he *felt*, she put them into a semblance of logic; all of which strengthened Paul's emotional devotion to the Negro cause.

The Robeson household became a happier home. As soon as he was old enough, Paul, Jr., was sent to Austria and later to Switzerland to school. Essie and Paul took a flat in London,

* The Sunday *Times* (New Brunswick, N.J.), October 27, 1935.

where Essie pursued her studies and Paul studied languages, singing, and comparative philology. When Pauli was in London he lived there, too, but since the flats were so small, he actually occupied one across the hall, with Grandmother Goode as his guardian.

Paul's trips back and forth across the Atlantic in the 1930s were like those of a commuter, and so were his concert tours of Europe and the British Isles. Concerts were his mainstay. He was extremely conscious of the limitations of the Negro actor in a white world, and he was not particularly eager to seek out stage or film roles. The Robesons had plenty of money, and Paul's way of life was so simple that they spent very little of it on themselves. They dressed well. The society columnists of the London popular press often commented on Essie's costumes when she appeared at Mayfair parties. But they did not own a car and they did not indulge themselves in many luxuries. Essie was her own cook. Visitors to their flat said it had the bookish, untidy, lived-in look of that of a professor.

In the middle 1930s, Paul began to extend his repertoire beyond the Negro spirituals. He added Mexican songs, Scottish and Russian songs. He continued his study of languages (and eventually developed some familiarity with some twenty-five tongues, ranging from Chinese to Arabic, with especial fluency in Russian). He also made it a point to acquire working knowledge of a number of African dialects.

Paul became very much interested in Africa as his social consciousness grew. He was like the man who goes back to the birthplace of his grandfather, looking at the headstones in the cemetery. In Paul's case it was not so simple. Brought up an American, second-class or not, Paul was not conscious of his African background until he began studying Africa. Soon, however, he felt a surge of affinity with the people who spoke the tongues of black Africa. In London, with Essie's active assistance, Paul sought acquaintance with a number of African students. He met Kwame Nkrumah and Jomo Kenyatta and a number of other leaders who would one day become the chiefs of state of independent nations. The Africans of the British Empire had organized a West African Students Union, and they maintained a clubhouse. Paul and Essie were made honorary members of the Union. The reason for the honor was that Paul had become the most prominent colored man in Western society, and he was looked up to with awe by Africans in the Western world. One reason for this awe was that Paul was a black man, not a tan man or a brown man. The Negroes of Africa, whose black skins indicated the purity of their ancestry, had a private and secret contempt for the American Negro with light skin. This contempt became apparent to white Americans only after African nations became free, but it had always existed. The Africans felt less kinship to the American Negroes, by and large, than American whites did to the English. It was a source of humiliation to the African racists to see the brown skins that represented mingling of white and black races.

In the early 1930s and in the middle of the decade, as Africa was emerging from the stone age culture into modernity, many Africans were coming to England and to other countries to study medicine, the law, economics, and other disciplines of a twentieth-century society. They mingled freely with Chinese and Indians and the colored peoples from many other lands, but the Africans had deep-seated feelings of inferiority to whites which had been thrust upon them by a hundred years of British rule. Where Paul went to sing, the Africans came out to see him and hear him, and to be awed by him. He was the epitome of an African, with his dark skin and huge stature. His success indicated to the black Africans as nothing else could that here was a man of pure African descent (he was anything but that, of course) who had triumphed in a white world.

Paul became a celebrity in white English circles, as well. At the universities in the 1930s, the Socialist clubs were extremely active and very popular among energetic young radicals who saw about them the shards of capitalist society. To the young, one appealing virtue of Socialist theory was its absolute negation of racism. Paul came to represent the ideal of western European, or at least of English upper-class Socialist thinking, as the representative of the downtrodden who had succeeded.

He was asked to speak to the Socialist Club of Cambridge University, though up to this point he had not indicated any political leanings. Willy, nilly, Paul was being forced into social consciousness by the responsibilities imposed on him, even though they might be masked as honors.

Chapter 6

RUSSIAN INTERLUDE

Late in 1934, at the invitation of Russian film director Sergei Eisenstein, Paul and Essie Robeson left England for a visit to the Soviet Union. Eisenstein was considering Paul for the lead role in a film he wished to make about Toussaint L'Ouverture, the Haitian revolutionary. Paul was eager to go to Russia to see the results of the social experiment there, in which his Indian and African friends took such an interest, and Essie was even more interested. In such matters as political and general social theory, Essie was the leader of the Robeson family. (Later she would become spokesman for the family.)

The Robeson trek took them through Hitler's Greater Germany. It was December 1934. Christmas was but a few days away, and one might have expected that Germany, of all places, would be ringing with sounds of Christmas joy. Not so. This was the second year of the Third Reich. In the summer, Adolf Hitler had conducted his blood purge, and the heads of scores of Nazis and enemies had rolled. A month later, at the end of July, Hitler had seized Austria, and less than a month after that a plebiscite had shown that 88 per cent of the German people wanted Hitler to be dictator of Germany. The Nazis had never before ridden so high as they did in this Christmas time of 1934, and their arrogance and their racism were coming to a peak.

Paul was traveling with Essie, who could always pass for white, and with Marie Seton, whom they had asked to join them on the trip because she was familiar with Moscow. After this trip Essie was to tell Rebecca West how Paul had been importuned on the street by homosexuals of the master race. That experience, however, was not all the story of their brief, unhappy visit to Germany.

Paul was prepared for a troublesome visit, knowing what he knew about the Nazis from newspapermen who had visited London, and remembering the call on him to play the benefit of *All God's Chillun* for German Jewish refugee relief. He had played in Germany in 1930, in a brief engagement of *The Emperor Jones* staged at Max Reinhardt's Berlin theater. Now, four years later, that progressive stage and screen director had fled the Reich, a victim of Nazi oppression. Most of Paul's other friends in Germany were gone, too, by 1934.

This German interlude was not to be much of a visit: the Robesons had only to stay one day in Berlin, between trains. But in that visit Paul was to have a sharply focused glimpse of Nazi racism. He was always intensely sensitive to atmosphere; as they arrived in Friedrichstrasse station, Paul squirmed beneath the evil glances of the blonde young Nordics who proclaimed themselves members of the Master Race. Striding along the streets of Berlin to the hotel, Paul was extremely conscious of the odd looks of even the mildest people. They looked at him, and then they looked away. The feeling of race was everywhere in the air, and this was the one subject calculated to drive Paul Robeson to the point of distraction.

Marie Seton later reported that Paul was nervous and upset during the few hours they spent in Berlin. Essie telephoned an old Jewish acquaintance, who came to the hotel, talked to them of the horrors of Hitler's concentration camps and left abruptly, saying he preferred to talk on the streets rather than in rooms. Paul refused to go out onto the street; he paced his room like a caged animal and whiled away the time until they were to leave. He insisted that they eat in the hotel dining room to avoid the streets again. They spent the afternoon in a motion picture theater, viewing a travelogue of Africa.

At the railroad station, waiting for the train to the East, came the beginnings of a racial incident. Paul, Essie, and Miss Seton stood on the platform and storm troopers began moving in close to them. Paul, who understood German, said the Nazis thought these were German women with him, and the troopers were working themselves into a frenzy, preparing for what Paul said would be "a lynching." The tension grew nearly unbearable on that platform before the train came chugging in. Paul hustled his group aboard their car, although their baggage had not arrived. He was prepared to leave without the baggage, to escape this malevolent atmosphere before an incident developed. The baggage came at the last moment, the train departed, and nothing happened, yet the feeling of violence and hatred just under the surface affected Paul deeply. Here, in one afternoon, Paul had been shown a glimpse of the future Germany. Nazi control was already complete. The Nazis had the people enthralled and fearful, and they dared to indicate that they would assault foreigners in public places if they pleased.

The Berlin incident had enormous effect on Paul as a political man, just because in that one quick capsule he had been exposed to unmitigated evil. Now, immediately to follow, came one of the most pleasant interludes of Paul Robeson's life, and one that was to affect him every bit as deeply in quite a different manner.

It was apparent that the Paul Robeson who arrived in the Soviet Union just before Christmas 1934 was not a political thinker. His friends, and his wife, were working toward this end, but Paul was still insisting that he was an artist and that he must learn how to live as an artist in a difficult and changing world. He was wedded to the concept of Negro separation from the white world. One might say in a sense that, twenty years before Elijah Muhammed and Malcolm X, Paul had adopted the theory, although not the trappings, of the Black Muslims. Shortly before Paul's trip to Moscow, he had told reporters that he wished to devote himself to the cause of Negro culture for the rest of his life. He called it a

"Renaissance of Negro art and culture." He wanted this culture to be entirely separate from that of the white world. He intended, he said, to go to Africa in 1935 and see what could be done about establishing a Negro homeland, similar in concept to the Balfour proposition of 1919, by which Britain backed the theory of a homeland for the Jews in Palestine.

Paul could not have chosen a more opportune moment for his visit to Russia. The year before, the United States had recognized the official existence of the Soviet State, and there was considerable friendliness to Americans in Russia. With the emergence of the Nazis in Germany, and their announced anti-Communist policies, the friendliness to the Western democracies was growing stronger at the moment of his visit. The Russians were beginning to feel a certain degree of security; the Communists had purged their party of a million members the year before and no longer had the fear of counterrevolution they had exhibited in the past. Soviet Russia was for the first time gaining prestige among nations; in this autumn of 1934, Russia had joined the League of Nations. Shortly before Paul's arrival, Serge Kirov, one of Stalin's closest associates, had been assassinated. Stalin was now searching within the party for his enemies, and soon another bloody purge would ensue, but at this Christmas season, Moscow gave the appearances of a city of joy. Christmas had been deprived of its religious significance by the Communists, for all but the most stubborn Christians, but the social trappings and many of the old Russian customs continued. So the atmosphere into which Paul moved from Germany was a happy one, by and large. Another key to Paul's reception in Russia and his attitude toward the Russians was his mastery of languages. He spoke some Russian, and he was able to sing in that language with some fluency.

The visit gave signs of beginning inauspiciously. The train stopped at the border station at Negoroel, and here the passport officers discovered an error in the Robeson visas. Paul was told that they would have to go back to London. They could not be admitted into the Soviet Union because their papers were not in order.

Frantic calls were placed to Intourist, the Soviet Official tourist agency, which handled all the affairs of foreigners in Russia. While the party and the officials waited for decisions from Moscow, the customs men discovered that Paul had brought a phonograph and records with him, and they began to play them. They recognized Paul's voice (Pavel Robesona, he was called in Russia) and soon they recognized Paul. Paul's music was very well known in the Soviet Union because he *was* a Negro. Soon the difficulties about passports were adjusted, and a laughing and very gay crowd bundled the Robeson party on to the train for Moscow. What a different reception than the one they had received in Germany!

In Moscow, Paul and his party were met at the station by a large crowd. Sergei Eisenstein led the delegation, and on their meeting the big muscular Negro and the short, chubby film director smiled and shook hands.

Paul was to spend two weeks in Moscow, accompanied by Eisenstein most of the time. He met many other people, Russians and foreigners. He met Chinese and Americans, including a Negro actor named Weyland Rudd who had come to Moscow from America to study with Eisenstein, and many, many others. Eisenstein screened his own movies and those of other Russian film-makers for Paul.

Paul and Eisenstein roamed the streets, talking with people on the trams, on buses, and on street corners. Paul visited the new subway that was then being built beneath the city. He talked with representatives of the Commissariat on Public Education, and learned that the Soviet child was instructed from the beginning of his school years that there must be *no* barriers of sex, race, language, or color. Religion, of course, was ignored by the Communist educational system, except to be discouraged as mythology. But, although his father was a minister, Paul was not a religious man.

One day Paul went to the Children's Theater to see a play called *The Negro Boy and the Monkey*, a Communist propaganda play to be sure, but one dedicated to a theme dear to the heart of Paul Robeson. In this play a Negro boy finds himself in Moscow and grows up to work in a factory, and becomes a leader. He has left a pet monkey in Africa. (The monkey's connection with the play is strictly to provide motivation for trips back and forth to Africa.) The monkey appears in Moscow in a circus and he and the boy are reunited in spite of the miserable, evil, private entrepreneur of a circus owner, who is a Russian Simon Legree. The boy and the monkey return to Africa with gifts for all the boy's little Negro friends, and a speech:

"These presents are from the children of Moscow," said the boy, "to the children of the dark forest. For the Moscow children wish every child in all the world, be his color white, red, yellow, or black, be his race what it may, and his language what it may, to enjoy the same full richness of life as Moscow children now enjoy."

Paul had been prepared well for his visit to Moscow. He had spent some time with the Dean of Canterbury, who was very favorably impressed with the Soviet experiment, and who had suggested that in their advocacy of the brotherhood of man the Soviets were fundamentally Christian in concept.

Thus, slowly, the conditions were created for Paul to become a political man, and the sights he saw in the Soviet Union aroused his sympathies because the Soviets proved themselves dedicated to dealing with the colored peoples of the world on a basis never before attempted by whites—the basis of actual, true equality. No Negro who came to Russia, if he were sincerely concerned with the condition of his Negro fellows, could help but be favorably (how weak a word) impressed by what he saw in Moscow. With Paul, the cause of the Negro had become a personal crusade. His eyes were wide open, taking in what he saw and heard about him.

The Russians are a friendly people, once they know to whom they are talking, and Paul found open-handed friendliness all about him. Even less than the English did the Russians have familiar relations with black peoples, for Russia had never ventured into African colonization. The Russians had no racial prejudices, and greater Russia was such an amalgam of racial varieties that any kind of prejudice could not be tolerated. Of course, speaking politically, it was absolutely essential that the

Soviet State wipe out any vestige of racism, in order to hold
the Union together, but except for anti-Semitism, there never
had been much racism in Russia, or in European Russia at
least.

Paul was taken wherever he wanted to go. The American
Negroes in Moscow all told the same story: they were treated
with absolute equality. There was no discrimination in the
Soviet Union.

The interest Paul showed in this matter transcended all else.
He visited the government bureau which handled the affairs of
the Russian national minorities. He heard the story of equality
there, too. Soon he was convinced, and when he became
convinced that here, at last, was a European, civilized country
which accepted the Negro for his personal worth, Paul was
overwhelmed with affection, the feeling of need to identify
himself with this progressive nation. To the white American,
the cultural and social values of the U.S.S.R. would always be
subsidiary to political and economic values, but Paul had no
reason to think in that manner. The Negro problem in America
was a social and cultural problem. The Negro was not complaining so much about being poor or deprived of the physical
niceties of an industrial civilization. Like any other human
being, the Negro liked to dress well, live in a clean, well-
lighted, warm house, and drive a new car; yet these matters
were not even to be considered by the average American
Negro; before he could worry about such luxury, he must first
achieve status as a full human being in the United States. Paul
Robeson could not be expected to identify himself with the
white Americans of the year 1934 in his attitude toward the
Soviet Union, or even perhaps at any other time in his life,
given the Negro view of life, and Paul's chosen mission in
behalf of the Negro.

In 1934, when Paul went to the U.S.S.R. for his two-week
visit, he was not embarked on that mission. He was always
slow to act; in 1934, Paul was considering the role he might
play in the affairs of the colored world. The associations with
Kwame Nkrumah, with Jawaharlal Nehru, and with scores of
other colored people who would one day be rulers, were

making themselves felt in Paul's consciousness, and very much so through the constant discussions with Essie. But they were feelings—no more than that.

Paul was very well treated by the Russians he met. He was kissed on the cheeks and embraced by men and women, in the traditional friendly Russian gestures. What impression this must have made on the American Negro, with his inherent fear of rejection by people with white skins! He visited the Kamerny Theater, which had added *All God's Chillun Got Wings* to its repertoire. He was greeted with embraces by theater director Tairov and his wife, although they had never seen him before. He visited the house of Maxim Litvinov, the Soviet Foreign Minister, who welcomed him in a darned pullover sweater and carpet slippers, and who slapped him on the back and made him take off his coat. There was a huge Christmas banquet at the Litvinovs, turkey and caviar, wines and vodka, and before the dinner was ended the party became very gay. Paul sang Negro spirituals for them, and then danced with the ladies. Here he was, an American Negro, rubbing elbows with Soviet field marshals, the foreign minister of the country, the foremost movie producer, and all their families.

During this trip to Moscow, Paul visited William L. Patterson, the Negro leader of many radical causes, some racial and some not. Patterson had recently led a defense of the Scottsboro Boys, that group of Negroes condemned by whites in America for an alleged assault on a white woman. In that defense organization, Patterson had been allied with the official policy of the American Communist party. To another American, a white one, Patterson's allegiances might have made him suspect, but to Paul the important matter was that William L. Patterson was working for the betterment of the Negro. Patterson, being an intensely political figure, importuned Paul to return to the United States and carry the fight for Negro rights. Paul was not yet a political character. He was silent. He had no wish to go home to America and live in an atmosphere of racial tension.

Paul did some singing in Moscow. He sang for the workers at the Kaganovitch ball-bearing plant. He sang on Christmas

Day for the film workers in Sergei Eisenstein's organization, at a party given in Paul's honor by the Soviet director. At this latter party he sang in Russian—the song of the dying Boris Godunov. The Russians in the audience, and, of course, it was a very informal audience, went wild when he had finished singing the song they knew so well, but which they did not expect a foreigner to know. They swarmed around Robeson, embracing him and calling him by the diminutives of his name that the Russians use to show affection. In the streets, too, he was stopped by small white children who clasped his legs in their arms and grinned up at him. The feeling was very warming and very pleasant; it would have been so for any American, white, yellow, or black; it was exceedingly pleasant for a black American who had never known such open friendliness from whites.

Early in January it came time for Paul and Essie to go home, but Paul had new plans. He confided in the press that he would spend little time in England or the United States in the future. He would go to Africa the next year, he said, but he also would come back to Soviet Russia. He hoped to spend part of every year in the Soviet Union from this time on. It was not a question of politics. When he was asked to comment on the Communist political and economic experiment, he said he knew nothing about politics and was not competent to comment. He was friendly to the Russians and to their way of doing things, however, and to the Soviet experiment, he said.

During Paul's trip there was one sour note—although he probably never knew anything about it. Because he was in Moscow, various officials of radio stations in charge of programing made it a point to play Robeson records over the airwaves. Among these were a number of spirituals, such as "Steal Away to Jesus." That particular song became very famous. The Western press picked it up, amused at the anomaly of Soviet anti-Christian government radio stations lauding Jesus. It was said later that some heads rolled at some radio stations, too, for this lapse. Such an incident would not have come to Paul Robeson's attention, and if it had, it would not have meant anything to him. If the Dean of Canterbury could justify the Soviet experiment, then who was Paul Robeson to question it on a moral basis? Besides, these two weeks in the Soviet Union had impressed Paul more than any other fortnight in his life.

"All I can say," he said later, "is that the moment I came there I realized that I had found what I had been seeking all my life."

Chapter 7

AFRICAN
ADVENTURES

By January 1935, Paul was emotionally bound to the Soviet Union with such strong ties that they would be hard to sever, for he had received none but the most favorable impressions of Soviet society. There were no political overtones to Paul at this time, and any newspaper reports that attributed political feelings to him were very much biased or represented reporters who were misinformed.

Paul's real feeling was that he would like to ignore the white world; this much was apparent in his hope that he might somehow help establish a home for the Negro people and bring about a flowering of Negro culture. The real difference between Paul and other Negro Americans, to say nothing of white Americans, was that he did not think in terms of recreating the American system, but he accepted that system for what it was and wanted Negroes to escape.

He wrote later in the year: "Africa does not realize that it has something to contribute, that it has a culture as clear as the European. Africans, instead of preserving their own culture, are fighting the ideas of 'be what you are' and go European as soon as they can."

Paul also said the Negro could not develop his culture until he was free, but Paul was talking about the African Negro, who now interested him much more than his fellow Americans.

Paul also said this: "Russia is the father of experiment. The Russians will save the white world from complete destruction when the black man and the yellow man rise up to avenge themselves. They will show that men are equal; that difference in color does not make men the enemies of one another."*

Many years later, in discussing Paul Robeson, editor James Hicks of New York City's Amsterdam *News* said that in his study of Robeson's career he had suddenly realized that Paul was saying all the things that American Negro leaders were saying in the 1960s—and saying them twenty years earlier when no one in America was listening.

Paul received a lesson in the economics of capitalism in 1934 and 1935 in London, one that touched him deeply, because quite beyond his control, he was pushed into a position of giving a public performance that was not true to his own spirit or his conception of his role in life.

The lesson began in the summer of 1934, when Paul was approached by London Films to take the role of Bosambo, the Negro tribal chief in the film adaptation of Edgar Wallace's novel, *Sanders of the River.* Paul was attracted to the project because it was described to him as an opportunity to show much of the true African culture. London Films had sent Zoltan Korda, brother of director Alexander Korda, to Africa to record tribal music, and he said this music would be used in the film. For five months Korda had tramped through Uganda, the Sudan, and the Congo, taking many thousands of feet of motion picture film of African background, and more thousands of feet of film of native dances and rituals. The sound engineers had recorded African sounds, from the noises of the jungle to the speech of the African peoples.

Paul liked the idea of showing reality in Africa that was proposed here. He liked it more when he was given some of the African recordings and played them at home on his phonograph. He particularly liked the music: the war songs, river songs, and tribal chants of the Africans, and he considered this to be a marvelous opportunity to associate himself with Africa. The movie was also outlined to Paul as a heroic drama of African life.

* Marie Seton, *Paul Robeson* (London: Dennis Dobson), p. 94.

Paul agreed to take the part of Bosambo. The motion picture producers found scores of Negro dockworkers and other black men to play in the crowd scenes, and Paul began learning his lines. The part was dignified and reasonable. He enjoyed working with the extras, because they were real Africans. He told of one incident during the filming of the motion picture when he overheard one of the Africans speaking his native language—and found that he could understand a few words although he had never studied the language. The man came from the Ibo tribe in Nigeria, to which Robeson's father's family owed allegiance, Paul said.

Paul filmed most of his part for *Sanders of the River* before he left for Moscow in 1934. When he came back to London early in 1935, he learned that certain retakes were necessary and he went to the studios to continue the work. In the meantime, he was also appearing in *Basalik,* a London play, in which he played the part of an African chief of considerable dignity. During the retakes for *Sanders of the River,* Paul learned that the focus of the film had been entirely changed since he had been in Moscow. Instead of a cultural triumph of African sounds and sights, the film had been cut back to become a mundane tale of British colonial superiority. Paul's part had been reduced to make him a subservient African chief, bright dream of the colonialist; the music and all that Paul had loved in the film were gone. New scenes had been written into the film to glorify imperialism, this last the farthest from Paul's desires.

Paul tried for a time to escape altogether by breaking the contract, but the contract had no escape clause. He had to finish the film. In April, when *Sanders of the River* opened at the Leicester Square Theater in a gala premiere, Paul and Essie were there, suffering, for the whole was worse than its many parts from their point of view. At the end of the program, Paul was called to the stage to make a speech. In protest against the film, he refused to perform. The protest was the first he had ever made against the misuse of his art. He began to become a protester. Biographer Seton says that at this point in his life, Paul began to study Marxism for the first time.

Perhaps it was the *Sanders of the River* role, or perhaps that mischance caused Paul only to accelerate ideas that had been gestating in his mind since the Russian visit, but he took an active interest in Russia and Communism in the spring of 1935.

One might call 1935 and 1936 the Robesons' African years. Paul was talking about making a trip to Africa. He had been invited to visit Uganda by a cousin of the King of Toro in that colony. Essie had been studying anthropology at the London School of Economics and London University, and she had chosen to do her independent research in Africa. The family planned to leave immediately after the premiere of *Sanders of the River*. Yet, in the end, Paul decided not to go to Africa. He had several commitments in London. Perhaps these would not have stopped him at another time, but on the heels of the disaster to his psyche of the *Sanders* film, he decided to remain and work on a play and a film that depicted Negroes as he wished them shown.

The play was *Stevedore*. The film was *Song of Freedom*.

So, shortly after the release of *Sanders of the River*, Essie and Paul, Jr., made their plans to leave for Africa. They went in 1936. Paul, Jr., was now eight years old and a remarkable child. His languages included French, German, and English because he had spent much time on the European continent. As a child he had been subject to respiratory ailments, and the doctors had advised a drier climate than that of England. Paul, Jr., and Grandmother Goode had gone to the Austrian Tyrol for a time, where Paul, Jr., acquired the nickname Pauli that was to stick to him. There had been a year of school in Switzerland; now he was to go to Africa with his mother.

On May 29, 1936, Essie and Pauli took the boat train from Waterloo Station, and they were gone on the great adventure, while Paul stayed home to work.

Paul played in several theatrical performances, one of them *Stevedore*. This play was another of the experimental plays at the Embassy Theater. Paul had some hope that this production might mark the beginning of an all-Negro theater in London. Most of the characters in this production were Negroes, which marked another departure, an advance from Paul's point of view. There was considerable trouble in assembling the cast, because it was an American play, and the Negroes in London were mostly Africans or West Indians. Some of them objected to playing the parts of American Negroes. Three Americans played roles: Paul played the male lead, Lawrence Brown was dragooned into service to play a role, and so was John Payne, an old friend of Paul's.

Stevedore was a serious play, social commentary, presenting the Negro in a heroic role against white exploitation and mistreatment. The play opens with a white woman quarreling with her white lover. The lover knocks her down and to conceal her adultery and account for her bruises she says a Negro tried to rape her. The police pick up Negroes, including Lonnie Thompson, a stevedore (Paul), but the white woman fails to identify any of them. Lonnie is involved in organizing the dock men for a union, and he is warned by the company representative to stop it. He does not. He is framed for the "rape," and a lynch mob comes after him. He rallies the Negro community against the white mob. In the end, Lonnie Thompson is shot at the barricades, but white and black workers band together to fight off the mob.

Paul had complained for many years about the paucity of parts for Negroes that showed them in roles other than what the Negro community would later call Step-N-Fetchit, after the movie actor in Hollywood who always played a shuffling, stupid Negro. Now, in rapid succession, Paul sought and found roles that portrayed the Negro as a serious and dignified person in plays that came to grips with some of the Negro's problems.

Paul hoped to go back to Moscow in the summer of 1935 or 1936 to film *Black Majesty*—the story of Toussaint L'Ouverture, but, in the spring of 1935, Sergei Eisenstein began work on another film, and the opportunity was lost. Paul's services were very much in demand, even though he made himself very hard to get. He developed a habit in London that he was to continue for many years—he did not answer letters and he did not answer the telephone. The way to be in touch with Robeson was to find someone who was intimate with him and send a verbal message. If Paul was interested in the project, he would make it easy for a meeting to be arranged.

In August 1936, Essie and Pauli came back from their tour of Africa. They had gone by steamer to South Africa and had then come up the continent, overland, to Egypt, stopping along the way for visits and studies by Essie. She kept a journal, and from her journal she prepared a book describing the trip and the reactions of an American Negro to it.

When the Robesons went back to the United States, Paul decided that Pauli ought to see something of his own country, and he was put in school in America. Paul had spent several months there, in concert tour, and had appeared as Joe once again, this time in the film version of *Show Boat.*

Even in the autumn of 1935, before he reported to Hollywood, Paul had the next few years of his life mapped out, or thought he had. He had still intended to go to Russia for a time, when he finished *Show Boat.*

"I visited there just before my last concert tour in England," he said, "and it is the one place in the world today where one can live as a human being without prejudice entering into the scene at all. In Russia you feel the vitality of a people who are building a new world; in comparison other countries are dead. I hope in a few years to be independent of the box office, free to do as I choose, and then I want to live for several months in East Russia among the Caucasians to learn their songs and explore their music."

Here was Paul Robeson again, Paul Robeson who had no particular interest in the politics or economics of Soviet Russia. He was interested in Russia as a human being and as an artist.

School in the United States did not work out for Pauli Robeson. Paul talked about sending him to Russia to be educated.

"I want the boy to be brought up in an atmosphere like the Soviet's if possible," Paul said, "that is, to be brought up as a free human being. I don't see why he should have to bear the burdens of racial prejudice—the world is too big for that today. In France, in England, and in fact here in America, too, I have no difficulty personally. Yet France and England have definite deadlines racially, and while New York is better than Georgia in this respect, I feel that as long as this burden of race is borne by any of my brothers, I, too, bear it."

In this period, the middle 1930s, Paul's views did not upset
very many Americans. They were stated with quiet logic, for
one thing. For another, the United States in the middle 1930s
was so deep in economic depression that there was very little
super-national prattling about radicalism.

The American way was very much on trial, and only by
severe modification could the economic system, and thus the
political system, manage to survive the trials of the 1930s.
Paul's criticisms were so simple and so obvious that they
passed accepted or unnoticed. It was not pleasant for America
to be told by an American Negro that he would prefer to have
his son raised in a foreign country to avoid the stains of
prejudice, but the truth of the charge was so obvious that who
could object?

Paul's interest in Africa kept raising its head, even on the
American tours of 1935 and 1936. He was called on to defend
his leopard-skin role in *Sanders of the River*, and he did
defend it in those years, even though he was ashamed of it and
later said that he had been misused. In the Bosambo role, he
said, he was "the spirit of an authentic forthright race with a
language good enough for the Bible and other heritages of
English literature to be translated into."

In the 1930s in America Paul faced some new problems—
family problems. He regarded himself, without particular
pride, as a "folk-song singer," and he was content with that
role, although he wanted to extend it. He was interested in
Negro art.

"And yet my mother's people, who are in Philadelphia, and
who were educated, the intellectuals of my family, think that I
am just playing some game when I tour as a concert singer or
appear in plays abroad or here.

"They want me to have done with such 'nonsense' if you
please, and return to Philadelphia and practice law. You see?—
Like the white man. Believe me, I have no such intention. I
shall keep on as I have till the day I die."

"All Negroes are exhibitionists," Paul said, "and I say this
with no intent to slight myself or my race. Rather I mean that
we have a natural ebullience. And this, too, stems from Africa

and not from Harlem. Thus I have no call to the law, challenging the white man. I have a definite call to delineate the Negro and to dispense, so far as my talent may permit, his art."*

What a change seven short years had made in Paul's life and in his approach to life! He had gone to Europe in 1928 as an American seeking refuge from the disappointments and unpleasantnesses of segregation. Essie's loud complaint of that era had been that her husband, a burgeoning star of concert stage and theater, could not enter a decent restaurant. Nearly all of Paul's early press interviews in some way touched on the race problem in a personal way. He praised life in London early in the 1930s because he did not encounter discrimination. By 1936, he said he *could* eat in restaurants in midtown New York without difficulty, and he said he no longer had personal problems of discrimination. But, by this time, Paul was no longer talking like an American. He had not given up his American citizenship, but he had become an international man. He had chosen to cast his lot with the Negroes of the world, in Africa or wherever they might be, and he had decided then that Russia was the country of all in the white man's purview where he would prefer to live. The change had come over Paul because of his personal accomplishments and his personal struggles. It had been a creeping change, but it was none the less definite and purposeful for that.

* New York *World Telegram*, October 15, 1935.

Chapter 8

SONG OF FREEDOM

In the middle 1930's Paul made several motion pictures, although he objected very much to being asked to portray Negro figures who did not live up to his own heroic proportions. One film that pleased him was *Song of Freedom,* which had sprung from discussions on the set during the filming of *Sanders of the River.* The story told of a West African queen who betrayed her tribe during the days of the slave trade with Europeans, and allowed the Portuguese to enslave many of her followers. She was killed and her descendants fled to the Portuguese for protection. Instead of protecting them, the Portuguese made slaves of them.

In this film Paul played the part of the last of the queen's descendants, a role that called for a certain dignity and again explored the difficulties of the modern Negro. Paul was a dockhand born in London who had an odd possession about which he knew nothing. It was a carved disc, handed down to him by his father, who had received it from his father. (The disc was actually the talisman of the wicked old queen, but her last descendant did not know that.)

Paul becomes a successful singer, meets an anthropologist who traces the origin of his talisman back to the African tribe, and Paul gives up his career to go to the African island of his ancestral past and convince the people that he is their ruler and that they must come out of the stone age. The title, *Song of Freedom,* comes from a tune that runs through Paul's mind, a tune that his ancestors handed down to him. By singing it, he establishes his identity.

Melodrama? Of course, but the kind of melodrama that might have been written by Paul Robeson had he been a film writer. The story line fit Paul's private dreams, and he was delighted to play the role of John Zinga, the lost prince.

This was, in a sense, Paul's picture. He dominated the set and he had his way about everything; in his contract he even had the right to approve the finally-edited version of the film. He had learned much from his experience in *Sanders of the River.*

Filming had begun in the autumn of 1935, and, in the early months of 1936, a camera crew traveled to Africa to secure background pictures and sound track that were typical of Africa. Paul was in America part of this time, and then in London, where he appeared that spring in a new play. He was a very busy man. Immediately on his return from American filming of *Show Boat,* Paul had gone on concert tour, and on ending the concert tour he had opened in the play *Toussaint L'Ouverture* in London. The play had been written by a young West Indian Negro named C. L. R. James. Paul announced that *Song of Freedom* would be finished and then he would give serious thought to establishment of his repertory theater for and by Negroes.

In August 1936, the *New Statesman and Nation* published a brief article comparing Western society and that of the African people and the Far Eastern people, an article supposedly written by Paul. Perhaps it was, but it showed a great deal of Essie in it, with her studies of anthropology and her particular interest in unearthing the positive aspects of Negro primitivism. Among the many points to be made (some of which contradict other anthropological works) were the fundamental ideas that Western man thinks in terms of abstractions and the Negro thinks in terms of concrete symbols—which seemed to Paul in this article to make all the difference between their mentalities. Western or white man was given credit only for achieving applied science; all other accomplishments of hu-

manity, "the full flower of the highest possibilities in man,"
were credited to a mentality shared by the dark men, such as
Africans, Mayans, and Chinese.

Within the white society, Paul said, "mathematical thinking
has made them so intellectualized, so detached and self-
conscious that it has tended to kill this creative emotional
side." Only a handful of rebels among the bourgeoisie, and
some from the proletariat, had managed to escape this stunting
of man's growth, he said.

And here was the key to Paul's thinking in 1936: "Perhaps
the recognized fact that over-intellectualism tends toward im-
potence and sterility will result in the natural extinction of that
flower of the West that has given us our scientific achievements, and to the rise of the more virile, better-balanced
European, till now derided and submerged. Some people think
that in the European proletariat this new Western man is
already coming to birth.

"It is some such solution as this which I imagine will solve
the problem of the further progress of the world."

Paul kept pounding at one theme that attracted him: a
common root for Negro, Asiatic, and prehistoric American
civilizations. He pointed to the music, which he had studied.
He pointed to the languages, which he had also studied, and
he found many similarities between various art forms and
symbols. Earlier, Paul had tried this theme out on Sergei
Eisenstein and had received sympathetic encouragement. So
Paul's social philosophy was now acquiring an underlay: he
was building for the Negro a base for civilization, which would
remove him from the "stone age" category. He was also building, in that same mind, a case for Negro superiority in many
fields: music, art, and literature. He called attention to the
Negro antecedents of Pushkin, the Russian poet, of Alexandre
Dumas, the Negro writer, to show that the Negro was not
inferior. At last, too, in 1936, Paul was finding a political
philosophy to fit his social theory. Western technology, said
Paul in this *New Statesman* article, did not function "except in
a socialist framework."

Paul's progress, it might be called, this gentle movement
toward a Socialist philosophy. He had come to Europe for

personal reasons, to make a career, to earn a fortune, and to escape discrimination because of his race. But, like any man of intelligence, he discovered that success, once achieved, was not enough, and that he must have a goal. Slowly, he chose the goal of helping his people, beginning first in the abstract concept of helping all the colored peoples in the world by his own successes, then turning to pointed demonstrations of colored abilities. In eight years Paul had achieved the position on which he rested in 1936.

It was still a very personal and very narrow position. Paul was not out to revolutionize the world; he was not yet a revolutionary; he was seeking to direct and help only one segment of society, the Negro world, and in this he was not making any effort to change the social or political systems of the world.

Personally, he admired the Soviet system, following his two-week visit to Moscow in 1934 and 1935. The reason was almost all racism—but not *entirely* that. He came back, noting that Sergei Eisenstein was quite free to take six months or two years in making a film. Under the Soviet system, Paul said with some envy, the economic problems that existed in the capitalist world were not present. He was very much conscious of this difference after the release of *Sanders of the River*—for the excuse given him for the change of emphasis and the disfigurement of what he had hoped would be a work of art was the commercial need of pleasing an empire-minded public. He did not choose to look into the restrictions placed on Sergei Eisenstein in another sense: Eisenstein dare not, did he wish, criticize the Stalin regime.

Had this latter point been suggested to Paul, he would have regarded it as red-baiting. Why should Eisenstein wish to waste his talents on carping when there was so much positive to be done in the building of this new society? Paul Robeson's view of the Communist world, as his view of the white world in general, could be understood by whites only if they disassociated themselves from their own traditions. The white traditions of capitalism, political freedom, social justice, and economic opportunity meant absolutely zero—nothing—to Negroes, simply because, in Western society and particularly in

American society, Negroes enjoyed the fruits neither of capitalism, political freedom, social justice, nor economic opportunity, and the Negro in America saw this absence of truth
around him every day. The exceptions were so few—bankers,
insurers, Negro gangsters, Robeson, that they scarcely needed
to be cited in 1936.

With this attitude in mind in the summer of 1936, Paul
Robeson's experiences of that year could be seen to be leading
him along a definite path.

First, in September, he began work on a new film, *King
Solomon's Mines*, which was to star Sir Cedric Hardwicke as
an explorer who sets out to discover the lost mines of the great
king, located somewhere in the wilds of Africa. Paul was to
play Umbopas, an African chief who helps the white searcher
in his quest. Paul had hopes that this film would again allow
him a dignified performance, but from his point of view (and
that of many English critics) the film turned out to be another
melodrama. The story—H. Rider Haggard's novel—was so
melodramatic it seems hard to believe Paul could have had
much hope, but he did propose to make of Umbopas a real,
living character, instead of the usual stereotype of the African
chief. His hopes were dashed on the cutting-room floor.

Later in the year, Paul undertook a new film role, not so
much because he was the Phoenix who rises from its own
ashes, as because he was not yet in the position he hoped one
day to achieve: to be "free of the box office," as he put it. Yet
the new film, called *Jericho* in England and *Dark Sands* in
America, did promise much. Paul was to play the part of
Jericho Jackson, who is court-martialed in the accidental kill-
ing of a bullying Negro sergeant. He escapes and meets a
white soldier who is also fleeing. They go to Africa. An officer
who has befriended Paul is disgraced and imprisoned, and,
when he is freed, he comes looking for revenge, but relents
when he sees Paul married to a Sudanese princess, leading an
upright life.

Paul's hopes were again high. The Negro role he was to play
showed him as a soldier, as the leader of his tribe of Africans
on a dramatic trek across the Sahara Desert. The story gave

promise of racial equality for mankind—by showing the friendship between black man and white man. Paul was also excited by this idea because part of the film was to be shot in Africa, and he would be able to make his first trip to his ancestral homeland. Paul stated all these hopes publicly. It was apparent that his feeling of the separateness of the Negroes of the world was not aggressive in the sense that he wished them to rise up and dominate the whites; rather, it was a feeling of longing and a search for a basis on which the whites would accept the Negro as offering something unique to the world.

In this mixed emotional atmosphere of hope and color consciousness, growing political feeling and excitement, Paul again visited the Soviet Union, in December 1936 and January 1937. One purpose of the trip, from his point of view, was to have a glimpse of Soviet Asia and the Caucasus, where the backward, primitive peoples of the U.S.S.R. lived. He gave concerts in Moscow and concerts in factories in European Russia, but he also had his wish and he went East. He saw what the Soviets had done to promote the transformation of primitive peoples to a level of industrial civilization in one generation. Some of these peoples had been herdsmen, living in a stone-age society as did the herdsmen of Black Africa, and twenty years later they were working tractors across the land, reading newspapers where before there had been no written language, attending schools and universities, and writing, producing, and staging their own dramas.

At the end of this trip to the Eastern Republics of the U.S.S.R., Paul made the final decision that Pauli would go to Russia to school as soon as he had mastered enough of the language to make his way. Paul was convinced that the Soviet system offered minority peoples their chance to come into the twentieth century, not as supplicants but as equals.

". . . I found the real solution of the minority and racial problems, a very simple solution," he said. "Complete equality for all men of all races."

He reasoned that if the Uzbeks and the Yakuts could do what they had done in less than twenty years, aided by European Russians, so could the Negroes in America and so could the Negroes in Africa. "I saw with my own eyes," he said, "that people are not 'backward' because of color, but because they are kept back."

Paul could not imagine, he said many years later, how any Negro could fail to be pleased to see what he had seen in the Soviet Union in 1936. How effortless it seemed for the colored peoples of the U.S.S.R. They "walked secure and free as equals," and this was all that Paul wanted for his son and for his people.

After renewing old friendships in Moscow, Paul returned to London and then went to Egypt for his first look at Africa. The purpose was to film scenes for the new motion picture, but this was only part of Paul's purpose. He wanted to see for himself some indication of the Africa of which he had dreamed for so long. In his years of study of African languages at the London School of Oriental Languages, he had discovered bits of Negro philosophy and epic poems that had been handed down, generation after generation, as with those of the Greeks Hesiod and Homer, which were told long before they were written down.

"It is astonishing and, to me, fascinating to find a flexibility and subtlety in a language, like Swahili, sufficient to convey the teachings of Confucius," he had written, ". . . and it is my ambition to guide the Negro race by means of its own peculiar qualities to a higher degree of perfection along the lines of its natural development. Though it is a commonplace to anthropologists, these qualities and attainments of Negro languages are entirely unknown to the general public of the Western world and, astonishingly enough, even to Negroes themselves. I have met Negroes in the United States who believed that the African Negro communicated his thoughts by means of gestures, that, in fact, he was partically incapable of speech. . . .

"It is my first concern to dispel this regrettable and abysmal ignorance of the value of its own heritage in the Negro race itself."*

For two years this idea had been gestating in Paul's mind, pushed and pulled by his personal desire for peace and quiet.

* New Statesman and Nation, August 1936.

Paul was, as Essie Robeson had said, just as lazy as he was allowed to be.

The trip to Africa was not inspiring. Africa looked much like other lands. The Arabs he met were not Negroes for the most part, and he spent much of his time around Cairo, in Arab territory. He saw black people, and he saw poverty, and he saw the white man's colonialism at work in Cairo—more brutalizing to the subject peoples than American treatment of its Negroes. But he did not see Black Africa.

Paul went back to London, thinking, and saying very little, as was his habit. One part of his mind wanted him to go to live out his life in Soviet Asia where he could be an equal among equals, perhaps even a teacher. Here he would find the peace he sought, and still be challenged by the awakening of a colored people.

He was persuaded by Essie and others, and by his visits to the U.S.S.R., that this was not the way for him to fight the battle of the colored man. And now he decided that he must fight that battle. One important factor in this decision was Paul's look at the world around him, a world where the forces of endorsement and oppression seemed to be gaining ground rather than losing it.

In 1934, Benito Mussolini had embarked on a program of aggression against Ethiopia, a colored kingdom. Two years later, the Spanish military had rebelled against the Spanish Republic, and had organized to fight under the Falange, a party organized along fascist lines. Fascism was on the march in Europe. There must have been many moments of agony and indecision for Negroes in the Spanish war, because large contingents of black Moorish troops adhered to the Spanish Insurgent cause under General Franco. But the Russians supported the Loyalists, and the fascist dictatorships of Mussolini and Hitler supported the Insurgents, so the line was drawn, if the issues were not exactly clarified.

In the summer and autumn of 1937, Paul Robeson decided that it was his role to bring the sense of equality to men. He could never do this job in England and the British Isles by appearing at concerts for the middle and upper classes. He decided to forego further dress-circle concerts and to appear in the music halls and motion picture theaters that were frequented by the common Englishman. Admission prices in these places were as low as sixpence. Paul thus sacrificed high earnings and undertook a program of heavy work—too heavy according to some critics, who noted that his voice was suffering. He appeared three times a day in some places, and he did so in many cities and towns in Great Britain.

"I want to reach a wider audience," is all that he would say.

Soon he was appearing without thought of profit, in places that the Paul Robeson of 1928 would not have considered working. He associated himself with the British labor movement. One night he appeared with the daughter of Wellington Koo of Nationalist China and the daughter of Emperor Haile Selassie of Ethiopia in a program arranged to raise money for defense and relief in their two countries. Paul sang without charge. It was his contribution to the fight for freedom on which he was now embarked.

Paul no longer confined himself to spirituals. He sang in Hebrew, in several of the Soviet languages, in Spanish; at the trade union halls and at the Christmas Tree Fund for the poor of Birmingham. He would sing anywhere for a good cause—and, generally, to him a good cause was a humanitarian cause.

What he had seen in Egypt, what he had seen in England, and what he knew about Spain and Russia had persuaded Paul that all the world was indeed the stage and that all the people on it were the players. Before, Paul had been concerned with the Negro exclusively. But now he was convinced—perhaps by Essie, perhaps by recollection of his conversations in Moscow with William Patterson, more likely by a combination of factors in the topsy-turvy world of 1937—that the cause of the Negro and the cause of the common white man were one against the mutual enemy of oppression. The alliance might be temporary, but it was definite in Paul Robeson's mind, and he set out to work for the common cause of white and black.

Just before Christmas 1937, Paul and Essie Robeson attended a mass meeting called by the leaders of Britain's labor movement at Albert Hall, where Paul had so often appeared before audiences clad in white ties and tails. The purpose was to hear Labor's Clement Attlee describe his recent visit to the Loyalist front in Spain, and to raise money to support the Republic in the Spanish Civil War. Paul sang a bowdlerized version of "Ol' Man River," the line changed from "I'm tired of livin' and feared of dyin'" to "I must keep fightin' until I'm dyin'"—and with the change Paul's life changed, too. The roar of approval from this sympathetic audience impressed Paul. His art suddenly became the servant of his politics, and Paul Robeson was drawn swiftly into the political web. A month after the meeting at Albert Hall, Paul and Essie went to Barcelona, the port of entry for Loyalist Spain. They saw parts of the International Brigade there, and they were impressed with what they saw: Spaniards, Italians, Frenchmen, Germans, Poles, Englishmen, even Americans, giving their lives in a cause that did not directly concern them, men and women convinced that they were right, so convinced that they were willing to die for the cause.

The depths of the emotions of the people involved in the Spanish Civil War on the Loyalist side were understandable to Paul. For the first time he saw whites aroused to what he knew were the emotional capabilities of his own people. For the first time he saw whites and blacks in the Western world living and working and fighting in equality. He was impressed. Paul sang in Barcelona. He went to Madrid, ringed around by the Insurgents, and he sang there, too. He heard the bombs of the Insurgent planes, and he heard the shells of the Insurgent guns, and he went back to France and to England to sing some more for the cause of Loyalist Spain. The Republicans, to him, carried the cause of suffering mankind, including the cause of Negro people everywhere.

In 1938, Paul put aside his dreams of a Negro theater, and began helping a group of young workers in what was christened the Unity Theater. The group found an old chapel near St. Pancras Station in London. It became a Workers' Theater, with membership fixed at a shilling a year and seats at a shilling a performance. Paul became dedicated to what the Marxists called the "class struggle." He volunteered to appear in *Plant in the Sun,* a labor play written by the American Ben Bengal. He played the role of the union organizer in this play for several weeks. Then he and Lawrence Brown set off on a tour of the provinces, to give concerts for the working classes. Pauli, who was eleven years old, finally went to Moscow that year to go to school. He had been studying Russian in an English school for two years, since Paul's decision to send him to Russia, and he had been going to a Russian camp in the summers to better his Russian. Now he was ready, and he traveled with Grandmother Goode to Moscow to enter a special school, where he rubbed shoulders with Josef Stalin's daughter and Vyacheslav Molotov's daughter, and the sons of many of the new upper class of Russia, the ruling Communist leaders.

In January 1939, Paul participated in a great mass meeting at the Empress Hall at Earl's Court to greet the survivors of two British battalions that had fought in the Civil War in Spain on the side of the Republican government. Paul sang, singing now militant songs, labor songs, songs of the mines and the labor wars of America. He joined with ten thousand others who pledged their full continued support to the Loyalist cause—just two weeks before Barcelona fell. The war in Spain ended three months later, with the Franco Insurgents victorious. With its ending could Paul have gone back to his previous insulation from the politics of nations, cloaking himself again in the concern over his Negro people? It was too late. He was committed to achieving Negro freedom through political action.

What was he to do? What role would he now occupy in the white society of England?

Paul was forthright—as he always had been—in his criticism of the governments of the Western democracies for their part in letting Loyalist Spain die before the guns of the Insurgents. "Republican Spain has been fighting the battle of progressive civilization," he said, "and it should be clear that because support was not given, many more Americans, Englishmen, and Frenchmen will have to die."

The statement was made just six months after the Munich agreement which was supposed, according to the British government, to assure "peace in our time." Paul's remark was not popular in England or in America, and it cost him many friends. He believed what he was saying. He also "adopted" a hundred Spanish Loyalist children. But see the change! Paul Robeson, concert artist, sometime actor, student of philology and militant leader of the Negro people of the world, had suddenly become a political man.

In the spring of 1939, the new political Robeson went on tour of Scandinavia with Lawrence Brown. He was greeted so warmly by the Norwegians, Danes, and Swedes that he said he felt as one with them, too. Perhaps this was a part of Paul's political story: sometimes he felt like a Negro, ready to lead the Negroes against the whites; sometimes he associated himself with the working classes of the world. He would come to some tentative conclusion about the peoples of the world, and then it would be blasted by a new experience. He had not expected the people of Scandinavia to greet him with such fervor.

In the summer of 1939, Paul agreed to take what he considered to be the most important film role of his career. It was to be the part of a miner who lived in the coal-mining Rhondda Valley of Wales. The part was that of an ordinary worker—the hero of the film. This role appealed to Paul on several levels. First it was the role he was seeking, to show the Negro as the equal of the white man, in an ordinary situation which might be in San Francisco or Southampton. Second, the role appealed to his new-found political sense: it glorified the worker, the common men, whose daily life was a round of toil, with some heartbreak, some happiness, and whose mettle was tested in disaster.

Paul and the others, including director Herbert Marshall, moved to the Welsh mining district, shooting the scenes around the village of Mardy in the Rhondda Valley, and using real people and real scenes just as much as possible.

World War II began as the film was in the process. The filming was rushed ahead, and, before the end of the month of September 1939, it was finished. By that time, Paul had decided to return to the United States.

Chapter 9

AMERICA THE FREE

As late as the spring of 1939, the Robesons really had no intention of returning to America permanently. Essie wrote Alexander Woollcott late in May that 2 St. Albans Village, Highgate Road, London, was their "permanent" address. Paul was in New York at that writing, and was expected to return in a few weeks. "While I'm not exactly reeking American, I AM definitely Negro," she said.

When Essie wrote to Woollcott again in late summer, with the sailing date planned for September, it still seemed that the Robesons looked upon their trip to the United States as simply another visit. There had been many of these in the past eleven years, but at no time had Paul ever planned to stay in America. The principal object of this trip in 1939 was for Paul to appear in the play *John Henry*. This play, by Roark Bradford, with music by Jacques Wolfe, glorified a giant Negro worker, a legendary figure about whom many Negroes in the south had spun tales for years. Bradford and Wolfe had toured the south, even visited the Mississippi state prison farm at Parchman, to secure authentic Negro music for the play. The play and the music were put together for Paul, before it was certain that he would do the role. The producer was in touch with Robert Rockmore, Paul's New York attorney, and one day a meeting was held. It was the spring of 1939, while Paul was doing concerts in New York, and he was committed to finishing the Welsh mining movie that year. Paul came to a meeting, he liked the idea and the play, and he liked the music when he heard it. He agreed then and there to do the play, so the decision was made to return to the United States for a few months—no more. Pauli would go back to school in Russia. Essie and Paul would go to New York early in October for rehearsals of *John Henry*. There would be tryouts out of New York City, in Boston, Montreal, Toronto, and Chicago, and then the play would open in New York in January 1940.

Paul's welcome to New York was made happier by a gesture of Alexander Woollcott's. Woollcott had been an admirer of Paul's since those early days in the 1920s, and he had often looked up the Robesons in England during his almost annual visits there. In recent years, Woollcott had become the most prominent alumnus of Hamilton College in Clinton, New York, and he had joined the board of trustees of that institution. Now, in 1939, he suggested that Paul Robeson and Helen Hayes be awarded honorary degrees by Hamilton. The college authorities approved the idea, and Paul accepted enthusiastically. He was to have a degree as Doctor of Humane Letters with a citation honoring him for what he had done in the cause of mankind. Paul was particularly pleased by the wording of the citation, for he had a new mission in life—the spread of the concept of brotherhood.

Paul Robeson was pleased with the America he discovered on his return in 1939. The nation was, and had been, in ferment. The concept of racial equality had received more impetus in the Depression years under the Roosevelt Administration than at any time since the Reconstruction. The Radical Republican movement, which had controlled American politics for ten years after the end of the Civil War, had brought about the beginnings of a true social revolution in the United States, but that revolution had been abandoned in the compromise of 1876, and the Negroes had never regained the ground they lost that year, when first-class citizenship, once firmly in their grasp, was taken away from them. Until Franklin Roosevelt's day the Negro in America lived entirely on sufferance and half-promise. During the Depression, Franklin Roosevelt and Eleanor Roosevelt began to take steps to secure those rights. They were small steps, but they were noticeable. Roosevelt invited Negro reporters to his press conferences—for the first time. Eleanor Roosevelt invited Negro girls to the White House—for the first time. Equal opportunity became a word with some meaning in government quarters. In the past, Negroes had always been segregated in the armed services, and now this matter came under study and was to be slowly changed after America went to war.

So the Robesons came home this time to a new America, and one that offered much hope to the intelligent Negro. Conditions were far from ideal, they were not even so much changed in fact as they appeared to be, in the hopefulness of liberals and Negro leaders. But change was in the air, and this was the best sign of all. In labor, the growing unions were those of the Congress of Industrial Organizations, which rejected the philosophy of the conservative labor movement and opened the membership to Negroes. Negro and white man worked side by side in the Civilian Conservation Corps, in the Public Works Administration, in the Works Progress Administration, and in dozens of other areas of American life where Negroes had never been able to penetrate before.

After a short stay with friends, Essie found an apartment at 555 Edgecombe Avenue, overlooking the Harlem River. It was still a Harlem address, but a very good one. Why Harlem? Well, Paul Robeson would have been able to secure an apartment somewhere else in Manhattan other than Harlem, but, if he did so, he and his family would have endless difficulties with life. Things had changed in America since 1928, but they had not yet changed so very much that equality was acceptable among business people—and business people controlled Manhattan Island.

There was a racial incident almost the first day of Paul's return to the United States.

"I was invited to tea in one of the city's leading hotels," Paul said. "When I approached the front elevator I was told to use the freight elevator. . . . Several years back I would have smarted at this insult and carried the hurt for a long time. Now—no—I was just amused and explained to the elevator

boy that I didn't belong with the freight, that, as I was the
guest of honor at the tea, my hosts might be surprised to see
me arrive with the supplies. The elevator man caught the idea
very quickly. His colleagues would, too, if they were taught all
the facts. They will know, someday. In the meantime, I
know."*

Paul was questioned about the reasons for his return to the
United States. It became apparent that he *had* returned, when
he and Essie took the apartment, and Pauli was brought back
and placed in an Ethical Culture School.

Paul then explained his gradual development as a political
man. He had learned, he said, that the Negro was not the only
one oppressed in the world. He had learned that Jews and
Chinese and others were oppressed, in America and elsewhere.
There was no place in a democracy for such oppression, he
said, and the implication was clear that he would dedicate
much of his time to fighting it.

He had learned something else—or he thought he had. He
had learned that when he sang his American Negro folk songs
in Budapest and Tiflis, in Oslo or the Hebrides, peoples wept
and rejoiced and treated him and the songs as their own. He
said he had come to believe that the forces of oppression had
nearly always been the same everywhere, and that the people
of the world were all brothers under the skin, that this was the
reason for such general approbation of his work. (He had told
Essie that he was shocked to discover that the Scandinavians
had liked his singing and had cried and shouted and cheered
in his audiences. He had gone to Scandinavia afraid of his
audiences—afraid that in their blondeness they would prove to
be as racist as the Germans—and a year later he had not quite
overcome the pleasant surprise.)

He felt, he told interviewer Julia Dorn in 1939, that "when I
sing 'let my people go' I can feel sympathetic vibrations from
my audience, whatever its nationality. It is no longer just a
Negro song—it is a symbol of those seeking freedom from the
dungeons of fascism in Europe today. The same is true for the

* *The American Century,* July 1939, as quoted by Julia Dorn.

refugees with 'sometime I feel like a motherless child a long way from home—come my brother.' "*

Paul said now that his political attitude had come about because he kept close to the feelings and desires of the working classes of England—his primary audience. Thus, said Paul, he had been made anti-fascist, "whether the struggle is in Spain, Germany, or here."

Then Paul lapsed into a strange, confused statement: "This [awareness of fascism] in turn, has made me see that the pseudo-scientific racial barriers which had been inculcated in me from cradle days upward were false. Even though I had won honors in university years, somehow these honors, instead of proving that color of skin made no difference, emphasized the difference all the more, since I was marked out as an exception to the rule.

"The feeling that all this is wrong, a feeling which has come from my travels, from world events which show that all oppressed people cry out against their oppressors—these have made my loneliness vanish, have made me come home to sing my songs so that we will see that our democracy does not vanish. If I can contribute to this as an artist, I shall be happy."

The political man was not complete. Deep inside Paul lay the old yearnings and the old turn of mind. Essie and others had worked on Paul for a long time to bring him around to the Marxist point of view about freedom and the Western democracies, and they were still working on him, but Paul was conscious much more of his Negro heritage as a colored man than of his heritage as brother of all the oppressed workers in the world. The change to political man was fermenting within him, but it was not yet a complete change, even though Paul now tended to forget some of the honors that had been heaped upon him—not as a Negro—not as an "exception" but as a man of great personal accomplishment. Soon he was to go to Hamilton College and receive the new honor. Seven years earlier he had returned to Rutgers to receive an honorary

* *Ibid.*

degree as Master of Arts, and to hear the President of his old school praise his work.

"Seldom is it given to one man to bring joy into the hearts of his hearer by the arts of singing and acting as it has been given to you, and you have well discharged the trust which that gift implies. The lilt of your voice, its rich interpretations, have awakened sleeping souls, caused happy forgetfulness to others, thrilled yet others with a new appreciation of the place of beauty in a commonplace world. You have contributed richly to the happiness and culture of countless thousands . . ." said the speaker that June day in 1932. Had Paul accepted this as empty honor, and would he accept the honors to be given him at Hamilton as the empty accolades of a racist, undemocratic society? If this were true, then Paul, the honest man and honest artist, would be living a lie, and this seemed hardly likely. In all that occurred in the few months after the Robeson arrival in New York City in October 1939, it was apparent that Paul was coming to a point of decision, being pushed by forces that he did not totally understand.

Until 1939, or at least until the Spanish Civil War, Paul had been totally apolitical. He was still apolitical; the Spanish question had been for him an emotional and not an intellectual matter. From the heart welled now two decisions. One was quite predictable: a decision that as long as he remained in the United States he would not sing before a segregated audience. He never was to do so if he understood beforehand that the audience was segregated. The second decision, made from the same kind of personal loyalty, was less understandable to many Americans. Paul had barely arrived in the United States when the new partnership of Russia and Germany split Poland, and the Russians marched into little Finland to secure territory and to prepare for the future war they knew would come against the Germans. This action represented the most naked kind of *weltpolitik*, yet Paul, in his innocence, could not bring it upon himself to criticize the nation that had shown the highest degree of sensitivity to racial equality of any in the world. One might ask: why should Paul Robeson be called upon to comment on the subject? Paul felt that he must speak out among friends and acquaintances when Finland came up in discussion, which it did every day.

Paul spoke for his friends the Russians, saying that since they were good the Finns must be bad—hardly a polished or sophisticated argument, and one calculated to arouse annoyance on the part of liberals who believed they had been betrayed by the U.S.S.R. in the entire management of the German-Russian dealings of 1938 and 1939. Paul had spoken out often enough in favor of Russia; it was inevitable that this question would be asked of him whenever he met the press. Paul's concert manager and lawyer Rockwell pleaded with him to beg the issue, to turn the subject and refuse to comment on politics, but Paul could not be less than forthright. He was trapped by his very honesty into saying what he thought—without considering that perhaps he might not know the facts.

In the mid-1930s when the Works Projects Administration had provided employment for many in the theater, a poet named John LaTouche had written *The Ballad of Uncle Sam,* a poem in the tenor of those times, when radical ideas—such as true citizenship for Negroes—were making themselves felt. A composer named Earl Robinson had set the ballad to music and it had been sung in the WPA musical *Sing for Your Supper.*

In 1939, a young radio producer named Norman Corwin discovered this stirring, patriotic song, and decided to incorporate it into a program series he was preparing for the Columbia Broadcasting System, *Pursuit of Happiness.* Corwin decided he wanted to use the song, and he wanted Paul Robeson to sing it.

Paul's agent held out for so high a fee that CBS declined to pay it, until Corwin insisted. Paul's commercial fees had been high ever since he became successful; in England, on the white-tie concert trail, he had received £500 and more for a concert. He was committed to the common man but he was also conscious of his own commercial saleability.

The financial problem was adjusted. The artistic problem took even more time, because the music had been written for a pure baritone, and Paul's untrained voice could not handle it.

The music must be made to fit the voice if he was to sing the song successfully, and after much work it was.

Ballad for Americans, as the song was eventually retitled, was first presented on the Corwin program on November 5, 1939. The theme of the ballad was racial and social equality:

> Man in white skin can never be free
> While his black brother is in slavery.
> Our country's strong, our country's young,
> And her greatest songs are still unsung.

This was a part of it, a thematic part.

> Am I an American?
> I'm just an Irish, Negro, Jewish,
> Italian, French, and English,
> Spanish, Russian, Chinese,
> Polish, Scotch, Hungarian,
> Litvak, Swedish, Finnish,
> Canadian, Greek and Turk,
> And Czech and double-check American.

The song was slangy. It was sentimental. It referred to lynchings and gangsterism and political log-rolling pork-barrel, and many of the ills of America, but it ended on a note of hope, the belief that America would rise above its old self, rise "high as our mountains, strong as the people who made it."

The radio program closed with Paul's song, that day in 1939, and it was said that for a quarter of an hour the hundreds of people gathered in CBS' big New York studio applauded and the CBS switchboard operators could not handle the congratulatory telephone calls that came into the network offices from every point in the country. Overnight the song became the hit tune of America, the patriotic song of the hour, and it was sung by Communists, Socialists, Republicans, Democrats, and schoolchildren.

For the first time in a quarter of a century, Americans were becoming conscious of an international responsibility and a need for unity. A few weeks before the CBS broadcast the Roosevelt Administration had discarded the old neutrality act to make it possible to aid the allies in World War II. In an hemispheric conference with Latin nations, rough plans for defense had been laid, and there was a growing belief that this defense organization would be needed. The nation was still divided over the question of aid to the democracies, over the attitude toward Soviet Russia; and Americans were very conscious of the divisions and hopeful that they would be healed. This ferment, in part, accounts for the surge of enthusiasm for *Ballad for Americans*. It was the right song at the right time, sung by the right man.

Paul was now popular in all America and, if there were some who knew little about him, this ballad helped educate them. *Ballad for Americans* was sung at hundreds of political gatherings, and concerts (even though the song lasted for eleven minutes).

Ballad for Americans helped put the finishing touches on the political Robeson. He discovered that there were many in the theatrical world who were willing to struggle for the rights of all mankind. (There always had been these people, but they had never been so vociferous.) He discovered that the Communists and Socialists in America were more active and more open in their activity than they had been before, and he approved in general of the trend his country seemed to be following.

Paul's sense of well-being was increased late in January when he and Essie and Lawrence Brown went to Hamilton College for the awarding of the degree. At Utica they were picked up by Oscar, chauffeur to President Cowley of Hamilton College, and were driven to Clinton, then up the long, steep hill to the cluster of buildings that were the college.

Dr. Cowley made the presentation. "In honoring you today," he said, "we do not, however, express our enthusiasm for your histrionic and musical achievements alone. We honor you chiefly as a man—a man of tremendous stature, energy and physical dexterity; a man of brilliant mind, a man whose sensitive spirit makes possible your penetrating interpretations; and a man who, above all else, travels across the world as an exemplar of the humanity and greatness of our democratic heritage."

In the past, Paul might not have agreed with the last phrases of the presentation. He had never considered himself to be a

representative of America. Rather, in Europe, he had been the
refugee. In the past, Paul and Essie would have objected to
those last phrases as patronizing; indeed, Paul had complained
many times that the fact that he was the great exception
among Negroes in America was a sign of America's disgrace.

It was a sign of Paul's softening toward what he saw in his
own country in 1939 and 1940 that he accepted the Hamilton
award with considerable grace. He and Essie came home from
Clinton filled with enthusiasm.

"The good DOCTOR sends you his love and thanks," Essie
wrote Alexander Woollcott, who could not be there himself.
"Thanks, of course, isn't the word. But it will have to do until
we can find a better one. He made a little speech when he
received the degree and then he and Larry sang quite a bit.
The student body tore the roof off. It was heartwarming. Paul
was so moved, and so proud, that he could hardly speak after
the citation was read. He actually blushed so I could see the
color from the center of the Chapel."

With people they liked, the Robesons felt no racial overtones. Tina Cowley, aged three and a half, daughter of the
President of the college, asked Essie at the top of her lungs
during the ceremony "Why is your Daddy so BROWN?" and
Essie had to shush her up before a thousand people, managing
only by promising to explain later. Later she had to explain,
too, "I made it a very elementary lesson in geography," she
said.

A week after the Hamilton investiture, Paul's calm was
shattered by involvement in the argument his lawyer and
manager had so feared. He had not sought trouble, he had not
trumpeted his belief in the Soviet Union, but the issue of the
Russo-Finnish War was brought to him early in February and
in his open way he did not try to escape.

Former President Herbert Hoover was leading a drive to
bring relief to the hard-pressed civilian population of Finland.
Finland occupied a special place in the hearts of Americans
during the years between the two wars, because Finland had
been the one nation of Europe to pay its World War I debt to
the United States in full. The Russians, having temporarily

neutralized Germany in the Russo-German pact, set about strengthening their defensive position on the European front. The Russians forced upon Estonia, Latvia, and Lithuania new alliances which gave Russia the right to establish bases and occupy the countries with military forces. They made similar demands on Finland. Finland refused those demands, and the Russians took the position that Finland would not refuse unless her government were inimical to the Soviet Union.

The Russo-Finnish War was important in the United States, however, because it became another of the stumbling blocks in the road charted by Communists and liberals toward the common front the Soviet Union and its followers sought with liberals and conservatives.

Here in America, just a little more than a year after Paul had seen Russians in Barcelona and in Madrid helping the cause of liberals against fascists, he was told by some liberals that he must believe his Russian friends were no better than the fascists. He could not believe it. He would not believe it. He was distrustful of the sources, in the first place. Too often had Paul seen inaccuracies in reportage about the Soviet Union, too often had irresponsible writers and irresponsible newspapers distorted truths or fabricated untruths about the Soviet experiment.

At the end of January 1940, the organizers of the Herbert Hoover relief fund for Finnish civilians decided to raise money in New York by staging a theatrical benefit performance. They sought Paul.

Paul was known in theatrical circles as an easy touch for benefits, ever since the day that he had made the decision to sing for the Jewish refugees in London in 1934. He had sung for the Spanish Republicans, for the Birmingham *Mail's* Christmas Fund, for Ethiopian relief, for Chinese relief, and for dozens of other defense funds and charities.

He refused now to sing for the Finns, making his famous remark about reactionaries.

Preposterous as his statement was, Paul meant every word of it. He sacrificed logic for love, and politics won over humanitarianism.

For once, the press let Paul feel the steely edge of its unfriendliness. The Associated Press dispatch on the interview noted that Paul was "the foremost Negro baritone and actor, a Phi Beta Kappa, and football all-American from Rutgers, who was awarded a doctor of humane letters degree by Hamilton College ten days ago. . . ." The implication was that Paul, who owed all his successes to America, suddenly was turning against his own. "Robeson," said the dispatch, "who has lived in England for the last ten years and whose son was educated in Moscow, said he was not personally a communist . . ."

Did one have to be a Communist to sympathize with the Soviet Union? True, the war against the Finns was naked aggression. True, the war had caused many liberals to drop off the bandwagon of the United Front against Fascism. Here was the first emergence of an issue that would separate Paul from white America for the remainder of his life.

Paul was far from alone in his reaction to the cause of Finnish relief. The world of the theater had always been emotional. Men and women were successful there not because of what they believed but of what they could do, and since by nature theatrical people were outgoing, generous, and usually free from prejudice, there were many in the 1930s who were very sympathetic to the announced internationalism and humanitarianism of the Communist revolution.

So, although Paul was condemned by many Americans for his views, among the people with whom he associated he found considerable support for them. Challenged, too, he became more steadfast in his support of his new loyalty.

Paul was not yet pilloried in America for his political views, nor did these views dominate his life. The incident regarding Finnish relief was no more than one incident in a busy time.

Paul had gone into rehearsals for *John Henry.* He was to be written up in *Collier's* this year,* in a most complimentary fashion, the first major article about him in a major American magazine. Said the *Collier's* article:

* May 15, 1940 issue.

Paul Robeson is America's Number One Negro entertainer. His performance in *Emperor Jones* fixed him in that position as a dramatic actor; his performance in *Showboat* settled the matter of his place as a singing actor. Meanwhile concert audiences had named him their favorite male Negro singer.

There have been, since, great Negro actors and singers who have sat upon the pinnacle for a brief moment. But when the final curtain falls upon a show in which some colored actor has achieved stardom, or when a concert artist has rounded the circuit and the electric thrill of the final note has died, there is still Paul Robeson. . . .

Paul went on the tryouts of *John Henry,* and then, in the winter of 1940, the play was brought to Broadway. It lasted only five performances, then closed, a dismal failure.

"It is something to see Paul Robeson again and to hear the cavernous roar of his voice. . . ." said critic Brooks Atkinson in the New York *Times.* But that was about all the good he had to say for the play. "It serves chiefly to remind us that someone ought to write a musical drama that would rouse Paul Robeson's spirit and keep him on the stage."

That winter the Robesons continued to live in the apartment on Edgecombe Avenue. Paul was on tour, giving concerts with Lawrence Brown. Essie and Pauli were living in New York, Essie studying at Columbia University. Her courses were playwriting, radio writing, film writing, and elementary Russian.

Essie said (in a letter to Alexander Woollcott) that whenever anyone wanted to take her out for an evening they took her to *The Man Who Came to Dinner,* the Kaufman and Hart play about Alexander Woollcott. She must have seen it a dozen times, she said. She saw many celebrities, including Vincent Sheean, who that year was working on a play for Ethel Barrymore.

Essie was very much interested in, and also very much annoyed by, Robert Sherwood's *There Shall Be No Night,* a play whose theme was the Russo-Finnish War. Yet, even in her annoyance, there was something mild, something idealistic, and nothing of the usual Communist and pro-Communist propaganda approach.

"I saw the new Sherwood play, with the Lunts," she wrote
Woollcott. "I wouldn't have thought it possible to have a play
come off so well, with all that talk. Long islands of talk. But all
the talk interesting, stimulating, provoking, and beautifully
spoken and beautifully played. I could have wrung Mr. Sherwood's neck when . . . I listened to all those lies and inaccuracies about Russia! And I was deeply gratified to hear protests, audibly, from the audience here and there, when we
listened to some of those most annoying misrepresentations.
But on the whole it was worth my $3.30."

Paul continued with his concerts. At the end of June, he
gave a concert at New York's Lewisohn Stadium which was
attended by 13,000 people—the largest audience to which he
had ever sung. He sang *Ballad for Americans*.

The next month Paul went to Cleveland to sing before the
convention of the National Maritime Union, one of the most
militant and left-wing unions in America, and also one of those
that boasted a large Negro membership. There was a reason
for the growing association between Paul Robeson and left-
wing organizations, and a very simple reason it was, too. In the
1930s and early 1940s, radicalism and social integration went
hand in hand, as did conservatism and segregation. Paul would
naturally be a radical in America if he took a militant stand in
favor of Negro rights NOW, not Negro rights at some distant
time in the future.

And on the race question Paul was militant, there was no
mistake about that: while on tour in San Francisco, Paul sang
at the Opera House, and then went out with a party of friends
to a fashionable restaurant. Five members of the Robeson
party were white, and four, including Paul, were black. The
restaurant refused to serve them. Thereupon Paul insisted that
the restaurant owner be sued under the California civil code,
which barred discrimination in public places because of race or
color. Suits for $22,500 were filed against the restaurant.

In America in 1940, Paul became an active member of three
separate organizations. One was the Committee to Aid China.
It would be hard to remember in the 1960s that, twenty years
before, support of Nationalist China was regarded in some

quarters as radical, but this was the case. Chiang Kai-shek's Kuomintang *was* a revolutionary government. Another organization of Paul's was the Joint Anti-Fascist Refugee Committee, which was helping Spanish Loyalists escape from punishment by their enemies or from neglect by the unconcerned. This committee, not regarded as particularly radical after the war, had as its purpose the settlement of Spanish refugees in the Western Hemisphere. Paul's third organization was the Council on African Affairs, of which he was chairman. The council was dedicated to the development of new relations between the Western democracies and the black regions of Africa. It also stood for "Victory over Fascism," a common enough slogan then for organizations in the Western world.

Sometime during the summer of 1940, Paul and Essie Robeson decided to make their home in America. It was not really feasible to return to an England at war, and take Pauli back to face the Luftwaffe, or even to send him to Russia again. Essie decided to move out of New York, to escape city and ghetto. She began house-hunting in Connecticut.

After some time Essie found a house that would suit her and her family in the little town of Enfield, Connecticut. It was more than a house, it was a country estate, overlooking the valley of the Connecticut River and the hills beyond, set in two and a half acres of land. But it was badly run down and even the grass had gone to seed. For eight years before Essie decided to buy the house, it had been unoccupied, and although it had its own swimming pool, tennis court, and bowling alley, the house and grounds needed much repair.

Essie did not simply buy the house. She went to the bank which owned the property—and was most eager to sell it—and made some inquiries. There was only one Negro family in all Enfield, and it was the family of a worker. How would the well-to-do whites in the neighborhood take to ownership of The Beeches, as the place was called, by Paul Robeson, a Negro? The bank said there would be no difficulty, but Essie was not willing to let it go at that. She insisted that the bank ask the neighbors how they would feel about living next door to a Negro. The neighbors had no objections, she discovered, and so the Robesons bought the house.

Paul spent much of this time on tour, as Essie set to work supervising the installation of a new roof, a new heating plant, a new septic tank and a new hot-water system. She brought the family's furniture from their New York City apartment and added a number of seven-foot beds, because her six-foot-three-inch husband spent most of his nights away from home cramped into beds too short for him and had a fetish about such matters in his own home. Too rooms were for Paul's private use, so that he could shut himself away from all the family for study, singing, or contemplation.

As it did for Paul Robeson in America, the war brought new openings, new opportunities, new freedom for all American Negroes. They entered the armed services, and not all of them were segregated. Fair employment practices committees came to life in many states. In the West, and in the South, the demand for Negro labor grew as the nation went on a war footing, and not all these laborers were unskilled.

Paul, in 1939 and thereafter, found himself often in the company of Communists and fellow-traveling left-wing leaders in public activities. For example, he was asked, in September 1941, to join a Citizens Committee to Free Earl Browder (the Communist leader who had been jailed because of his activity against the war. Until Russia was attacked that June, the Communist line had it that the war was an Imperialist war, and not one in which America should become involved). Paul worked with the committee. He spoke and then he sang before a crowd of 20,000 people at Madison Square Garden.

Paul appeared in a motion picture called *Native Land,* an exploration of the plight of the Negro in the South, and in this he came to the unfavorable attention of Martin Dies, chairman of the Un-American Activities Committee of the House of Representatives. In the autumn of 1942, for the first time, Paul was branded "Communist" by the House Un-American Activities Committee—a charge that was based entirely on guilt by association.

In 1942, that particular charge made by that particular committee was not very important in America. The reputation of Martin Dies was not high among thinking Americans, and his committee had comported itself with so little dignity that it had sacrificed much of the respect of the nation. The charge of "Communist" in 1942, coming from that source, was not particularly hurtful to Paul Robeson.

Chapter 10

CITIZEN OF HONOR

With the exception of a handful of Americans, few people looked askance at Paul Robeson and his family for their pro-Russian attitude in the early years of World War II. One reason was that, on June 22, 1941, without warning, Hitler's armies opened a new 2,000-mile front by invading the Soviet Union, and suddenly Russia became the ally of the Western powers. Six months later the United States was propelled into the war, and Robeson's view on Russia was not regarded as odd at all. Rather the Robesons were respected as Americans who had visited Russia and knew something about the people there, and Paul, Jr., need make no pretenses about his interest in the Russian war effort and Russian victory over the Germans.

Paul was as busy as he could be. If he was not on concert tour, he was appearing on a radio broadcast with Andre Kostelanetz, or appearing in motion picture roles, such as one in a movie called *Tales of Manhattan*, which featured some of the most famous of the motion picture players: Charles Boyer, Rita Hayworth, Ginger Rogers, Henry Fonda, Charles Laughton, and a dozen others. Paul sang, and he sang again. Everywhere he was singing, it seemed, to a tremendous emotional response.

In June 1942, Paul appeared again at Lewisohn Stadium in an Interracial War Bond Rally. Such rallies were sponsored by the government, and by many public-spirited groups, for, faced with the greater danger from without, it was not difficult for white Americans to forget their prejudices and call for a united defense of America by Americans of all creeds and all colors.

Paul sang at war bond rallies and at war plants. He appeared on an endless chain of broadcasts. Paul's story, written once by Essie, was written again, this time in a novelized form by Earl Schenck Miers, manager of the Rutgers University Press. Miers portrayed Paul's college years, and Paul helped him with the novel. Here was Miers' evaluation of Paul in the summer of 1941.

> As a man he is every inch a Negro—black of skin, possessor of a gift for quick infectious laughter, sensitive, kindly, loyal, and affectionate. As an artist he has known happiness, as a good husband and devoted father he has known happiness, but as Negro he has not been immune from the tragedy of his race, and so sadness has been his troublesome companion on many a lonely hour.*

A complementary, even flattering evaluation, that, and not a well-rounded one. But it did show a part of Paul's character which at that one moment in American history appealed to the whites of his native land. The Miers' view of Paul Robeson was the view of millions of well-meaning white Americans.

Paul's political views of the war years were clearly explained in an interview he gave Richard S. Davis of the Milwaukee *Journal* in October 1941, after Russia had been attacked by the Nazis, but before the United States entered the war. Paul said,

> As I see the war, it is fundamentally a collision between conservative and liberal forces. It is a clash between those who would enslave the common man and those who would give him freedom. In such a battle, the forces of slavery can never win.

Paul spoke at length of the Russia he knew at a time when the Germans were pressing ahead, and no one knew if Moscow

* The Sunday *Times* (New Brunswick, N.J.), October 27, 1935.

would stand or fall, or what would happen if Moscow did fall.

> I think Russia will fight on, and on, and still on until somehow victory is won. If Moscow falls, there will be another line back of the Urals. There will be no collapse . . .
>
> You see, it is this way: the man we so glibly place "in the masses" sees something ahead. He sees ahead and he remembers. It is ridiculous to believe that this man will ever submit to slavery. He will die, as he is dying, but he will never submit.
>
> If these Russians down at the roots did not have faith, they could walk over to the Germans and quietly sit down. That was what so many people in this country expected them to do, and great is the surprise at their eagerness to fight, but it is no surprise to me.
>
> There will be the fiercest kind of guerrilla warfare in the country held by the Germans. There will be sabotage to make child's play of the destruction everywhere else in the world. It is absolutely certain, to my mind, that Hitler will meet defeat in Russia.
>
> Some observers babble of the chance that a new order will come in Russia after the war—re-establishment of the Kerensky regime or something like that. It is absolutely unthinkable. Any such system would not have a ghost of a chance. I tell you, and I know, that the man of "the masses" in Russia has hope and he will not give it up.

Paul impressed Reporter Davis as he had impressed so many other men and women in the world, as "a huge black rock of a man" with "the world's most disarming grin." It was the Paul of years before, the relaxed, friendly Robeson of whom a number of whites had commented that the greatest faculty of the man was his ability to make whites forget that he was black after a few moments of conversation.

The fact that it mattered whether he was white or black was the problem that still concerned Paul Robeson.

"It means little," he said, "when a man like me wins some success. Where is the benefit when a small class of Negroes makes money and can live well. It may all be encouraging but it has no deeper significance.

"I feel this way . . . because I have cousins who can neither read nor write. I have had a chance. They have not. That is the difference. And I believe that no political philosophy that does not include a chance for all of them can possibly endure.

"The reason I mention the Negro problem in America is to explain my feeling about Russia. The kernels of the situation are the same. I mean this: in Russia the people who are 'the masses' feel they have been given their chance. They may be wrong, but that is their conviction.

"People who feel that way will never again be enslaved. Hitler hasn't a chance."

Paul was speaking then of the hope of Russians, peasants and sons of peasants, serfs and sons of serfs, who had progressed and had learned to read and write under the Communist regime. He contrasted this sadly with his own cousins, who were held back, who had no education, under the democratic republic of the United States. To Paul the argument was very simple.

In a way, the war years were happy years for Paul, although he was pained to think of friends fighting and dying in battle. He made some three hundred records, he appeared in hundreds of concerts; when he could manage it, he escaped back to The Beeches in Connecticut, which he called "de ole plantation." He was a little shamefaced to admit that he owned a swimming pool, tennis court, private bowling alley, and billiard room.

Paul's rededication to the cause of the *American* Negro came in these years. When he went to Kansas City, and was greeted by a segregated audience, he continued the concert, but he was shocked and he said so on stage. He refused to tour the South on concerts, except to sing at Negro institutions, where the Negroes were kind enough to let the whites in.

For years, since the London production of *Othello*, there had been talk about staging the play in New York. Some producers had thrown out trial balloons, but always those balloons had burst on the sharp rock of prejudice. Now, in 1942, actress and producer Margaret Webster decided that she wanted to stage an *Othello* with Paul Robeson in the lead.

Race prejudice had become unpopular; for the second time in the century, the Negro was needed to help protect the white American. In the federal area, segregation was prohibited by FEPC laws, and that worked for Miss Webster. When she announced her plans, there was shocked comment, and the negative, hateful prediction that the play would fall of its own weight; remarks could even be heard that *Othello* was not one of Shakespeare's better plays. But the prejudice could not be stated openly.

Miss Webster went ahead with her plans buoyed by Paul's enthusiasm. The first tryout came in August of 1942 at Cambridge. It was decided to take the play to Princeton, then to New York.

As the war years wore on, Paul became more determined than ever to fight discrimination, and more strident about it. He was sure that the end of the war would bring about a social revolution in America. The Negro would have his freedom, he said, and Paul would fight for it. As he traveled, as honors were heaped upon him—even though when he went through the South he was forced to obey the Jim Crow laws—Paul chafed under a system that allowed two standards. He felt that his success was being exploited by the white community to its own ends, to keep the mass of Negroes from achieving the equality they deserved.

In the spring of 1943, Paul went south to present an award to the President of Tuskegee Institute, one of the most prominent Negro educational institutions. He was forced to travel in segregated cars: the dining car of his train was separated into one section for whites and one for Negroes. The waiting rooms and washrooms of the railroad stations were separated into special facilities for whites and Negroes—with the Negro facilities nearly always inferior to those of the whites.

Paul accepted Jim Crow conditions for himself, if not gladly, at least with the feeling that he was sharing (in a way unusual for him) the deprivations of his race in the United States of America. In his speech of presentation, Paul traced the history of the struggle for freedom. He indicated that out of this great World War must come the rise of the common man to greatness, and included in this grouping of common men, especially dear to his heart, was his own race in the United States.

"People of America and of the world have their great chance," Paul said, "in the winning of this war to see that a true new world begins."

On that Southern trip, Paul received an honorary Doctorate of Humane Letters from Morehouse College, another Negro institution, located in Atlanta, Georgia. It was the first special award he had ever received from members of his own race. The award referred to the leadership he had given, as a man "who embodies all the hopes and aspirations of the Negro race and who despite crippling restrictions, breathes the pure air of freedom."

There was a six-week tour to help sell war bonds, in which Paul flew across the country, stopping for brief concerts at many places. He sang at the Great Lakes Naval Training Station. He sang at a Negro Music Festival in Chicago, sponsored by the Chicago *Defender*.

Paul's singing and his public appearances in 1943 began to assume an even more militant appearance than they had during the days when he was turning to the workers of England. In Chicago he chose a public gathering to turn over a check for $2,000 to William L. Patterson, his old acquaintance from Moscow, who was organizing the Abraham Lincoln School for adult education, an interracial school whose orientation was very much to the left of center. In San Francisco, Paul sang and spoke for the Council on African Affairs, which was becoming known as very left wing, and the Minorities Committee of the CIO, which was also accused of being dominated by left-wingers.

Given Paul's absolute convictions about the place of the colored man in postwar society, he must turn to the left wing of American politics. Left wing did not mean in 1942 and 1943 what it was to come to mean later. A few months before this tour, Paul had attended a dinner of a thousand persons, at which four hundred more were turned away, a dinner sponsored by the American Committee to Save Refugees. Paul had spoken at that meeting, quite unlike himself. He had described his world travels. He had described his growth as a "fighter against fascism." He told of his first concert for Jewish relief, his trips to Germany and then to Russia, and his visits to Barcelona and Madrid. He had closed with an appeal for all-out war against Fascism in Europe and Asia, and then he had come to the point that concerned him above all others: he called for the postwar emergence of a world of free men.

Now what did this mean, this call for a world of free men?

It meant an end to world colonialism, for one thing. Japan had unleashed this force in Asia and in the rest of the world with her Greater East Asia Co-Prosperity Sphere. When the Japanese marched into the various countries of Asia and the Pacific, they ousted the existing governments. For the most part, these countries were under colonial domination. Indo-China was a French colony. Malaya was a British colony. Burma was a British colony. The Philippines was an American protectorate, not yet given full independence. The East Indies was a Dutch colony. Thousands of islands in the Pacific were governed by various Europeans in behalf of their governments. Siam, alone, among the East Asians, was an independent entity, and it had been long dominated by British and French colonial interests.

The Japanese, because they had to do so, created native governments for most of these areas, and for the first time the peoples had an element of self-government. It was government under the Japanese, and in the final analysis it was not independence, but it was closer to independence than some of these people had ever known. Further, the Japanese move changed the world. It could never be again as it had been in 1939.

Many Americans recognized this fact, among them the leaders of this dinner at which Paul made his long and impassioned speech. Dorothy Parker, the humorist, was the chairman of the dinner. Why Dorothy Parker? Because she had visited Spain during the Civil War, and she knew the horrors of that war. Other speakers at the dinner were Erskine Caldwell, Lillian Hellman, and Quentin Reynolds. Left wing?

Of course the dinner was left-wing, because the world not dominated by the Germans and the Italians and the Japanese was left-wing.

These people knew of what Paul spoke. As he spoke, the Kwame Nkrumahs and Ho Chi Minhs of the world were laying plans to secure the independence of their peoples.

The stage for a peaceful revolutionary change in the world had been set by President Franklin Roosevelt and Prime Minister Winston Churchill, meeting aboard a warship. The United States was not yet in the war, but already the United States was feeling the pressures of colonial peoples. Britain was under tremendous pressure from her colonies, such as India, where there was grave doubt that the adherence of such Indian leaders as Mohandas Gandhi and Jawaharlal Nehru could be assured unless specific concessions leading to independence were made. The Indians wanted independence and they wanted it immediately.

Thus, on August 14, 1941, was issued the Atlantic Charter. The charter was a joint American-British declaration of postwar aims. It promised that the United States and Britain wished no territorial aggrandizement, and desired no territorial changes *without the consent of the peoples involved*. It announced respect for the right of nations to choose their own forms of government and indicated that self government and sovereign rights should be restored to people who had been deprived of them.

The United States and Britain also favored equal opportunity for all nations, and economic aid and access to raw materials. They wanted friendly cooperation among the peoples of the world without economic exploitation of any peoples, the abandonment of war as a means of policy, and the disarmament of aggressor nations.

The Atlantic Charter was a truly revolutionary document, and the oppressed peoples of the world looked to it with hope. That was why it was issued, to give hope to peoples under the yoke of Germany, Italy, and Japan at a time when the aggressors seemed to be holding all the winning cards.

In East Asia, Ho Chi Minh read the Atlantic Charter and took hope. In a hundred colonial nations in a dozen regions of the world the reaction was the same.

Paul shared the position of such men, a perfectly normal position for anyone concerned with the freedoms of oppressed peoples. In the United States, however, the ramifications of the Atlantic Charter were not fully understood. Only those who could see that there was no freedom in a colonial world were able to see what the charter meant to the world at large. There were a number of such people, writers, travelers, foreign correspondents, and during World War II the prestige of these people was high.

Although political and racial affairs were taking up ever more of Paul's time during 1942 and 1943, he did put them aside enough to begin rehearsals for Margaret Webster's *Othello* under the sponsorship of the Theater Guild. By taking the play into summer stock for two seasons, and playing it in Cambridge and in Princeton, they had proved that out-of-town audiences, at least, were as sympathetic as anyone could wish to a portrayal of the blackamoor of Venice by a black man, and specifically to the playing of that role by Paul Robeson.

In spite of the doubters, they were proved right on Broadway. When the play opened in October in New York it was immensely popular. The major New York newspapers spoke highly of the play and of Paul. He had matured as actor, and his performance was far more artful than in the London production. The record for consecutive New York performances of *Othello* had been held by the production starring Walter Hampden; now the Theater Guild production with Paul in the lead ran five times as long, for nearly a full year.

This period, 1943 and 1944, marked the prime of Paul's rise in America, and the height of his personal popularity. He found that when he spoke, people listened.

Earlier, Paul had shown how strongly he felt about racial matters when he turned down an offer of $10,000 to make a brief concert tour of New England, in order to go to San Francisco and appear without pay for the Council on African Affairs.

The ambition that had taken shape years ago, on his visit to Asiatic Russia, was sometimes enunciated in interviews with friendly reporters. He told a writer for *The American* magazine that he did not intend to be a public performer all his life:

"I work harder in one performance of *Othello* than I ever did in three concerts," he said, "but I have only one ambition— to be a great scholar, a teacher, and I'll die with it. I want to teach Negroes, for I've always felt that education is the only solution for our problem. Some day I'll give up the theater and join the faculty of a college."

Paul had high hopes for the Negro. He saw that in this war many peoples were fighting battles similar to those of the Negro. "All over the world," he said, "colonial peoples are seeking and demanding freedom and human dignity." He also saw in the American government signs of a growing liberality in matters of race and freedom, and he applauded it publicly. Such applause always served to take the edge off his criticisms of his own country.

His success in *Othello* having created for Paul a more respectful audience in the summer and autumn of 1943, he began to use that new respect to expound on his philosophies. After *Othello* opened on October 19, at the Shubert Theater, he was invited by the New York *Herald Tribune* to participate in its forum on current problems of the world.

On November 16, Paul spoke. He gave a clear and forthright exposition of the position at which he had arrived in 1943: ". . . I visited the Soviet Union where I found new life, not death, freedom, not slavery, true human dignity, not inferiority of status."

He spoke of his realization that the problems of the Negro were shared by other minorities and other nations. Paul spoke as one who had discovered these facts immediately on his return from Moscow to London in 1935—although actually his political awakening was another three years in the process.

Yet there was something new in Paul's manner of making formal pronouncements: he seemed to speak in the jargon of the Communist party. Never was this more apparent than in the prepared address Paul made before the New York *Herald Tribune* forum.

Paul usually spoke informally, with a warmth and honesty that impressed all who listened to him. A few days before his appearance on the forum, Paul had been interviewed about his early life by Robert van Gelder of the New York *Times,* and he had talked of his fears and frustrations. For example, he told how he had faced one of his problems as a Negro:

"When I set up as an actor," he had said, "I didn't know how to get from one side of the stage to the other. When I started playing *Othello*—in London, that is—I was almost as bad. And I wasn't helped a bit when Hannen Swaffer—you know about Swaff, anything for a headline—brought up the question of how will the public take to seeing a Negro make love to a white woman and throw her around the stage. Now probably most people that didn't bother a bit—but it sure bothered me. For the first two weeks in every scene I played with Desdemona, that girl couldn't get near to me, I was backin' away from her all the time. I was like a plantation hand in the parlor, that clumsy. But the notices were good. I got over it."*

As opposed to that charming reminiscence consider the formal words of a part of his New York *Herald Tribune* address:

"Other people, however, besides the direct victims of Axis aggression also have a genuine awareness of the democratic significance of the present conflict. Their awareness is born of their yearning for freedom from an oppression which has predated fascism and their confidence that they can have a stake in the victory of the forces of democracy.

"The American Negro has such an outlook. It dates from the fascist invasion of Ethiopia in 1935. Since then, the parallel between his own interests and those of oppressed peoples abroad has been impressed upon him daily as he struggles against the forces which bar him from full citizenship, from full participation in American life."

* New York *Times,* June 6, 1943, Drama section.

The sentiments were Paul's. The words were scarcely his. Essie was now, she said, acting as secretary to Paul, handling his multifarious business and social affairs. Essie also was helping direct Paul's thinking—not his basic feelings about the racial question and the future of the colored peoples, but the manner in which he stated these feelings and the associations he made with them. And very much, the tenor of Paul's public addresses began to coincide with that of the Communist jargon of the day.

Yet Paul spoke only what must, a quarter of a century after World War II, be regarded as truth when he talked to Americans about the attitudes of American Negroes in 1943.

"There are three things in the American scene which today arouse the bitterest resentment among black Americans and at the same time represent the greatest handicap upon his full participation in the national war effort. First is their economic insecurity which they know to be the result of continuing discrimination in urban communities such as Harlem.

"Second is the segregation and inferior status assigned to Negroes in the armed forces, and their complete exclusion from most of the women's auxiliary services. Added to this are the insults and acts of physical violence nurtured by the segregation policy, which have been inflicted upon them in many of the camps and camp communities, even in areas which before the coming of the army camp had been free from racial prejudice . . .

"Third is the poll tax system of the South, which operates to maintain undemocratic elements in places of authority not only below the Mason-Dixon line but in our national life as a whole."

Paul explained, in this speech in 1943, hopes and fears of the American Negroes that existed almost unchanged twenty years later.

"The Negro," he said, "asks that we be clear about the great moral and practical issues involved. Do we want to fulfill our historic destiny and build a good wide world and a good life for the many (as is clearly possible?)—abolish inequalities in great measure; provide tremendous opportunities for the hitherto oppressed, or shall we follow the fascist idea of dog eat dog and let the many starve—deny the fundamental equality of all men (we'll excuse genius) and their equal potentialities given equal opportunities."

Paul indicated the direction of Negro thinking in 1943:

"Today's militant protest of the Negro people, as illustrated in the recent election of the Negro Communist [Ben Davis] to New York City's Council and the general trend of the Negro vote towards acceptable candidates rather than party labels— this militant protest represents the development of a clearer understanding among Negroes of their goals, their allies and their enemies. Negroes know that their rights can only be achieved in an America which has realized all of its democratic ideals. They know that their own struggle is bound up with the struggle against anti-Semitism and against injustices to all minority groups. They know that those sections of organized labor which have enlisted membership on a plane of strict equality constitute the Negro people's chief allies in the struggle for democratic rights, and they know, too, that the winning of the war against fascism is the first and fundamental requirement towards the realization of a democratic America."

Paul was saying something that every intelligent Negro accepted: Communist, Republican, and Democrat were all on trial before the Negroes of America. Labor leaders Harry Bridges and John L. Lewis and George Meany were all one to the Negro—how did each stand on the question of Negro rights? The heroes would be those who favored the Negro, whether or not it be Harry Bridges, with his Australian twang and his deep sympathy for Communist causes; the villains would be the Negro haters, no matter how secure their position or their professions of Americanism.

Paul also mapped his own future:

"Let me read to you something that a Negro leader in South Africa recently said," he remarked, and then he read: " 'I know, like anybody else, that although we are fighting for Democracy, we do not enjoy democratic rule in this country, but I look with hope to the influence that will be exerted by America and Russia towards our rights as I think that if the Allies win a new order of government will be brought about . . .' "

"This last quotation," Paul said, "brings to mind that once again as in Munich we stand at another crossroad in this Fascist struggle but this time the lessons to be learned and the ever present danger are much more easily comprehended, and a great responsibility lies with us here in our great America. I feel it my duty as an American to press the need for collaboration and friendship now and in the postwar world with the great peoples of Soviet Russia for Negroes hate Fascism to the death, and of all its destroyers the Soviet people have been the most potent and self-sacrificing. In their blood they are wiping much of this monstrous thing from the face of the earth. We either collaborate with the Soviet Union, England, China (our decisions must deeply influence the other nations concerned), or we can pursue a selfish path which can only lead to further imperialistic ambitions and wars which in my belief could well lead us to disaster."

So here was Paul's credo, and Paul's warning to his countrymen, expressed clearly and as honestly as he could make it in the autumn of 1943. He was an American. He had an abiding love and respect for the Soviet Union, because there and there alone among white nations he had discovered an absolute freedom of the colored man from discrimination of any kind. This fact cannot be repeated too often if one is to understand the character of Paul Robeson and the tragedy that became his in the years that followed World War II.

Not too much attention was paid to Paul's *Herald Tribune* forum speech. He had said many of these things before, singly. He had not been the only one to say some of them.

The *Worker,* the Sunday edition of the Communist party newspaper, picked up the speech a few days later and ran it in full, noting that Paul was chairman of the Council on African Affairs. True, he was, but he also was Paul Robeson, and everything he said could be directly related to the experience of Paul Robeson.

Paul was speaking out openly, and often in this same vein, and the public was listening to the star of *Othello.* He spoke at the New Jersey College for Women.

"We cannot follow the old path if we are to establish decent living in America after the war," he said. "We must keep pace with the progress of the world. We are fighting to blot out racial inferiority. That is the essence of the war and the historic period in which we live."

These words were well received, but elsewhere such forthright speaking out against oppression was not so well received.

Paul was in Boston during an outbreak of anti-Semitism in which several Jews were attacked by hoodlums. "To attack the Jews is to attack the colored race, and I trust that Negroes in Boston are as outraged as though the attacks had been on themselves," he said. "I want to see Governor Saltonstall go to the roots of this."

One statement was picked up by the newspapers. The article described Paul's words and his views, and yet there was something out of place about the emphasis. "Paul Robeson, noted Negro singer and actor, has demanded a full investigation of the recent alleged anti-Semitic incidents in Boston," said the lead sentence. Was this raising the question: what right did a singer and actor have to comment on such affairs? Probably not, but of such questioning is the enmity between popular heroes and the press built up. Paul felt that as a public figure he was impelled to speak out. Not all newspapers nor all reporters agreed that what he had to say was germane or newsworthy.

Nonetheless, the years 1943 and 1944 were good ones for Paul. He lived, during the run of *Othello,* in an apartment on Park Avenue, far from the ghetto of Harlem, and he had no difficulty in securing service in midtown Manhattan restaurants. Of course this "exceptionalism" never appealed to Paul. He knew that he was accepted as the exceptional Negro. What he wanted was to be accepted as a human being, without regard for his color. To some it seemed a fine or ridiculous line as far as he was concerned. To him it seemed completely real.

Paul and Pauli were written up by *Yank,* the serviceman's magazine. It was a very favorable, nonpolitical discussion of the two as athletes. Pauli was attending Cornell University, where he played football as his father had at Rutgers. When Pauli was sixteen years old he played end on the Cornell team.

Paul received a number of awards. He was given the

Abraham Lincoln Medal for notable and distinguished services in Human Relations in 1943. He was given the Donaldson award for "the best acting performance" in 1944. He won the 1944 Gold Medal presented by the American Academy of Arts and Sciences for the best diction in the American theater.

No matter where he went, there were hundreds and thousands of people, white and black, brown and yellow, ready to greet him and make much of him.

Somehow, because of Paul's views regarding the Soviet Union, a rumor got about that he was to be denied a passport if he applied for one. At least one syndicated columnist carried the rumor. The State Department denied the tale, or that there was any thought of refusing Paul Robeson a passport because of his political beliefs. There was nothing amiss, officially, with those beliefs in 1944, so it would have been most unseemly if the State Department had frowned on Paul's position that the Soviet Union was a home of freedom. There were some in America who wondered how Paul could completely overlook the political repressions of minority groups, even ethnic groups, by wholesale deportation from their homelands to other parts of the Soviet Union, but there was no official remonstrance or official feeling on the subject.

Paul was working hard all this time for Negro rights. He was exceedingly conscious of his position as spokesman for the American Negro. Had he not been conscious of it, he would have been made conscious of it by white America. He appeared on platforms with Henry Wallace, vice-president of the United States and with other prominent citizens. It was important to the United States that the war effort be shown to be national, and Paul Robeson lent his efforts to this task, warning all the while that the price of Negro patriotism would be Negro freedom.

Chapter 11

END TO GOOD WILL

The year 1944 opened with Paul participating in war bond drives and a special broadcast over the Office of War Information radio facilities in commemoration of Lincoln's birthday, with Vice-President Wallace speaking from Illinois at the tomb of Abraham Lincoln in Springfield. Paul was much in demand, and he was much honored; a birthday party was celebrated publicly at the 17th Regiment Armory in New York on April 9, attended by some 7,000 persons. It was given by the Council on African Affairs. The guest list included many people prominent in the theater and entertainment worlds, writers, columnists, journalists. Paul was forty-six years old, and he was happy, surrounded by friends and well-wishers.

Not all the world wished Paul Robeson well in 1944. In March, he planned a recital in Baltimore, but canceled it after he was refused the use of the Lyric Theater in that city when he insisted that the audience be seated without segregation of races.

Paul had learned a long time before to roll with that kind of punch; he expected nothing else from the South, until action was taken by the people of the United States to put an end to what he said was dishonor. Paul in 1944 was the political man, which he had not been until this time. Acquaintances noted that he had lost what some called the old "shyness," what Rebecca West called his "curious langour." It seemed that, as a

128

public figure of the Negro in America, he accepted the role wholeheartedly as a full-time occupation.

When Paul was able to escape from New York to his home at The Beeches in Connecticut, he lived a quiet life, seeing few of the townspeople, and entertaining mostly people from New York, if entertaining at all. But most of the time in these years he was not at home but traveling, either appearing in concerts, in the road show of *Othello*, which began in the fall of 1944, or in political meetings and defense effort meetings. *Othello* played in forty-five cities, and ended up with a month's run in Chicago at the Erlanger Theater, where it opened on April 10, 1945.

The Chicago experience marked another change in Paul's life. Two days after his opening, President Franklin Delano Roosevelt died suddenly at Warm Springs, Georgia. That was part of the change, although Paul did not know it at the time. There was another kind of a change. Paul's discussions of racial and international problems became defensive and negative rather than expostulatory and expository. There was reason for this change, too. The war in Europe was not yet over, and yet some in America were talking about "driving straight on to Moscow." A conference of the United Nations—the Allies against Germany—was called for April in San Francisco, and some voices in America were raised against the conference as so many had been raised against the League of Nations a quarter of a century earlier.

Paul became shrill in his demands for immediate Negro equality and immediate freedom for "oppressed peoples everywhere." When the war was won in Europe the political maneuverings of the victors began almost on the day that war ended, and with the arguments between the Russians and the Western Allies over methods of occupation, territorial question, and nearly every other matter of mutual interest, Paul's world of unity was shattered.

Some good-will still existed. In the summer of 1945, as the war ended in the Pacific, Paul and Lawrence Brown went to Europe under the auspices of the American military forces, to give a five-week tour of concerts to troops in the American

zone of occupation in Germany, to France and to Czechoslovakia. They went to Nuremburg and to Munich and to Pilsen,
to Paris and to a dozen other spots. In all, they gave twenty-
five concerts for the troops. Special services officers at the
various bases reported that these Robeson concerts were the
best received of all programs given that year by traveling
groups of the United Service Organizations.

The fact that Paul was invited on this tour indicates that he
was not yet in trouble with his own government. Most Americans were extremely sympathetic to Paul's aspirations for his
Negro people. In the South he was detested for his attempts to
interfere with social custom, but elsewhere in America Paul
was allowed his say. Not all Americans would agree with his
stalwart defenses of the Soviet Union's social structure, and his
defenses of the political system (which were always secondary
to Paul). Yet these same Americans who disagreed with Paul
usually defended his right to say what he pleased. He was not
held down, or at least there was no indication that he was ever
censored in any way in his defense of Russia or his attacks on
various American policies during this period at the end of
World War II.

In 1945, Paul represented the dreams and hopes of the
American Negro community, and that community was dream-
ing and hoping much in the manner of colored peoples all over
the world. When World War II ended, these colored peoples
expected immediate independence and immediate equality.
The Allies had indicated that immediate freedom and immediate equality would be forthcoming—at least this promise was
read into the statements of these governments (and not without reason) when the war was going on and the help of the
colored peoples was sought.

Africans, Indians, Annamites, Malays, and scores of other
peoples expected immediate establishment of free governments. In Korea, the people who had been subservient to the
Japanese for half a century met the Americans and the Russians as they came into the country—having formed already a
provisional government of their own. All they asked was the
privilege of taking over and running their own country. They

were intensely shocked when American and Russian governments in Korea established military government and ignored
their free government.

There were to be similar shocks everywhere in the old world
of colonialism. Ho Chi Minh met the incoming Chinese and
French, he was in possession of the government of Hanoi, and
ready to take over all Indo-China. He was sadly surprised to
discover that the French had every intention of restoring
colonial rule, and that the Chinese Nationalists had no interest
in stopping it, nor did the Americans.* In the Dutch East
Indies, the Japanese left a native government, and the British
sent troops in to take over and put it down. In the Philippines,
the Hukbalahaps decided that they would establish a government, and the returning Americans put it down.

In the United States, Paul Robeson and other militant Negro
leaders hoped for and demanded immediate full equality for
the American Negroes. Paul had earlier worked on such
matters as the securing of Negro participation in professional
baseball. (Satchel Paige, who had been appearing in the bush
leagues for years, and Jackie Robinson, the UCLA football and
baseball star were two of the very earliest to get into big-
league baseball, partly through Paul's interventions.)

Paul came back to America from his tour of Europe and did
not like what he saw. He became angry, and for the first time
his tongue began to run away with him.

In October, the National Association for the Advancement
of Colored People paid Paul Robeson its highest honor. He
became the thirtieth recipient of the Spingarn Medal, which
was given every year by the association to the Negro American
making the noblest and highest achievement among all those
of his race. Walter White, the head of the NAACP, presided at
the banquet at the Biltmore Hotel where the medal was given
to Paul, and Marshall Field, the liberal publisher, was on hand
to represent the white community. Marian Anderson sang. It
was a happy and impressive occasion.

Then, a few weeks later, Paul's tongue was unleashed. He
made the mistake of charging before the Central Conference

* Ho Chi Minh in interview with author, September, 1945.

of American Rabbis that the United States "stands for counter-revolution all over the world."

This remark did not go down well, either with the rabbis or with large segments of the people of the United States. It was understandable to Americans that Paul Robeson could be critical of the American treatment of the 10 per cent Negro minority, or for that matter, of all colored minority groups. The treatment of all these people—Nisei, Chinese-Americans, Negroes, Mexicans—left a great deal to be desired, and most Americans of the majority white ruling group knew it, lamented it, and were willing to take steps to put an end to this mistreatment, given adequate leadership. But Paul's way of putting it lent an edge to American thinking, the thinking of the majority. The trouble was that Paul was equating the American series of racial and religious problems with colonial problems abroad. The fact was that America and American policy did not stand for counterrevolution. Suddenly, at the end of World War II, it became apparent that the Soviet Union was seeking expansion of its territorial control and of its influence on the states surrounding it. The Comintern might be dead, but the idea of international revolution was not, and it was revived as a Soviet offensive measure in 1945.

The end of the honeymoon between Russians and Americans came very quickly at the end of World War II. It was apparent in Europe in the occupations of Hungary, Rumania, Bulgaria, and the various zones of Austria and Germany. It was apparent in the swiftness with which the Russians put down all attempts to organize an independent government in Poland, and the controls and stern measures they took to assure pro-Soviet returns in the Polish elections. It was apparent in Korea, when suddenly, in November, two months after the occupation began, the Soviets closed the border at the 38th parallel and would not permit either Americans or Koreans to travel north and south between the two occupation zones. It was more apparent in Greece, Italy, and France, when the Communists tried to take control of government.

At first the Americans abroad and at home were stunned by Soviet and Communist measures. Then Americans began to realize that the old pressures and old ways had not been wiped out by the war. Many Americans had begun to believe that the Soviets would be made less suspicious and less hostile by the victory in World War II. Quite the contrary. The Russians took the point of view that they must now build twice as fast for their own protection against a hostile Western world. The Russians began to do just this. They stripped Manchuria of its industrial resources, taking them to Russia—though by all standards those spoils of war belonged to the Chinese.

There were, in other words, two sides to the coin when American and Russian policies were compared. The problem for Paul was that he *had* become the political man. His associations, by and large, were now with people active in the left wing of the labor movement, revolutionaries, and the social reform movement. Among these people it had become lese majesty to remark on the vagaries and hostile attitudes of the Soviet Union, and this was a trap into which Paul fell. Why? One need not say why, for he was not alone. Thousands, even millions of Americans accepted the ground rule laid down by the Communists for those who would be friends of the Soviet Union: *thou shalt not criticize.* They accepted, and having accepted, they lost their influence almost immediately with the vast majority of the American people. Americans—white Americans—were usually willing to listen to criticisms as long as they were tempered and as long as they believed they were getting a fair picture. It is not within the power of any totalitarian state to accept criticism of the negative type, and consequently, particularly under the proven viciousness and terror of the Stalin regime in the late 1940s, the Soviet government pursued a policy which would be used by psychiatrists to describe an individual as paranoid—one who suffers from delusions of persecution, and who, therefore, lashes out indiscriminately against all around him.

Paul was no different from thousands of others who came to be known as fellow-travelers of the Communists. That was the trouble. His friends expected more of him, they expected him to be different. He had for so long shown a smiling, positive face to the American people—the whites—that they expected

more understanding than he was willing to give to his own
country.

The fact was that Paul Robeson did not know his own
country very well. He had not lived in that country in its hour
of trial—the years between 1929 and 1939, years in which the
hates and fears of the past were tempered, and in which the
old capitalistic economy was tempered. Paul had been living
"high on the hog" in Europe while millions of his fellow
Americans, white and black, struggled to achieve the social
changes that he now demanded so vociferously. As long as
Paul kept his temper and his head about him, and showed
himself to be a positive American, fighting for betterment, he
would be listened to by the white community. He had that
much respect from most Americans.

The tragedy that began in the autumn of 1945 was largely of
Paul's own making, and yet, given his background and his
associations, it seems doubtful that he could have escaped his
fate. Too early had he seen the rosy side of Soviet life—rosy
for him. Too strongly had he espoused a cause that might be
only partly his—the cause of the international revolution of the
common man. He could not believe that there could be a
common man who could fail to benefit from the coming of a
social revolution, but he quite failed to differentiate between
an independent social revolution, brought about from within a
country, and a foreign-sponsored political and social revolution
brought about from the outside.

And, finally, to understand Paul's turnings at this point in his
life, those who would judge him must understand the importance to Paul of the social revolution that would bring absolute
equality of races and men of all creeds. One could never say
that Paul Robeson was a dishonorable or a selfish man. He
earned millions of dollars, and he sacrificed millions of dollars
in earnings or gave his money away. Paul was, as the donors of
the Spingarn Medal had said, a noble man, a man of the
highest spirit. Had he been any less than that, there would be
no tragedy of Paul Robeson worth writing, but only the
grubby story of a Negro revolutionary, dedicated but persis-
tently wrong-headed.

Paul did much traveling in the United States in 1945 and 1946, and he was disturbed by what he learned. Sometimes he hoped that the Negroes of America were going to be given their absolute equality. Suddenly he saw, in the actions of state, local, and federal administrations, an alarming tendency to return to the ways of the days before the war.

This yearning for the old days came on every level of American society. At the end of the war there were loud cries in Congress for the immediate return of American troops overseas, without regard to American commitments to maintain peace and order.

To accompany Soviet suspicion, in America there arose considerable suspicion of the Soviet Union. One reason was the U.S.S.R.'s insistence on plunging into the war against Japan in the last week of that war and then grabbing billions of dollars in loot from Manchuria and Korea. There was suspicion in America that U.S. underlings of pro-Soviet view had influenced the Yalta Agreement, which fixed occupation lines at the end of the war, and gave Russia back territories and privileges she had lost in the Russo-Japanese War of 1904–1905.

The suspicion grew between the two nations. Perhaps, had Franklin Roosevelt survived, he might have bridged the gap— even with the paranoia of Josef Stalin. But Franklin Roosevelt did not survive, and the man who replaced him was not schooled in foreign affairs or familiar with the grand design for freedom that Roosevelt had drawn.

Roosevelt's successor, Harry Truman, was an honest and capable politician and he had in him the makings of a statesman, as he showed in the next few years.

President Truman's primary responsibility was to the government and people of the United States of America, just as Winston Churchill's and Clement Attlee's was to Britain, and as Josef Stalin's was to the Soviet Union. In the negotiations at the end of World War II, each negotiator played his role and represented his own nation. Each represented a recognized selfish interest; although all nations masked their interest as unselfish. Strangely enough, of all the nations, the United States had the least to gain in any way from maintaining order,

as opposed to disorder, and it wanted no territorial aggrandizement—at least not in the beginning. As matters wore on,
the problems of American bases grew to the point where the
military wanted that kind of territorial aggrandizement, but
these conditions did not exist in 1945 and 1946 to any marked
degree. The United States' selfish interest was far less than that
of the Soviet Union, which insisted on territorial grabs and
huge reparations. One need not argue that the victors were
entitled to the spoils—a traditional concept in war—but by
demanding the spoils of war, the U.S.S.R. certainly showed
itself interested in its national problems above and beyond
those of other nations.

It was this period of 1946, not yet ready even twenty years
later for the calm judgment of history, in which Paul Robeson
and white America parted company. Paul was intensely critical
of British slowness in granting full independence to the black
nations of Africa. He said so in May 1946, speaking as chairman of the Council on African Affairs. One could understand
his impatience. One could sympathize with it. But one could
not always go the whole way in sharing his deep suspicion of
the motivations of the British labor government.

The simple fact was that the British labor government
symbolized the hopes of a shattered Europe. The end of the
war meant an end to the old capitalism in Europe. Its successor, by all accounts, would be Social Democracy—or democratic Socialism—whichever one wanted to call it. The elements of democratic Socialism were the strongest and most
appealing of all, offering as they did the breakdown of the vast
accumulations of private capital, with a modicum of personal
freedom of movement.

Another simple fact is that the Soviet Union set out to
destroy Social Democracy or democratic Socialism and to a
very great extent the Soviet Union succeeded. Certainly that is
the story of every nation on the Soviet border in Europe. One
could always justify by saying that the Soviets feared the re-
ascendance of the old ruling classes in the guise of Social
Democracy. The fact is that it never happened or ever came
near to happening. The Soviets and their minions crushed

democratic Socialism, and in doing so they incurred the growing, deepening suspicion of the United States as to all Soviet aims and promises.

Reaction in America grew slowly, then speeded, and, by 1947, the suspicion was deep and probably insurmountable. By 1947, Soviet espionage organizations were being uncovered all over the world, with the first major unveiling in Canada. True, the Soviets had been denied access to the secret of the atomic bomb by American, British, and Canadian leaders meeting in solemn discussion in Canada. So the Russians decided to steal the secret.

All this is germane to Paul Robeson's story—this general political recollection—only because it explains why white Americans were moving away from the idea of honest friendship with the Soviet Union, and why anything made in Russia —a manufacture or an idea—immediately became suspect.

For his part, Paul was singularly immune to this suspicion. Really, he showed a one-track mind. He was concerned about the betterment of the Negro in America. He could expand this concept to include the Africans in Africa and to associate Negroes with underprivileged everywhere and thus "the working class." Yet one listened in vain and searched the printed word in vain to see Paul's praises when, on July 4, 1946, the Republic of the Philippines became an independent nation, backed by the might of the United States of America. Was not this a colored people getting its freedom almost on the dot of the schedule promised, given allowances for a world war? Why was this not worthy of comment by those so concerned with the welfare of the colored people of the world?

In July, when the Philippine Republic began trying its wings, what was Paul talking about?

He was wiring President Truman to protest a lynching of a Negro in Georgia, and demanding federal action to protect the Negroes. An excellent cause, and one could not blame Paul for his concern. But was there not a moment to say something positive about the Philippines?

It was not that Paul was so concerned with domestic affairs. He found time to complain about the Union of South Africa's strong actions against striking black gold miners. He found time to go before the most militant left-wing unions to talk of race and similar matters. He buttressed the opinions of the militants that the American government was mistreating its own people, and they buttressed his opinions that the American government was turning fascist and colonialist abroad.

Was this last charge true? If there was any truth in the charge, then the complaint must be laid straight at the door of one man: Mr. White American. There was no point in trying to blame President Truman, as the people of the left wing did. There was no point in trying to blame Congress or other government officials. The fact was that the tenor of the United States was very conservative at the end of World War II—conservative in the sense that Americans did not wish to see the Communist revolution triumph all through the world, and when that revolution was forced on people in various countries, the people of America reacted sharply. Thus began the intense American public suspicion of Communists everywhere; it was not engendered by the federal government and it did not grow by leaps and bounds because any government official ordered it. The suspicion by Americans of the American Communist party came about because the Russians took actions that Americans found it impossible to justify. Had such actions been taken by America, they could not be justified to others. Americans, by and large, were not willing to accept two standards for conduct in the world, one honorable standard to be followed by the United States and one less than honorable to be followed by the Communist world. Unfortunately there was no way to drag the lowest standard up, so the United States reduced itself to fighting the Communist threat to coexistence with the Communists' own weapons. One need not agree with this official American government policy to understand how it came about.

The country that gave the world billions of dollars without strings through UNRRA also gave the world billions through the Marshall Plan. The Russians were invited to join the Marshall Plan, but they refused, because the United States had also begun the Truman Doctrine, which was a very stiff defensive measure against Soviet expansionism in Greece and Turkey. The Marshall Plan did its job without Soviet participation. More than any other measure the Marshall Plan brought about the split of Europe into Eastern and Western Europe—those participating and those not participating in the Marshall Plan. The Truman Doctrine was equally effective. The Soviets, who seemed very likely in the spring of 1947 to achieve control of Greece and Turkey through exterior-inspired revolutionary movement, did not achieve that control. The Truman Doctrine was immediately recognized by the Soviet world as the most effective weapon that could be used against Communist revolutionary movement, and the outcry against it was immense.

That was 1947. By the spring of 1947, Paul Robeson had gone far, probably he had passed the point of no return in his adherence to the cause of the enemies of white America.

Several events vital to the life of Paul Robeson and to the cause of Negro Americans occurred in the autumn of 1946 and the spring of 1947, months when Paul was traveling across the country on concert tour. He learned of many racial incidents, of murders and violence against Negro veterans who had dared assert their rights as citizens of the South. Who wants to read of the South Carolina sheriff who gouged out the eyes of an "uppity Nigger?" Each incident made him shudder, as it would make any sensitive human being shudder.

Paul was upset. It seemed that he was almost constantly upset by the direction of events in 1946, but all his pronouncements were not confined to the matter of the Negro cause. In the fall of 1946, after the An-ping incident, in which the Chinese Communists in the Peking-Tientsin area picked an open fight with America by ambushing an American marine convoy, Paul began complaining that American policy in China "strengthens Fascism." Here he assumed the Communist line, there was no question about it. There was no question, either, that affairs in China were called to Paul's attention by someone other than himself. He was getting some very careful advice—and he was taking it. His problem was that he was taking advice from people who had very little concern with the

welfare of Americans, white or black, unless they could gain
control of those Americans.

The American Negro in 1946 was unhappy with the trend of
events. He felt that he was being thrust back into the life of
darkness he had lived forever, at a time when it seemed that
there was hope, or had been hope.

And there was much in what the Negro believed. During the
gearing-up of American industry, prior to the American entry
into World War II, thousands of southern Negroes had moved
north, to Detroit, to Cleveland, to Indianapolis, and other
industrial cities. They had been confined to ghettoes in these
cities, but to many of them even ghetto life in a northern city
was preferable to life in the sharecropping South, where the
Negro saw no money from one year to another and no one
took responsibility for their ills or their children's education.
With the move to the big cities came hope. With other changes
in the lives of Negroes came more hope. With the interest
shown in the Negro as a voting entity in the North, the
situation changed even more, and Negroes slowly began to
become aware of their power as a voting bloc. That political
power was still extremely limited, and it was not always
readily translatable into votes. Yet, sometimes it was so translated, and with the growing influence of Walter White's National Association for the Advancement of Colored People, the
Negroes were learning how to use economic and social power.
Some were escaping the ghetto of New York for suburban life.
Life for the Negro was changing—not as rapidly as he hoped,
but it was changing. These were the years in which *Ebony*, the
Negro magazine, gained strength and scope, years when Madison Avenue's advertising men discovered the Negro "market."

Two important events occurred in Paul's life in the autumn
of 1946. The first of these was his attendance at a meeting of a
delegation of civil rights workers who went to call on President
Harry Truman and issue a formal protest. Paul led the group,
which called itself the American Crusade to End Lynching.

Paul and his delegation arrived at the President's office and
read a message calling on the President for a formal public
statement on his views. They demanded a definite legislative

program to end mob violence. They insisted on a public statement then and there. President Truman was not willing to give it. Paul then engaged in a sharp dispute with the President over American foreign policies. Mr. Truman noted that Great Britain and America were the "last refuges" of freedom in the world. Paul, who had once found Britain so fine a personal refuge, now said that Britain was no such thing, but "one of the greatest enslavers of human beings." He also said that it seemed "inept" for the United States to take the lead in the Nürnberg trials, and yet treat the Negro as Americans were doing as a white nation.

At this meeting, the President took the position that Robeson and his friends ought to keep domestic matters domestic and not tie them into the international situation. Mr. Truman said he was in favor of anti-lynching legislation, but that timing was all important in the matter. That was not the time to make a statement, he said.

Paul displayed both naïveté and political ineptitude in his demands and in the manner in which he made them. One should not blame Paul for his honesty—he was saying aloud what many American Negroes believed. But there were considerations other than President Truman's desire for a "fair deal." One such consideration most definitely was politics—the art of the possible—as was shown a few weeks later when the Republicans captured control of the United States Senate and the House of Representatives. In the Senate then, the Republicans held 51 seats to the 45 of the Democrats. In the House, after the elections of 1946, the Republicans held 245 seats to the 188 of the Democrats, plus the one seat of Vito Marcantonio, the American Labor party representative.

Among all these Congressional seat-holders, one of the best friends of the Negro was Marcantonio, and he was tarred already with the brush of being a Communist sympathizer.

In the 80th Congress, such an association was fatal to legislative leadership. The Republican-Democrat ratio did not mean very much in terms of the Negro situation because many of those Democrats came from the deep South and were bound to vote with many Republicans in opposing civil rights legislation sponsored by the administration. That is not to say that all Republicans were anti-Negro. Not at all. When it came to practical matters, the Party of Lincoln was fairly well divided in this respect. Added also to the various prejudices of the individual members of Congress was the basic struggle for power between the two parties and the desire of both to take credit for any social reforms.

Paul never pretended to understand the American political system nor to worry about its inner workings. He was an idealist. He wanted a revolutionary change in the status of the American Negro. It was apparent after the White House meeting with President Truman that the Negro would not have a revolutionary change during the Truman Administration. After the meeting with President Truman, Paul remained for a time, talking to reporters, and one asked him what would be a key question in the months and years to come.

"Are you a Communist?" asked the reporter.

"I label myself as very violently anti-fascist," Paul said.

To some in America that answer smacked of evasion of the issue. It was an evasion. Why? Paul did not like the question. He felt that, by asking the question, the reporter was changing the focus of the interview. Yet, Paul was not a Communist. He so told a California State Investigating committee under oath the following month. This committee was called the California Legislative Committee on Un-American Activities. The reason for its investigation was ostensibly to see who had been burning Ku Klux Klan crosses in California. The investigation developed into a hunt for headlines.

Paul then swore that he had not been a member of the Communist party and was not then a member of the party. Having said this, and knowing that it was an insulting question, he decided that he would not answer it if he was asked again. He was on record. If there was a Communist conspiracy —which he denied—he was not a member of it. His political beliefs were his own. In this testimony, Paul again showed how and why he stood where he did on all issues of politics. He was asked why he was so interested and friendly in his interest in the Soviet Union. The Soviet Union had long ago established racial equality, Paul Robeson said.

Very simple. This was the story of Paul Robeson's life from 1946 on, a simple story. Paul became a man obsessed with a single concept, and from it sprouted all kinds of peripheral statements and peripheral arguments. But the concept was single and simple, and it had not changed from that of 1938: Paul demanded racial equality *now* for the Negro people. As long as the United States denied the Negro that equality, he would compare the United States unfavorably with the Soviet Union. He did not trouble himself about the political prisoners in Soviet labor camps. He did not worry about the suppression of freedoms by Soviet power in countries along the Russian border. He did not concern himself with reports of Communist espionage. He was concerned with the freedom of the Negro, and that alone.

The other vital change to come to Paul Robeson's life in the autumn of 1946 occurred that September. It came at the fall meeting in New York City's Madison Square Garden of the Political Action Committee, a New Deal organization. The principal speaker was Henry Wallace, secretary of commerce in the Truman Cabinet. Secretary Wallace had long been known for his efforts to help the Negroes and other minority groups in America and abroad. He had called for the development of the century of the common man, with America leading the way. Now Wallace came out against the tough policy that America was following regarding the Soviet Union. At that same meeting, Paul spoke out against lynching and against racial violence in New York State, citing specific cases that Governor Thomas E. Dewey had not followed up with official action.

The Wallace speech and the general tenor of the meeting caused a sharp reappraisal in Washington, but not of the kind Paul would have wished to see. Wallace's address had been submitted to the White House and had been cleared before the Secretary spoke but it had not been read very carefully, and when the newspapers made much of the apparent *volte-face* of the administration on its declared tough policies in the face of Soviet aggression, President Truman had to take his choice: either repudiate Wallace or repudiate his own policies. Naturally he chose to do the former, and the Democratic party was split—its farthest left wing torn away to follow Henry Wallace.

Paul's political activities now moved into a circumscribed area. That statement does not characterize his musical activities. He was very popular as a singer. He had many admirers among conservatives, and if they lamented his attitudes and his associations these days, they did just that, they "lamented" the activity. After the interview with President Truman, in which Paul spoke his mind so openly (and so rudely), the little Perth Amboy *News* of New Jersey put the matter succinctly from the point of view of American whites who liked Robeson, honored him and respected him, but did not approve of his political associations.

The newspaper mentioned Paul's strong statements to the President, including one that indicated that if the federal government did nothing to stop lynching, the Negro would do something about it. (Here was the first instance of open advocacy or warning of Black Power.) The newspaper did not like the mention by Paul that if the federal government did not intervene soon there would be riots that would require the intervention of federal troops. (Here was the militancy of the Negro, the threat of armed uprising and racial violence from underneath that all whites secretly feared and detested.)

The *News* had this comment, quite a restrained one under the circumstances:

> Newspaper accounts of the meeting of President Truman and Paul Robeson, Negro singer and All-American football star from Rutgers University, carried a note of disappointment for those who have come to respect Paul Robeson for his success in the world of music, the theater and politics. . . .
>
> Such speeches are not worthy of such a recognized leader of a minority group. The approach used by Robeson in appealing for his cause was strictly the attitude of a rabble rouser. His acknowledged communistic feelings, as evidenced in his statements, certainly did not further the crusade to end lynching.*

* Perth Amboy *News*, September 2, 1946.

The whites began to preach at Paul about his "communistic leanings" in 1946, but he paid these preachments little heed. He was not consciously setting out to be a rabble rouser. He did not have any ambition to become the Moses of the Negroes of America. Had he possessed such ambition, he would have chosen safer companions. Paul's companions were chosen by circumstance. He liked the people who stood up with him for Negro rights, not stopping to wonder what their motivation might be, if their motivation was morally superior, or who might be directing that motivation. Was the purpose of his new friends in America the freedom of the Negro, as it was most certainly his purpose?

The question has never been answered satisfactorily. Long after his departure from the Communist party in disgust, Howard Fast retained a strong respect and love for many of the people with whom he had associated in the party. They were the most sincere men he had ever known, he said. Fast stuck with the party for many years, until he became thoroughly sickened and disgusted by the tales told out of Russia about the excesses of Josef Stalin and his henchmen. The point was, of course, that, in this period of the 1940s, the American Communists were either fooled or foolers, and no one knew which, inside and outside the party. Obviously the men and women of good will who were not Communists were among the fooled, not the foolers. In their work for the betterment of the Negro (including the Black Belt idea, in which a part of the United States was to be turned over to the Negroes for their separate control and life) the Communists did what they were told. They helped the Negro very little, if at all. They hurt Robeson. They destroyed him in the end. But all the while they worked with him as friends, demanding his confidence, bolstering him in his excesses, and leading him into further temptations, all in the name of the betterment of his people.

Chapter 12

YEARS OF TRIAL

Those who tend to oversimplify American political trends point to the campaigns of the House of Representatives Committee on Un-American Activities and the activities of Senator Joseph McCarthy of Wisconsin as establishing the mood of "witch hunt" in America during the late 1940s. The fact is that these activities were symptomatic, not causative.

The cause of a surging American anti-Sovietism and anti-Communism was the realization in 1946 and 1947 on the part of millions of Americans that we were not to have a peace in the world after all. During the war years, after Russia was attacked in 1941, she became "one of the democracies" in the oversimplifications of wartime propaganda. Suddenly she was one of the democracies no more, but the same old totalitarian state about which Americans had so many reservations. Further, it became apparent in a number of espionage cases that she was out to use whatever means she could to protect herself. In that connection, one must remember that the United States had no tremendous espionage organization such as that which became the CIA. All this was developed in the twenty years following the "victory" over Germany and Japan, as a necessary means of keeping up with the world as it changed.

A central source of discontent among Americans was the Department of State, that bureau entrusted with responsibility for political reportage and diplomatic relations. It was generally believed that the State Department had let America down somehow in failing to keep Americans abreast of the aims of Soviet Russia and her methods of attaining them.

All this was in the air in 1946, when Paul was conducting his frenzied drive for Negro rights. The rights were not forthcoming, and as one failure piled atop another, Paul became ever more disturbed and more suspicious of those in power who failed to grant the rights. He took the position that too many southern Bourbons were being brought into government by President Truman, and, shortly after their acidulous conversation in September 1946, Paul turned against Truman and the administration. One of his bêtes noires was James F. Byrnes, of South Carolina, who became Secretary of State in the Truman Cabinet. Byrnes was a southerner; Paul was deeply suspicious of him because of that; and it was no trick for Paul's left-wing friends to persuade him that the Byrnes who would oppose Negro rights would also oppose the rights of all other men.

It is an oversimplification, but this is the kind of reasoning that was extremely effective among good-hearted Americans who wished for the century of the common man, Social Democrats at heart, who looked with suspicion on the privileged classes and their accumulations of great wealth. Oversimplification is one of the curses of American politics; it occurred now on both sides, to the detriment and sometimes destruction of many men and women of good will. Old friendships were destroyed and new enmities created among people whose sole differences amounted to the question of faith in the direction in which the United States was heading, at home and abroad, in 1946 and 1947.

"My views concerning the Soviet Union and my warm feelings of friendship for the peoples of that land, and the friendly sentiments which they have often expressed toward me, have been pictured as something quite sinister by Washington officials and other spokesmen for the dominant white group in our country. It has been alleged that I am part of some kind of 'international conspiracy,'" Paul wrote later.

Of course he was not part of any conspiracy.

But Paul exhibited in 1946 a curious deficiency of understanding.

The United States government did not declare war on him: he declared war on the government of the United States, and the date was September 24, 1946, when he went to the presidential office as head of the committee representing some fifty organizations in thirty-eight states, to protest about lynching. On that day Paul began to practice excess in politics.

Afraid of Paul's excesses, a Democrat named Charles R. Howell of New Jersey, who was running for reelection, asked Paul not to come to Trenton, where Paul was scheduled to appear in his behalf. It was becoming most unacceptable to the majority of Americans when men praised the Soviet Union and attacked the philosophies of government that were being followed in the United States.

In 1946, Paul's political views did not upset his professional life any more than he wished them to. He was welcome as a concert singer nearly everywhere that he wished to go, except in the white halls of the deep South, and there it was the same old story of Robeson *vs.* segregation.

Paul was not led quickly into the arms of the Communist party. It was the Marxist unions and the Marxist organizations that wooed him. There were equal opportunity groups where Negroes were welcomed as full members, such as the United Auto Workers Union, but these unions did not make the fuss over Paul that the Communist-dominated unions did. From the Communist point of view this was simple good sense: Paul represented the Negro race. He was the most important Negro in America in 1946. Capturing him, the Communists would, they thought, develop the entree into Negro life in America that they had always sought and always failed to obtain.

So the Communists set to work to convert Paul Robeson to their views, and their adherence to the U.S.S.R.

Paul began to join picket lines when the pickets were demonstrating against racial injustices. He began to sing revolutionary songs—and, musically, the trouble was that some of these were neither tuneful nor particularly interesting. He took his singing of these songs into the heartland of the nation, too.

By the spring of 1947, anyone who remembered Paul Robeson as a singer of Negro spirituals would have been quite surprised at his concerts. He sang in Chinese. He sang in English, French, Italian, and German, old songs for the most part. He sang Russian arias and German arias. He still sang spirituals in a small part of his program. Now he added revolutionary songs—songs of free men he called them—when he made a recording for Columbia records during the war.

Later, Paul was to say that his songs of free men made him many enemies. He told of the time, in the spring of 1947, when he sang the ballad of Joe Hill at a concert at the University of Utah. It was particularly appropriate to Paul that he sing this song here (he had sung it many times before in London and elsewhere). Joe Hill was a union organizer who had been executed in the Utah state penitentiary for a murder his friends in the union said he never committed, and he had become a hero to the hard-bitten, much mistreated miners and smelter workers of the copper country of Utah.

Paul closed his program that night with the ballad of Joe Hill, and then he announced that from that day forward he was giving up the concert stage. "I shall sing, from now on," Paul said that night, "for my trade union and college friends; in other words, only at gatherings where I can sing what I please."

He had made this announcement earlier, in January, when he stood on a picket line protesting the segregation of Negroes in the American Theater of St. Louis. Now, he was taken at his word. The next month, when Paul was scheduled to sing at the Shrine Mosque in Peoria, Illinois, his use of the hall was canceled by the Shriners of that southern-oriented city. Paul had now associated himself with the very left-wing Civil Rights Congress. He had attended a dinner dedicated to the defeat of Senator Theodore Bilbo, the South's leading racist, and Bilbo had put his supporters against Paul. He had made a speech at the Southern Negro Youth Congress, which the southern white supremacists had used to have him brought under investigation by J. Parnell Thomas' House Un-American Activities Committee for "Communist" affiliations.

The Communists were growing daily more unpopular in the United States, and Paul's nearness to them was affecting his reputation with other Americans.

The reaction to Paul's visit to Peoria was not all negative. Various union leaders and others concerned with civil liberties were indignant when the Shriners' canceled the contract for the use of their hall. They demanded that the mayor allow the concert to take place and a reception to be held in the city hall. The American Legion of Peoria, quick to condemn those accused of "un-American activity," protested Paul's appearance. The ground of protest was that Paul was "an advocate of Communism," and of course he was. Later, Paul had this to say:

"On many occasions I have publicly expressed my belief in the principles of scientific socialism, my deep conviction that for all mankind a socialist society represents an advance to a higher stage of life—that it is a form of society which is economically, socially, culturally, and ethically superior to a system based on production for private profit."*

Paul was not a card-carrying Communist. He was a philosophical Marxist with a strong personal leaning toward the Soviet Union. He had achieved this position by the spring of 1947. But could anyone, Paul included, expect the citizens of the American Legion of Peoria to make the differentiation between a philosophical Marxist who loved Russia and a Communist?

Nor could Paul very well expect the American Legionnaires to have greeted him with open arms if they had understood him and what he stood for. He stood for the destruction of private capital. Every businessman in Peoria would quarrel with him on that, and so would many workmen, particularly the skilled tradesmen of the American Federation of Labor who usually had hopes of becoming shop owners and contractors, and, in a small way, capitalists themselves.

A man who came to Peoria bringing so startling a theory and wanting to be accepted wholeheartedly on his own terms,

* Paul Robeson, *Here I Stand* (London: Dennis Dobson, 1958), p. 47.

asked a great deal of Peoria in 1947. Paul always did ask a great deal of Americans, white and black, and when they failed to respond, he was puzzled, confused, and eventually embittered. He had lived abroad so much of his life, he had seen so many different systems of government in operation, and had learned so much about the basic similarities of all peoples everywhere, that he did not understand that his audience was afraid of what he had to offer. He had no way of estimating the lack of information, lack of basic understanding of the one-ness of humanity that existed in Peoria in 1947. He knew that his Russian friends were good people, and he thought he knew that the Russian government had no evil designs on the lives or property of any Americans. But his knowing and thinking he knew had no effect on people in Peoria, no matter how much they honored him as an American Negro who had gone far, or how much they enjoyed the magic of his voice.

Paul's failure, in one sense, began at Peoria, when Paul failed to show any understanding of the temper of the American white people in the hinterland. America's failure to Paul began here, too, as will be seen in a recital of the events of that unhappy week in the history of America.

Paul had chosen a city known in America for gangsterism, lawlessness, and earlier—in the 1920s—as a particularly horrible headquarters of the Ku Klux Klan. Peoria and, indeed, many towns in Illinois belong to the North of America only on sufferance, their hearts and many of their customs are closely allied with the South, and have been since days long before the Civil War.

On April 13, 1947, the Shriners canceled the contract for use of the hall for Paul's concert. Unionists and others then demanded that City Hall be made available. Mayor Carl Friebel, who had called for the barring of Paul Robeson from Peoria as a matter of public safety caviled. He said yes and then no. On April 17, the American Legion protested Paul's coming appearance, and, when the Mayor refused to allow the sponsors the use of City Hall, there seemed to be no place for Paul to come to hold a concert.

On that morning Paul arrived in Decatur, a town not far from Peoria. He was to give a concert there, and then go on to Peoria. Reporters came to talk to him, because the controversy made a good news story. Here, also, began Paul's difficulties with the American press. Some of the reporters were unfriendly, and their questions made Paul's temper rise. He began engaging in argument with the reporters, and worked himself into a fine passion. He then announced that he would go to Peoria and speak on a street corner as a matter of principle because his civil rights were being infringed by the attempt of the Mayor and the American Legion of Peoria to keep him out of the city.

Paul indicated that he would take the afternoon train to Peoria. Thereupon the chief of police of Peoria sent eight detectives and six policemen to the train station. Their mission was to keep Paul Robeson from getting off the train.

What might have been an incident was avoided when Paul was driven to Peoria. Sometime on the ride, wiser heads prevailed over Paul's and he did not attempt to make his street-corner speech.

Paul was not alone in the Peoria incident, or accompanied only by his leftist backers. Far from it. The ministerial alliance of Peoria backed his stand and deplored the attitude of the American Legion and the city government. Their position was that he had the right of any American citizen to express his views, even though they disagreed with those views. The local newspaper did not come out to defend his freedom, and one of its columnists attacked Paul in print. The ministers invited him to speak under their auspices. And thus the matter passed into history.

What Paul would have said, if he had been allowed to speak, was that he disagreed with American foreign policy and that, in standing with the colonial powers (which the United States did not do, although Paul never came around to accepting that fact) and in failing to grant Negroes immediate, full rights and protect them in their exercise, the United States was not living up to its responsibilities. Well, in many ways what Paul had to say was true, and the actions of the city government and the American Legion of Peoria showed why. The white Americans were afraid. One reason that Paul was so unwelcome in Peoria was because he was a black man, and Peoria, with its large number of southern citizens and its large number of Negroes, was a very fearful town.

But the fact was that if Peoria was representative of America, then America could not have survived to win World War II, and if Paul Robeson did not know that, then some of those around him should have known it. Peoria was the kind of town in America where Paul Robeson would have gone for an incident if he was seeking it, because it was predictable that an incident could be arranged there as easily as in Biloxi, Mississippi, in 1947.

The Peoria action was largely misunderstood, and Paul's philosophical dedication to Marxism because it promised racial equality was also misunderstood. What decent American could object to a statement like this one, made by Paul in his book *Here I Stand:*

> I do not intend to argue here for my political viewpoint, and, indeed, the large question as to which society is better for humanity is never settled by argument. The proof of the pudding is in the eating. Let the various social systems compete with each other under conditions of peaceful coexistence, and the people can decide for themselves. I do not insist that anyone else must agree with my judgment, and so I feel that no one is justified in insisting that I must conform to his beliefs. Isn't that fair?*

Of course it was fair. Eminently fair. But in 1947, frightened Americans were not prepared to be fair. The great hole in Paul's argument was: how would he guarantee that "conditions of peaceful coexistence" would be maintained? Americans believed that the Russians were only waiting for an opportunity to attack the United States, overthrow the American form of government, and institute Communism. Those who worried about racial problems also added the codum that this Communism would be run by the blacks, and they had secret

---

* *Ibid.,* p. 48.

fears that were nightmares of racial integration by sexual mixture.

Five days after the cancellation of the Peoria concert, the Board of Education in Albany, New York, canceled permission previously granted for the use of the auditorium at Philip Livingston High School for a concert by Paul. Fortunately, in this case the cancellation came early enough that something could be done. The sponsors of the concert were members of the Carver Cultural Society, a Negro Methodist group. They appointed attorney Arthur J. Harvey to take the matter to court. These Negro Americans were as much insulted as Paul was insulted by this action. His politics did not matter to them. The aroma of his views would not remain behind in the auditorium to infect the schoolchildren, and, as their spokesman remarked: "whatever his political views may be they won't affect the tone of his voice."

During the next two weeks hearings were held in court with the Carver Culture Society on one side and the Albany Board of Education on the other. Other parties intervened, including a dozen clergymen who came out in favor of the Negro group. Finally, the judge prohibited the school board from revoking the permit to use the auditorium, and the concert was held. The American Legion again entered the fray, calling for a boycott of the concert and pickets to man the buildings. They had their pickets, but 1,100 people attended the concert.

Paul was really doing very well, considering what he had set out to do—which seemed to be to antagonize the right wing in America. Obviously that was not his real aim, his aim as always was to secure freedom for American Negroes and the downtrodden everywhere. He seemed to lose sight of that aim himself, in 1947, as he lumped it together with the causes of the extreme left wing, led by the American Communist movement. Being proud, irascible Paul Robeson, criticisms of his associations and his political views did not frighten him or in any way change his mind. Quite to the contrary, they may have driven him to an adherence to some positions he might otherwise have eschewed.

At the Albany concert Paul did not make a single political remark. He did not sing a song that could be regarded as radical. Had he confined himself thus at his concerts, people might have wondered what all the shouting was about. But Paul had no intention of being muzzled, and he had a very vague idea about the best method by which *he* might help the beleaguered Negroes of America. The Russians certainly did not help matters any, as far as Paul's relations with white America were concerned, by coming out on May 1 and announcing, as *Pravda* did, that Paul Robeson was one of the U.S.S.R.'s prime friends in America. It was almost fatal to be so labeled in the United States in 1947.

In the spring of 1947, Paul came home to New York and Connecticut. Soon he was off on a concert tour sponsored by the United Public Workers of America, a CIO union, and a left-wing one, which was seeking to unionize workers in American installations in Panama and the Canal Zone. Most of these workers were colored people, and it would obviously be useful to have Paul Robeson helping them. Tickets to the concerts were selling at a dollar apiece—this was part of Paul's announced program of reaching the masses of people. Enemies of the union and others did not understand or did not wish to understand Paul's philosophy about such matters and they hinted direly, indicating that at such low prices Paul must be subsidized by someone, and that the someone was Josef Stalin.

No subsidy was needed, as it turned out. The concerts, or some of them, drew as many as 10,000 people, which would pay expenses and leave Paul enough to live very comfortably for some time.

Paul made speeches in Panama, and they were speeches about the need for action of the subjected peoples of the world, including the American Negro, to bring about the human dignity to which they were entitled by virtue of being men. This was revolutionary talk. Twenty years later it would not seem very revolutionary, but in 1947 Negroes and other minority groups did not talk that way. They were not supposed to make demands, but were supposed to make requests and pleas.

Paul did no such thing. Earlier, in testimony before the Tenney Committee of California, Paul had made some startling suggestions.

"If Mr. Truman is going to raise the under-privileged third of the nation or the Negro one tenth, he'd better establish a dictatorship in the South," Paul had said. Anyone knowing Communists would know that such a statement would not be made by a member of the party, in connection with a discussion of Communism. Communists just did not talk that way in 1947—the term "dictatorship" went out of style when the word dictator became an evil one—in the days of Mussolini and Hitler.

Paul was not well-schooled in his revolutionary thoughts— his real trouble was that they always came from the heart. He was not yet filled with resentment in 1946 and 1947. He was hailed before the Tenney Committee because of his membership in a number of organizations that had Communist direction or Communist affiliation, or that gave indications of being Communist-led. Of course Paul would belong to such organizations for one simple reason: every one of them was on record as favoring the immediate guarantee of racial equality to all Americans. So he would belong to the National Committee to Win the Peace, to the Independent Committee of the Arts, Sciences, and Professions, the Civil Rights Congress, to scores of other organizations dedicated at least in part to freedom and equality for all Americans, Negro and white.

Birds of a feather flock together, the old saying goes. Paul found himself flocking with the International Longshoreman's and Warehouseman's Union that year, because that union was absolutely dedicated to racial equality. How could the ILWU be anything else? Its membership was loaded with Negroes, Chinese, Japanese, Mexicans, the underprivileged of the nation, and how could *that* be otherwise, for how many men with strong minds, good education, and other privilege choose to work as stevedores on the docks?

Paul went to Hawaii, to sing in Honolulu and in smaller cities and towns in the islands under the auspices of the ILWU. In 1947, when the United States government was still trying to deport Harry Bridges (as it had been since the San Francisco Longshore strike of the 1930s) association with the ILWU was enough to brand a man as pro-Communist in con-

gressional circles. That is how American politics was progress-
ing in the great wave of fear of the late 1940s and the early
1950s.

That summer of 1947, in August, came the first of the
Peekskill incidents—nothing like the celebrated incident of
that name, but indications of what might happen one day. The
American Legion of Peekskill protested the Robeson summer
concert of that year and urged a boycott. Shortly afterward
came a House Un-American Activities Committee report which
named Paul as sponsor of many Communist-front organizations.

The more he was vilified by the right wing in America, the
more he was lionized by the Communists, at home and abroad.
That autumn of 1947, Paul received an award and special
mention by the Artists, Writers, and Printing Workers Congress
of Bucharest, Rumania. Now what was the Artists, Writers,
and Printing Workers Congress of a country of 18,000,000—
about equal to the Negro population of the United States?
What did it mean to Americans or to Paul that he was so
chosen for honor? It should have meant very little, but to
many Americans such honor was proof of a conspiracy in
which Paul was a figure. The fact was that Paul was honored
by some of those Rumanians because they believed he should
be honored for his fight for his people—and by others because
Paul's struggle was proving very embarrassing to his government.

Embarrassment does not account for the attitude of many
right-wing organizations, such as the American Legion, toward
Paul Robeson and his activities in the year 1947. The only
emotion that could provoke the hatred and vilification to
which these people were aroused was naked fear. Paul, who
had never really been afraid, did not know this fear, and did
not understand it, and that did not help him come to grips
with his problem vis-à-vis white America. Nor were the events
of the next few months to endear Paul to either of the two
major political parties. For in the early months of 1948 Paul
became the complete political man.

Chapter 13

POLITICAL MAN

Paul's conversion to politics as an instrument of justice for the Negro was a natural outgrowth of his use of culture and polemics. By 1948, it was obvious that culturally he was not getting through with his message to the people who must be reached, and he had quite given up in that direction. By the end of 1947, singing, to Paul, was simply a means of maintaining an entree and earning a living. He was not trying to convince white America by singing that the Negroes should be freed.

Paul had also learned by 1948 that he would not be heard gladly or even with much tolerance if he opened his mouth to speak when he had gained entrance into the hall as a performer of music. Those who did not wish to honor what he had to say shushed him by indicating that as a performer he should perform and leave the thinking to others.

One might say, then, that given his mission in life, that of advocating the cause of the Negro as a full member of American society, Paul must turn to political means. He did not turn to the Communists—who wanted him very badly. He did not turn Communist in spite of the fact that one of his great friends was Ben Davis, a Negro leader of the Communist party and a brilliant man who had taken that path in the hope of serving the Negro people of America. Ben Davis might be hated and feared in white America; he was never hated and feared in Negro America until perhaps the end of the 1940s when some in Negro America began to have enough stake in American capitalism to worry. Paul knew Ben Davis well, yet he did not choose this course.

Those who would understand Paul and his relationship to the American Negro people should consider some of the incidents that occurred in Harlem in these later years of the 1940s. Paul had been known for many years as "king of Harlem." It was not a self-proclaimed title; one of the first to hang it on him was *The New Yorker* magazine in an admiring profile written in 1928. Paul represented every Harlemite's dream of success in a white society after he moved to England in that year; even before he was as successful as a Negro could be.

Paul's innate good manners and his decency appealed as much to Negroes as it did to whites. Further, there was always a bond that held together the successful Negroes of Paul's generation. After all, there were not so many of them outside the Step-n-Fetchit or Bojangles Bill Robinson or Jack Johnson schools. Three of the most prominent of these Negroes were Paul, Ben Davis, and Ralph Bunche. What different roads they chose! Bunche chose to become a lawyer and civil servant and eventually to advance the cause of the Negro through his work at the United Nations. Ben Davis became a lawyer and then an open, prominent Communist leader. Yet Davis had the respect of the Negro community of Harlem as much as did Bunche, and there should be no mistake about that. White man's law and white man's prejudice were not Negro law or Negro prejudice.

This standard, the whole attitude of Negro society, is indicated in one anecdote about Paul and Ralph Bunche.

The incident occurred on New Year's Day in one of these formative and frightening years of the late 1940s. It came out of the custom of Harlem society—and there is a definite Harlem society—to assemble at the Renaissance Ballroom in the heart of Harlem on New Year's Day. The ladies come in their finest gowns, the debutantes in their white tulle and even more spectacular costumes. Everyone is dressed to the nines and everyone is on his best behavior. It is the principal meeting day of Harlem society in the entire year.

The ladies come with their husbands and escorts to the Renaissance, and then they gather around and sit in chairs and talk, and some of the most honored of the men go back into the private office of Bob Douglas, proprietor of the establishment, and they look over the television and talk, and they watch some of the big football bowl games for a little while.

Among the members of Harlem society, the names of the Bunches and the Robesons have loomed large in recent years because these are Negroes who have been doing something for the Negro outside in the white world where so few Negroes have been able to break through.

On this particular New Year's Day, Ralph Bunche was in Bob Douglas' office, talking idly and watching a football game on television. Bunche was watching with the interest of an old football star. Bunche was at that time under consideration but not yet appointed to his very sensitive job with the United Nations organization as an American representative. This was not actually his role—becoming a permanent UN employee supposedly took him out of the nationalist role—but he had to be acceptable to the United States government as well as to the United Nations.

Suddenly the door opened and Paul Robeson walked in. All the room greeted Paul with great pleasure, and he walked up to Bunche and stuck out his hand.

"Hello, Ralph," said Paul.

"Hello, Paul," replied Ralph, taking the outstretched hand.

At that moment the photographer of the *Amsterdam News*, who happened to be in the room, recording this day's activities for posterity, took aim and fired with his flashgun and camera.

Neither Paul nor Ralph Bunche moved a muscle, and neither said a word to the photographer, although it was immediately apparent in the room that the photographer's action was much frowned upon by the Harlem community. Everyone there knew that this picture might cost Ralph Bunche an important job if it were to get out into white society.

The picture never did get out. James Hicks was there, too, James Hicks the bright, tough-minded editor of the *Amster-*

dam News, who knew exactly what the reaction of the white world would be. He sought out his photographer and took away the negative gently. He tore up that negative, before it could be ejected into an alien world that would not understand.

There is one more anecdote from Harlem during those years that again shows how highly Paul was always regarded in his home community, where there is no worry about many things that disturb the white man.

There is an old respectable bar in Harlem called the Red Rooster, which is to Harlemites what Toots Shor's is to the white entertainment world downtown and what Bleeck's Artists and Writers restaurant once was to the newspaper crowd. Paul was always welcomed eagerly, even feverishly, when he dropped into the Red Rooster for a half hour of yarning. One day in the 1940s, when all the political troubles were besetting Paul, he did come into the Red Rooster. There, sitting at a table, surrounded by admiring friends, sat one of the wonders of the Negro world of the season, the big brawny Don Newcombe, pitcher for the Brooklyn Dodgers.

Paul did not know Newcombe, for Newcombe was not one of the Harlem boys and Newcombe was of a different generation. Newcombe did not know Paul.

Some genial soul in the crowd bethought himself that these two important representatives of the Negro race ought to know one another and he brought Paul, who was still standing, to Newcombe's table to say hello. Paul, always genial in Harlem, did as he was bade and stuck out his hand.

Newcombe looked up at him coldly and refused to shake his hand. He didn't have anything to do with Communists, he indicated.

Well, that day, they nearly had to form a protective society to get Don Newcombe out of Harlem and back over to Brooklyn safely, because Harlem did not like young Mr. Newcombe's attitude towards its king.

By the end of 1947, Paul had become the complete political man. On December 20, 1947, for the first time in his life, he took a personal and public stand on the matter of the coming presidential election in the United States. It is questionable if Paul ever voted in national elections between 1928 and 1948. At least, it is obvious that he showed no particular interest in politics in the first decade of that period; in the second his interest was social rather than political until that point, reached in 1947, when he decided to give up the concert stage and devote his time to the political fight to aid the Negroes in America. The decision Paul made, on December 20, 1947, was to back Henry Agard Wallace as an independent candidate for President of the United States.

For many months, since the speech before the Political Action Committee that touched off his breach with the Truman Administration, Henry Wallace had been developing a new line of political thought. He had left the administration to become editor of the liberal journal the *New Republic*. In the pages of the *New Republic* began appearing alternative arguments against the current policies of the Truman Administration. The year 1947 was the year of many policy changes, and, in foreign policy, very far-reaching ones. It was the year of the Truman Doctrine, the year of the Marshall Plan, the year in which it was decided to ease assistance to a faltering Chiang Kai-shek government in China. It was the year of the beginning of the Cold War and the Iron Curtain which was characterized by Winston Churchill in a speech in Missouri.

In December and January, Paul met with a number of liberals, left-wing New Dealers from the Roosevelt era, and persons whose personal political beliefs were very much akin to those of the Communist party. From these meetings came the formation of a national committee to back Wallace as President, and from this came a six-man committee whose purpose was to persuade Wallace to run for President and to organize a broad political movement to back him. Paul became a member of this committee, along with C. B. Baldwin and Rex Tugwell, two New Dealers, E. A. Benson, who represented the old Progressive movement of the Middle West, and Jo Davidson, sculptor, and Angus Cameron, brilliant Socialist-oriented editor of a pubilshing house.

Paul was named co-chairman of the group. So, after forty-nine years of political celibacy, Paul became wedded to a new party, which was to be named the Progressive Party of the United States.

It would be some months before the Progressive party would be named, at the party convention in Philadelphia late in July. In the interim the organizing began, with Paul very much involved in the work. Unfortunately, almost immediately on receipt of the information that a Wallace party was being organized, the American Communists decided to try to take it over rather than put up their own candidate in the elections of 1948, and that is what they did do. Paul and other leaders of the Progressive movement went from one end of the country to the other speaking on college campuses, speaking to labor organizations. They secured the adherence of many students and many left-wing labor groups, but they did not secure the adherence of very many Negroes or very many liberal Americans. The Communist adherence hurt them deeply.

In April, a meeting was held in Chicago at the Knickerbocker Hotel to establish an embryo organization and Paul introduced Henry Wallace amid cheers and applause. At this meeting, a demand was made that Paul stand for the vice-presidency, but he refused. He also refused an offer to become chairman of the American Labor party, a left-wing organization confined almost entirely to New York City.

Paul Robeson, the political man, spent the months between April and July of 1948 on the stump, speaking for Wallace and the new movement. His position was that this new organization stood for the rights of man, which had been abandoned, he said, by the two major political parties.

As Paul spoke, so did others in America—public opinion was so badly split in America in 1948 that there were eleven parties on the ballots of the various states (not all on every ballot). Paul spoke for the rights of man, and in the South J. Strom Thurmond and other political leaders spoke for State's Rights —usually a narrow cover for the advocates of white supremacy, but possessing just enough logic about it to appeal to some good-hearted conservatives.

That was one trouble with the election of 1948—it was hard to separate the sheep from the scoundrelly goats. The enemies of the Progressives called them all Communists, and of course they were not that. (West Virginia authorities banned Shirley Graham's innocuous biography of Paul from its public libraries because of his political views, for example.)

Paul went on blithely. He was convinced now that the United States was heading directly toward Fascism, and his supporters and associates for the most part agreed. He spoke before the convention of the United Public Workers Union. He spoke on the steps of the Capitol against Jim Crow in the South. He spoke before many unions. And yet, suddenly, Paul was not as welcome everywhere, even among strong militant unions as he had been before he became an open political figure. Michael Quill, leader of the Transport Workers Union in New York City, blocked an attempt to have Paul address that union's convention. Quill was certain that Paul and his associates were in the hands of the Communists.

There came a serious split in the African Affairs Council that Paul had led for so many years, and a number of prominent liberal and Negro members withdrew from the organization, charging that it had become a Communist dupe.

Paul, it seemed, now set out to bait rather than convince. That summer Communism and Communist affiliation became a major American political issue. Before the country was a piece of legislation called the Mundt-Nixon bill, which would have placed serious controls on left-wing political organizations in the attempt to control Communism. The House Un-American Activities Committee was investigating Communism in America, and so was a Senate committee. From these investigations came the indictment of Alger Hiss for Communist affiliation during the 1930s (the indictment and conviction were for perjury, but the issue was always Communism). President Truman had been enough concerned about problems of Communist infiltration into the American government to issue a Loyalty Order, which provided for investigation of employees of the Executive branch of government on almost any pretext.

The atmosphere in America was very unhealthy for democracy in the spring and summer of 1948. In the air of hysteria in Washington, many people were brought forth to be questioned about their political views. Eugene Dennis, general secretary of the Communist party was cited for contempt for refusing to state his views. Ten Hollywood figures were cited for contempt because they would not answer political questions, and most of them went to jail and served out their sentences on charges that were purely political. It was not the first time that the United States government had harassed people because of unpopular political opinions, but it was the first time except during actual war that men had been imprisoned for holding unpopular ideas—and the laws under which they were imprisoned were regarded by the left wing as subterfuge. (The left-wingers did not take such a position a score of years later when the same Congressional contempt laws were unleashed against the Ku Klux Klan.)

The atmosphere was tense that summer, there was no doubt about that. There was no doubt, either, that Paul believed his country was far down the road to Fascism, goaded by its fear of Communism. Paul went to Washington to testify before the Senate investigating committee in June, and, as was popular among the left-wingers to show their defiance of the Congress, he refused to answer the question as to whether or not he was a Communist. He was asked the direct question: "Are You A Communist?"

"That question," he said, "has become the very basis of the struggle for civil liberties. Nineteen men are about to go to jail for refusing to answer it. I am prepared to join them. I refuse to answer it."

They could have sent Paul to jail. He was not a Communist. He had already told that under oath to the Tenney Committee in California, and he had not joined the party since. But he was stubborn, with the dedicated stubborness of a man who thinks he is right.

He was not cited and he was not sent to jail because it was an election year, and no matter what Paul might represent, to many he represented a large segment of Negro votes. Also, there were some wiser heads among the Senate committee who were certain that Paul was showing his stubbornness, and the sensible advisers won out.

Paul joined a Washington demonstration against the Mundt-Nixon subversives control law while in Washington. The demonstrators called for, instead, a law protecting the rights of Negroes. It was obvious that the Progressives, as they called themselves, and the conservatives of both major parties were not talking to each other at all. The Communists were using Paul and others to keep the issue from ever being narrowed to the single question of Communist subversion, and, indeed, among people of good will in America the confusion was very thorough in 1948.

Paul's singing in this period lost much of its musicality and gained a great deal of politicality. He sang a parody of *The Battle Hymn of the Republic* at a Communist party dinner in New York City. He sang and spoke at the American Labor party convention in New York. He planned a concert in Savannah, Georgia, and then called it off because the authorities demanded segregation in the auditorium. His action here left the definite feeling that he had set up a straw man to knock down.

In July, Paul went to Philadelphia to attend the convention of what would be the Progressive Party of the United States. "Jim Crow Must Go" was the chant in the streets. In the hotel rooms the talk was how the United States might placate Russia, by giving up its rights as conquerors in Berlin and making peace on any terms the Russians demanded.

On July 22, James Loeb, Jr., executive secretary of the Americans for Democratic Action, called on the Progressives to throw the Communists out of their party. It was too late. The Communists were in such secure control of the party that they were able to defeat a resolution by the liberals, saying that the party did *not* endorse the Soviet Union's foreign policy. When the Progressive party's platform was knocked together, it included every one of the recommendations listed two months before by the Communists except one. During those two months, a switch in Soviet foreign policy had outlawed the idea of a homeland for Macedonians, and this American political party then decided a homeland for Macedonians was not necessary either. So no provision was made in the Progressive Platform for dozens of Macedonians who might be interested.

Paul grew most unwise during this campaign, most ungenerous and most inclined to exaggeration. In September, he said the American Negro's plight was the worst of any peoples' in the world. Annamites, Moslems in Hindu India, and Hindus in Moslem India, Japanese prisoners of war in Russia might all dispute that statement.

Paul was brave, even foolhardy. He went on tour for Wallace *in the South*. True, he could be expected to pull large crowds of Negroes and white well-wishers in the South, but he could also expect to be a constant target for violence. The state of mind that had produced the Ku Klux Klan in the South at the end of the Civil War and again in the 1920s was always present in the South. The Klan could be revived on a few days' notice, for all it took to create a Klavern was a handful of sheets and a few words of advice about where the night riding and violence were to be committed.

Paul was threatened with lynching in Memphis by men who said they were members of the Ku Klux Klan. He went to Florida and to Savannah, to Charleston, South Carolina. Sometimes he was allowed to speak in a public place. Usually the police announced that public halls were segregated, so he spoke in Negro churches or in union halls, where whites were invited to come if they wished.

One incident of this trip was described by Lawrence Brown to Robeson biographer Marie Seton, and it does much to explain why Paul's feelings about racism were so strong.

Paul, Brown, and Clark Foreman, the white treasurer of the Progressive party, were in Jacksonville, Florida, waiting for rail transportation to Savannah, Georgia, one day. They were standing on the platform, where there were no signs declaring that there are two races. Foreman had the tickets for all three in his hand.

The train that arrived that day, at that time, was without private compartments. It was, as were all day trains, a segre-

gated train, with some cars set aside for whites and others for
Negroes only.

Foreman, a white southerner, decided that he was going to
stand on his constitutional rights and sit with his two Negro
friends. Paul told him to leave the colored section of the train,
but Foreman refused. When the white conductor came up, he
ordered Foreman into the next car—and only by claiming that
he was a "white" Negro was Foreman able to ride in the Jim
Crow car with Paul and Lawrence Brown.

That year the Progressive party did not have much chance
of achieving a high vote, for its support came from the radical
left. Had the Progressives confined themselves to domestic
issues, perhaps their fate might have been better. They might
have polled more votes, but the ideological slant of the party
was so obviously directed by the American Communists that
the domestic issues could not be brought forward above the
others. Had they gained in strength, the Progressives might
have forced the Democrats, in particular, to make concessions
to the Negroes. The Progressive party did threaten the Democrats seriously, because it drew support from some left-wing
voters who had supported the Democrats in the Roosevelt
years. The Republicans hoped that the Democratic vote would
be so badly split that the GOP would win—and this was
generally believed to be the trend by the press and much of
the public. The Republicans grew reckless and accused the
Democrats of being traitors, of having sold out the country to
the Communists; that is how ridiculous and heated the campaign of 1948 became.

Paul sometimes managed in 1948 to surmount the difficulties
he set for himself. In a concert for the Progressive cause at
Yankee Stadium in New York, for a few moments Paul made a
deep impression. He spoke out for the Negro and against
oppression, and he sang "Let My People Go" and "Ol' Man
River." When he pleaded his own people's cause, he was
irresistible. When he pleaded the Soviet Union's cause, his
words fell largely on deaf American ears. For the fact was that
the vast majority of Americans in 1948, no matter their political views and affiliations, had general good will toward the

American Negro, but they shared an innate distrust of the Soviet Union.

The Progressive party can be credited with one major victory in the election campaign of 1948: the party and particularly Paul did force the Democrats to give more attention to the matter of special federal legislation to guarantee civil liberties than might otherwise have been the case.

Paul should have been able to take some personal satisfaction in this victory. But, as for the party itself, it failed miserably to attract public support; it did not poll as many votes throughout the nation as Strom Thurmond's anti-Negro Dixiecrats did in the South alone. The Thurmond vote was 1,169,063. The Wallace vote was only 1,157,172. More Negroes voted for Harry Truman than voted for Henry Wallace, by far. In this was a simple fact, a simple warning to Paul if he intended to continue to be the political man. He had been to Russia and he said that Russia was free. Other Negroes in America, love him as they might, did not automatically accept his political judgments. American Negroes had the feeling that their problems would be best solved in America, and not on the broader canvas of world affairs. They would listen to Paul. They would love Paul. They would defend Paul against white criticism and attack. Some of them privately disagreed with him, and some of them felt he was doing the Negro cause disservice by such close associations with the interests of another country. In the election of 1948, there is no indication that Paul realized how matters stood, even with his own people.

Chapter 14

THE LONG
RUSSIAN JOURNEY

Early in 1949 Paul made a tour to the British West Indies. He was scheduled to go back into the concert field on a non-political basis, and some eighty-five appearances had been arranged in the United States for that coming season. Then, on January 29, Paul erupted again in another political statement about the widespread oppression of American Negroes in a way that suggested his continued adherence to the cause of the U.S.S.R. "The music Moguls," as Paul termed them, forced a cancellation of the concert series. (The idea behind the cancellation, Paul indicated, was to compel him to be silent or to give up his singing career.)

"There is no such thing as a non-political artist," Paul had said to a rally of Communist war veterans two years earlier. "Either the artist serves the people or he serves those who would throttle them."

Thus he had not made a formal concert since the concert held in Albany in 1947 that was first denied and then granted by court ruling over the objection of Mayor Erastus Corning II. On that occasion, Paul had said he was delighted to be out of the formal concert field for the next two years so he could speak and sing as he pleased. Now, two years later, he wanted to go back into the concert field, but he still wanted to sing and speak as he pleased while on tour.

Paul decided to go to Europe to resume his singing career. "I wanted to make it perfectly clear that the world is wide and a few pressures would not stop my career," he said.

He went to England. Two concerts were held at Albert Hall, seating eight thousand people, and both were sold out. Elsewhere there were also sell-out audiences. The concerts were financially and artistically successful.

Meanwhile, in the United States Courthouse at Foley Square in New York City, a number of Paul's new friends were going on trial in a case unique in American history. The United States government charged that eleven members of the executive board of the Communist party, U.S.A., were members of a conspiracy dedicated to the overthrow of the United States government by force and violence.

Paul's name was brought into the trial almost immediately. On March 15, a prospective juror was excused by Judge Harold Medina because he was acquainted with Paul Robeson. Paul announced that he would interrupt his concert tour to return to the United States and testify for the eleven defendants. Marxism, he said, was on trial in the United States—Marxism, the political theory. He said he was going to take the view that Marxism was a cultural philosophy.

Such was not a new view for Paul. It was always his view, and that is why he was in trouble with white America; he was totally unable to make whites realize how he could hold this view and be a loyal American.

There was a secret to it—but no secret at all to those who could understand Paul's general nature and general philosophy of life. Paul was a political man? There was certainly an attempt made by Paul and by many close to him, especially by Essie, to make Paul into a political man, but the attempt had been basically unsuccessful because Paul kept retreating to his own interests. Paul was a philosophical Marxist, and when he told reporters that Marxism was a cultural philosophy he spoke no more than *his* truth. That was his view. That is what kept him in constant difficulty at home. Paul was used as a political man, then and for the next decade to come, but the attempt was a miserable failure. He could not be made to remain political, he would not stand for office, he had none of the attitudes of a political man even though he was kept dangling in the political arena by the baiting of unfriendly reporters and officials, and by his never-ending search for the ideal of Negro Equality.

Paul worked for black equality while in London. He joined a meeting organized by Krishna Menon and he sang and led a protest against the apartheid policy of the South African Government.

In his effort to be a political man, Paul now moved to the edge of the abyss. In April, he went to Paris to attend the World Peace Congress which had been organized by the Partisans of Peace. In the United States it was said that the World Peace Congress of 1949 was organized by the Communist movement of the world as a weapon to be used against the United States. This attitude was generally accepted in the United States by white Americans.

Here is how Paul got to Paris:

That London meeting to protest apartheid was the beginning of an event that would bring Paul much grief in the next decade. The meeting was sponsored by the Coordinating Committee of Colonial Peoples in London, together with Dr. Y. M. Dadoo, president of the South African Indian Congress. This group, representing, at least in geographical distribution, some 600 million colored peoples, asked Paul to go to Paris the next day and address the World Peace Congress in their name, saying that they did not want war.

So Paul went to Paris.

Meanwhile, resentment against Paul had been growing in the white world. Following his address to the London conference against apartheid, the Union of South Africa's broadcasting company banned the playing of Paul Robeson recordings. On April 19, as he made ready to leave for Paris, he was cited by the House Committee on Un-American Activities in Washington because he had taken part in a Cultural and Scientific Conference for World Peace in New York. It was just another Communist front, said the House committee. Some white Americans nodded and became convinced that Paul was a card-carrying Communist conspirator out to destroy the United States government and bring Soviet Communism to America.

Of course, Paul, the political adolescent, had once said he thought Communism ought to be tried out in the United States. He told that to the Tenney Committee of California in 1946. He said the United States was the most developed nation in the world, and that Communism—Marxism—could thus have its best trial as a means of human social organization in the United States. Paul had been quite serious. Most people did not understand that he regarded Marxism as a theoretical philosophical question, perhaps akin to the endless discussions he had held with philologists about the similarities he thought he saw between the Chinese language and several of the African tribal dialects.

Paul arrived at the Paris conference, passed beneath the handsome dove of peace designed for the conferees by Pablo Picasso, another philosophical Marxist who thought he was a political man, and ascended the rostrum to make an *unprepared* speech.

"We colonial peoples," said Paul, whose experience certainly did not qualify him to use the "we" in this matter, "have contributed to the building of the United States and are determined to share in its wealth. We denounce the policy of the United States government which is similar to that of Hitler and Goebbels. We want peace and liberty and will combat for them along with the Soviet Union, the democracies of Eastern Europe, China and Indonesia."

This speech contained several fundamental errors, from the American point of view, in addition to Paul's misplaced use of the word "we." First, no matter what anyone thought of the policies of the American government, they were not similar in any way to the genocidal policies of Hitler and Goebbels. Second, when Paul referred broadly to the "democracies" of Russia, Eastern Europe, China, and Indonesia, he was not talking about democracies which were run by the traditional democratic method, and white Americans did not believe they were democracies at all. This much of Paul's speech might have been based on clippings from the *Daily Worker*. It was as nothing to the next part of Paul's speech:

"It is unthinkable," said Paul, "that American Negroes could go to war on behalf of those who have oppressed us for generations against the Soviet Union which in one generation has raised our people to full human dignity."

For ˙a long time the Communists had been raising the specter of a separate Negro movement in the United States. It was one of those matters that disturbed white America, but it was not openly discussed. The Negro was presumed to be an American and a loyal one. Now Paul Robeson, who pretended to speak for the black man, said the Negro Americans were among those whose primary loyalty was to the Soviet Union in case of any conflict between the U.S.S.R. and America.

The cables hummed that April day with the story of Paul's speech. Some newspapermen in the hall may have misheard it and some may have embroidered it, but the essential facts were correct. Paul had indicated that the black man must stand on the side of the U.S.S.R. in any conflict with the United States, and that the black man *would* so stand. Any misinterpretations about exactly what he said were unimportant. Paul had been taking the responsibility as major spokesman for the American Negro for half a dozen years. He could not escape that responsibility now, nor could the American Negro community. The American Negroes must go on record one way or the other.

The reactions in America were immediate. Paul probably did more to restore a lagging white confidence in the loyalty of the Negro than anyone else could have done. Of course, he did not mean to accomplish this, or to bring out patriotism in American Negroes, but that is what he did. He also, once and for all, destroyed his own position as unchallenged leader of the American Negroes.

After this startling Robeson statement was reported in the press, various prominent Negroes were asked to make comment. Rep. Adam Clayton Powell, Jr., the consummate Negro political man, said that Paul Robeson was not a spokesman for the Negro people of America. Meeting in conference in New England, the officials of the National Association for the Advancement of Colored Peoples said that Paul certainly did not speak for them. A Negro college professor said that Paul misrepresented most Negroes. A. Philip Randolph of the Sleeping

Car Porters Union, one of the senior statesmen of black America, said that Paul Robeson was completely wrong in his statements.

Paul went to Sweden a few days later, a land that had been the scene of so triumphal a tour a few years earlier that memory of it had brought happy tears to his eyes. He was greeted in a friendly fashion, by some thirty persons who brought flowers to him at the airport, and his concert was a success. Yet, this year the success was restrained, and the concert's ending was marked by a few boos because he sang a number of songs glorifying the Communist revolution.

In Oslo, the greeting was even more mixed, and here Paul was incited to further intemperance. He said he would abandon singing and take up political speaking entirely. He said he was sure his political views would one day land him in jail. He said other foolish things; he was an angry man, who was just beginning to learn that he was being disavowed by Negroes in America. That news did hurt him, probably more than anything had hurt him in his life.

In Copenhagen, Paul's temper got the best of him again. He learned that his concert was to be held under the auspices of *Politiken*, a very moderate and well-respected newspaper that was in favor of the Atlantic Alliance. He refused to sing until he had new sponsorship.

No political excess was now too great for Paul. He defended the slave labor camp system in the Soviet Union, even as he attacked Americans for daring to try Communists for conspiracy. He did not condemn *both*; he condemned his own country and praised the country his countrymen believed to be a potential enemy. His actions, whether he realized it or not, were rebukes to millions of white Americans who held different beliefs. It was hardly to be expected that he would be very popular in the United States.

Paul returned to London briefly in May, disgusted with the press of Europe and America. He felt that he had been misquoted, although, of course, the newspapermen had found the important points of his remarks, and they could not be blamed if he was inept. Paul claimed that when he spoke to the World Peace Conference he was thinking in terms of all Negroes, 40 million West Indians and 150 million Africans. Perhaps he was thinking that way, but he had stumped America, representing American Negroes, for the Progressive party a few months before, and then he was concerned with 15 million American Negroes. Paul might be able to switch gears that rapidly, but Americans could not.

It was quite within character for Paul, the adolescent political, to have considered the problem in this light. Again, it must never be forgotten that, to Paul, the Soviet Union, with its equal treatment of peoples of all colors, was the promised land. Nothing ever changed that concept in his mind. It would be inconceivable to Paul that Negroes could fight against the one nation in the world that had done away with color and religious and racial intolerance, by law and in fact, or almost in fact—barring the Jews.

Paul left England at the end of May for Prague, where he sang in concerts and in impromptu concerts for workers. He joined Africans and Indians in a concert in the Prague Stadium one Sunday. There he met Marie Seton again, who was to write a biography of him a few years later. He told her he was going to Warsaw and then to Moscow, to visit the people he loved. He said he would like to live among the Russians for a while before he died, and yet he was homesick for the United States.

In Moscow, Paul participated in the celebration of the 150th anniversary of Pushkin's birth at the Bolshoi Theater. He said he had changed the original words of "Ol' Man River" to mean "we must fight to the death for peace and freedom." In the United States, when Oscar Hammerstein learned of this ridiculous statement, he defied Paul to try it, to change the Hammerstein words. How times had changed since the old days of the 1920s when the song was written, virtually for him.

Paul Robeson came home in June by airplane, with sour words for press and public. He was greeted by a police escort at the airport—standard procedure in New York for people who might arouse crowds, as Paul certainly might after his

"Negroes will not fight" statement. He said he had found no liking for American policies abroad. (That, of course, was to be expected, considering where he had looked.) He assailed the American press for "distortions" and said he preferred to give his news items to newspapers like the *Daily Worker*.

Later, Paul became furious when the press questioned him about a forthcoming marriage—the marriage of his son Paul, Jr., to Marilyn Greenberg, a white girl Pauli had met while they were both students at Cornell University.

The wedding was held on Sunday afternoon, June 19, in the apartment of a Congregational minister, in Harlem. It was a family affair. Two newspaper women, both Negroes, managed to make their way inside the apartment to see the ceremony, but the white press was held below, with the big figure of Paul blocking the stairs. Paul became furious—something that came easy to him these days—and he grasped a camera, nearly smashed it, but he restrained himself. Such a wedding would mean nothing elsewhere in the world, and particularly not in the Soviet Union, he said. He could not understand all the excitement.

Paul was making no effort to understand. Not just the white press, but the Negro press, too, was interested in this marriage. It was a mixed marriage, to be sure, but that was not the primary reason for curiosity. Paul had made himself and his family public figures by his own attitudes. He had made an outrageous statement in Paris, and it had called even more attention to him.

Nor could one overlook the aspect of a mixed marriage. Paul Robeson, Jr., had accomplished what every Negro in America wished to accomplish. Not that he had married a white girl. That was not the point. He had married the girl he loved, and the fact that she was white had made no difference. This marriage was symbolic of all that Paul Robeson had fought for in his life, and he should have been generous enough to understand a legitimate interest in this marriage on the part of well-wishers, not just the maudlin and curious. Naturally the youngsters wanted their privacy, but there was a symbolism in this marriage that Americans realized and accepted. Of course, on the other hand, there were the racists, the hate mongers of the South, and those of the North who would call Marilyn a "nigger lover" just as they would sneer at anyone who married outside the white race. But these people were definitely in the minority. Paul's disturbance at what he considered to be the willful misrepresentation of his position, his growing paranoia about the press and general public, all combined to make him withdraw. He showed his ugly side to the press that day—and newspapermen are particularly unforgiving to public figures who spite them. Paul's was an unfortunate homecoming that June of 1949.

This summer was a summer of intense political, military, and revolutionary activity in the Western world, and relationships between the West and the Communist world were as tense as they would ever be outside of actual war. The Chinese Communists had defeated the Nationalists decisively that winter and occupied nearly all of the Chinese mainland: another country gone to Communism. The North Atlantic Treaty had been adopted by the Western powers: a new defensive measure which worried the Russians. Alger Hiss had been on trial, and, although the jury had not agreed, much information about Communist methods and Russian espionage in America in the 1930s had been revealed: a new basis for American fear of Soviet infiltration of American government by Communists. The Russians exploded an atomic bomb, putting an end to the monopoly of the Western powers over this new and disastrous weapon: greater fear of Americans that war was very near.

In this atmosphere, with the leaders of the American Communist party on trial for conspiracy to overthrow the government by force and violence, every day the newspapers were filled with items about Communism and Soviet maneuvers of one kind or another. The Cold War seemed, to Americans, to be going very much the wrong way. Consequently, Americans were not prepared to accept Paul's defenses of Communists and Russians. He was not prepared to understand the nervousness of his fellow Americans. He did not believe there was any Soviet conspiracy or that Communist parties around the world represented anything but a common belief in political and economic principles. It is fundamental to understand Paul's willful self-blinding to any facts that he did not wish to recognize.

As far as the Soviet Union was concerned that summer, Paul had many things to say. He greeted the Soviet atomic bomb explosion with pleasure. He repeated his statement that American Negroes (and others) would not fight the Soviet Union. He defended the existence of concentration camps in Russia. He said furious words against the American press for "misrepresenting" the Soviet Union.

"I never saw such a beautiful city as Moscow today. The correspondents—the turncoats—I don't see how they have the nerve to lie about the Soviet Union the way they do. How can you find a great people you love and then suddenly turn against them?"

He spoke of Soviet art: "The level of art in the Soviet Union is so far away from anything we can possibly see in this country that we can't begin to compare it, so I don't want to hear any more nonsense about the freedom of the artist."

He repeated his never-ending sense of wonderment at race progress in Russia: "I talked to anthropologists in London and New York about the peoples of Africa. They said 'It'll be a thousand years before you can do anything.' And I saw the Kazakhs in Moscow. It's a tremendous thing that these people could be there with their literature, music, theater (to attend the Kazakh art festival held in Moscow that year)—not after a thousand years, but in hardly one generation."

He reviewed his political development: "It was in 1939 that I came to see so clearly the tie between the Negro and the workers; I saw much more clearly after I had been in the Soviet Union that the Negro people must come to identify themselves with the workers."*

There—above—is probably the clearest and simplest explanation ever made of Paul's position a decade after he first came to "identify" with the U.S.S.R.

* *Time,* June 27, 1949.

This sense of identification was understood by American Negroes in a way that whites could never understand. After Paul had made his statements about the Negro and the U.S.S.R., many outraged Negroes came forward to challenge him. Among these was Jackie Robinson of the Brooklyn Dodgers, one of the first Negroes to be given a chance to play baseball on an equal basis with whites, when Branch Rickey broke the color bar. Jackie Robinson offered to go to Washington as a friendly witness before the House Un-American Activities Committee to refute the impressions Robeson had left about the loyalty of American Negroes.

The Baltimore *Afro-American,* one of America's most prominent Negro newspapers, took Jackie Robinson to task. The newspaper advised him to stick to baseball and stay out of politics.

"When Paul Robeson said he is not willing to fight against Russia, he is not thinking about himself. He is not thinking about Russia," said the *Afro-American.*

"He is thinking about millions of colored people in the South who can't vote, who are terrified by mobs at the least provocation, and cannot get a decent job or a decent education."

Paul increased his political activity that summer in America, and as he increased it he became unalterably identified with the Communist party and its sympathizers. There is no reason he should not have been identified thus, he was perhaps the most prominent Communist sympathizer in America. Certainly he was one of the most active in defending the Communists. He was not promulgating Communism for America, although he believed philosophically in the theory. He was defending the right of the Communists to hold their beliefs and to attempt to persuade others to those beliefs. He spoke at huge left-wing rallies in New York, Washington, Chicago. He picketed the White House with members of the United Public Workers Union, protesting alleged discriminatory labor practices at the Bureau of Printing and Engraving. He appeared as a defense witness for the Communist leaders at the trial in Foley Square—although the questions and his answers were almost entirely stricken from the record as irrelevent. He spoke before the Communist-oriented Civil Rights Congress. He said he would seek the impeachment of Judge Harold Medina, who was trying the Communist case. He also said he would protest to the United Nations about the trial of the Communists. He suggested that violence would soon break out in Harlem unless Negroes received their full civil liberties. In what seemed to be almost the next breath, he praised Eugene Dennis, general secretary of the Communist party.

America responded to Paul negatively in that summer and autumn of 1949. The newspapers sneered when he suggested that the words of "Ol' Man River" be changed, and they quoted Oscar Hammerstein. Of course they would. Paul was obviously losing all sense of proportion in his own anger against his fellow Americans, white Americans. Jackie Robinson and A. Philip Randolph and the editors of the Baltimore *Afro-American* understood the America in which they lived, and they understood the fears of the American who would come to be called "whitey" by the Negroes in a few more years. Who was "whitey" in Negro parlance? He was Mr. Average White American, not too well educated, not too much concerned with such matters as American Constitutionalism. He was not the Ku Klux Klansman or the professional racist, he was just America, the America that had so long ignored the black race's pleas for freedom and responsibility.

The conservative, "responsible" members of the Negro community understood the white man and his fears. These people were not content with what they had, but they were content to seek change slowly.

Paul was never in this group. He was always the revolutionary, seeking immediate change. The revolutionaries like Paul did not seek violence. If the change could be accomplished without violence, so much the better. But they were always willing to accept violence as the price of the change.

As long as Paul's revolutionary ideas were confined to ideas, and he represented himself or other Negroes, the white community did not fear him. Of course, he was hated and maligned in the South, but that was to be expected. But in the North and West Paul lost the sympathy of white Americans when he became an outright apologist for the Communists, because these white Americans feared that the Communists would come and take away what they had. It was a basic fear, and particularly that summer there was a psychotic aspect to it. The indications were, as far as white America could see in the newspapers, that the government was infiltrated by Communists whose dedication to the Soviet Union was unquestionable. Who knew or could guess, which of our secrets were in the hands of the Russians already? Who knew or could guess, whether his neighbor was a secret spy for the enemy? Add to this atmosphere of fear and suspicion the normal white fear of the black man, and one has an indication of the attitude stirred up about Paul Robeson in America in the summer of 1949.

The veterans' organizations, being by their very nature organized patriotic societies, took upon themselves the task of representing the feeling of white America toward Paul. When Paul appeared at a Civil Rights Congress rally in Newark, the VFW there picketed him. Earlier in the year, after his remarks about the Negroes and Russia, a Connecticut state official had suggested that Paul be barred from the state when he returned to America—that he not be allowed to return to his Enfield house. This statement was so ridiculous that it aroused sympathy; the New York *Times* had this to say:

> The suggestion that Mr. Robeson should be barred from returning to his home in Connecticut is, of course, fantastically stupid. The reasons for his present obsession with the Communist line are so clearly apparent that they should cause no surprise. He is mistaken and misled, as many other persons are and have been. We hope, profoundly, that his passion for a good cause will not lead him permanently into support for a bad one. We want him to sing, and to go on being Paul Robeson. *

It was a forlorn hope, and perhaps the patriotic organizations sensed more than the men of good-will in America how far Paul had gone in his support of the good cause—and

* The New York *Times*, April 25, 1949.

his unwitting tie to one that Americans regarded as bad. Soon the American Legion at New Haven urged Governor Chester Bowles to ban Robeson rallies in that state. All this was a prelude to the hideous display of hatred at Peekskill that was led by the American Legion.

The hysteria about Paul Robeson—and it became just that—built up all summer long. A Negro ex-Communist named Manning Johnson testified before the House Committee on Un-American Activities that Paul was a secret member of the Communist party and that he had set out to become the "black Stalin" of America. The young Robesons, Pauli and Marilyn, were booed on the streets, and when they came to the Robeson house at Enfield, to escape the crowds, they were deluged with hate mail—unsigned, defamatory, and vicious.

Then came the two weeks of Peekskill.

It is apparent that the newspapers and patriotic societies incited the riots. They had spoken out against the previous concert and the Peekskill Post of the Legion had called for a boycott, and as far as local residents were concerned, the boycott had been quite successful. Only about a hundred local people turned out in 1948 to hear Paul sing.

The Peekskill story tells much about the change in the emotional attitude of America towards Paul Robeson. The Peekskill story was told by Howard Fast in a booklet published by the Civil Rights Congress, a pro-Communist organization. Granted that Howard Fast's emotions were deeply involved in this affair, and granted that Fast's objectivity would be warped by his affiliation with the Communist party, Fast was a novelist and a very sensitive writer, and his view of the events at Peekskill gives one view of America—an America seen by Paul Robeson late in the 1940s—and a view of the attitudes of plain, ordinary Americans in a small town and rural area of the United States, toward the man who had once been lionized in such places. Fast need not apologize for his account of the Peekskill riots, for it was proved to be essentially an accurate account, supported by the general press, and confirmed in detail in an investigation by the American Civil Liberties Union.

The Peekskill Affair began on August 27, 1949. The events of that day and the days that followed are important to the story of Paul Robeson because those days marked, in a way, the complete revulsion of the white community against him.

The Peekskill concert was to be the fourth that Paul had given there in recent years. Each summer, thousands of workers in the garment trades came to this particular region of the Hudson, from Croton-on-Hudson to Peekskill and a few miles north. They built, bought, and rented summer houses. They created interracial camps and developments. As the number of interracial groups increased, the long-time residents of Peekskill objected to the fact that most of these summer residents were Jews and Negroes. They objected to the fact that most of them were radicals and many were Communists or fellow travelers. Egged on by local newspapers, the people of the region began to be aroused.

This summer's concert was to be sponsored by a left-wing organization of folk musicians known as People's Artists. Howard Fast was to be chairman of the affair.

The campaign against the concerts began in the third week in August. The Peekskill *Evening Star* noted the coming of the concert, and that its proceeds would go to the Harlem Chapter of the Civil Rights Congress. The association of those two entities—Harlem and the Civil Rights Congress, aroused considerable emotion in Peekskill. Harlem was not a popular word in Peekskill. The Civil Rights Congress was less well known, but it had recently been called a "red front" in California, and it was making a name for itself as the major fund-raising organization for the defense of the Communist leaders on trial in Foley Square.

Soon civic leaders began inciting the people of the area. The commander of the Verplanck Post of the American Legion sent a letter to the newspapers stating his opposition. The President of the Peekskill Chamber of Commerce did the same. The Junior Chamber of Commerce called for "group action" to stop the concert—which might have been regarded as incitement to riot, had the authorities been interested.

Three days before the concert, a meeting of the patriotic organizations of the area was called by an Assistant District Attorney for Westchester County—a law enforcement officer. He did not call the meeting in that capacity, but in his role as chairman of the Joint Veterans Council. At the meeting it was decided to organize pickets to parade past the concert site and show the feelings of the veterans toward Paul.

It was to be, said the Assistant District Attorney, a "peaceful protest."

Some who were connected with the concert became worried about the atmosphere that was building in Peekskill, and they protested to the Attorney General of New York State, asking for protection for the concert-goers. The Attorney General's office referred the protest back to the Westchester County District Attorney, who referred it to the Assistant District Attorney who had called the meeting in the first place. He, of course, said again that the picketing would be perfectly peaceful, and he probably believed this. So far the affair was largely a commentary on the average American's propensity for self-delusion.

Then came the first riot. On the day of the concert, friends warned Fast that there was to be trouble, but he said he did not believe it. He was told that the American Legion would be marching to protest, and that other citizens were coming out to make their feelings known about the concert. Focal point of the criticism was Paul Robeson.

"It appears," had said the Peekskill *Evening Star,* a few days earlier, "that Peekskill is to be treated to another concert visit by Paul Robeson, renowned Negro baritone. Time was when the honor would have been ours—all ours. As things stand today, like most folks who put America first, we're a little doubtful of that honor . . ."

Howard Fast was concerned that day, but perhaps not really worried. In the evening he drove along back roads near Peekskill to Division Street, a three-mile-long country road that runs between the town of Peekskill and the Bronx River Parkway which connects New York and various Westchester

County communities. Before he reached the entrance to the
Lakeland Picnic Grounds where the concert was to be held, he
encountered many parked cars, and at the entrance stood a
crowd of men who jeered and thumbed their noses at him as
he drove by into the grounds. Inside, about a hundred people
were assembled, many of them Negroes, but this was only a
handful compared to the thousands who were expected. The
concert was set for seven o'clock. Seven came and, although
there was no sign of trouble, neither was there a crowd.

Finally, a small boy brought the news of trouble. Fast and
perhaps twenty-five others ran to the entrance to the park and
discovered why no cars were coming in. One fork of the
entrance road had been blocked by a large pile of rocks and a
truck had been pulled across the other fork. The concert-goers
were set upon then by many scores of men armed with clubs,
brass knucks and rocks. Some of these men wore American
Legion caps. This brief fight ended when three deputy sheriffs
came up to talk for a moment. The deputies accused the
concert-goers of "making trouble," but they backed off to
consider their role, and Fast was allowed a few minutes to
plan strategy. He sent a runner to crawl through the bushes,
reach the road, and telephone. Who was he to telephone?: the
New York *Times*, the *Daily Worker*, and Governor Thomas E.
Dewey.

So the emissary left, and then Fast put his strategy into
effect. He was to try to hold the road, some twenty-five or
thirty men against a crowd he estimated to be three hundred,
armed men, swinging "broken fence posts, billies, bottles, and
wielding knives."

"Lynch Robeson," they shouted. "Give us Robeson. We'll
string that big nigger up! Give him to us, you bastards."

That cry was the signal for the battle. "We'll kill every
commie bastard in America," the attackers yelled, as they came
forward. Now there were forty-two defenders by Fast's count,
and they linked arms and held against the mass of oncoming
attackers. They beat off the first attack. The attackers moved
back and reorganized. The press arrived, but the police did
not. There was another attack, and soon it was eight o'clock

and the defenders were bleeding. Fast said that federal agents were on hand, but they did nothing to stop the violence. (Federal agents then had no authority, or thought they had no authority, to engage themselves in local situations.) The fight surged up and down a meadow, past the two thousand empty chairs of the amphitheater. Fast lost his glasses. Men were hit and cut with rocks. Eventually the police came, after the violence had run its course, and that was the end of the first night of violence. Paul Robeson had never come near the concert. Many who had tried to come in had their cars smashed by the Legionnaires and others blocking the road. Paul had been turned back miles from the concert grounds. It was an ugly performance. There was not a single arrest of a rioter. Law and order had lost its tenuous hold on the citizens of Peekskill.

Throughout America, the reaction to the first Peekskill riot was one of disbelief or disapproval, but there was not much serious reaction, for the affair had been more threatening than real for all but a handful of participants.

The day after that riot, those who had organized the concert met and organized the Westchester Committee for Law and Order, which was to be a protective organization, this time to be sure that Paul Robeson could arrive and could sing. He was invited to come again.

A few days later, a mass meeting was held at the Golden Gate Ballroom, at 140 Street and Lenox Avenue, in the heart of Harlem. This auditorium held an estimated five thousand people, and it was packed to more than capacity that summer night, with a solid crowd of Negroes shoving and pushing to try to get in or to show their feelings by just being on the street near the meeting place. The word was out in Harlem that an organized attempt had been made to lynch Paul Robeson. Fast wrote,

> He came into the hall then, and the noise was fused into a somber, angry meaning. He came in very proud and very troubled; and though I had seen him before in so many places in all the years our paths had crossed, I had never seen him

like this, so proud and so troubled, with the whole face of the future bare to him, waiting and challenging.

It was very hot there on that hot summer evening, and the manner in which that old, gilded ballroom was packed with humanity did not lessen the heat. Men sat in their shirt-sleeves, but the sweat ran off them, and the heat hung like a heavy cloud under the ceiling. But no one rose to go, and one after another, people spoke of *Peekskill*, of what had happened on Saturday night, of the meaning inherent in it. You could not watch that crowd of serious, troubled faces—faces of people who had known little else than trouble—and not understand that something new was in the making here. It was a bitter coming of age. "You have harassed our people so long, and now you go against this man whom we love and honor, because he is such proof of our seed of greatness.

Fast quoted Ben Davis, Negro Communist leader, as speaking out:

"Let them touch a hair of Paul Robeson's head," he cried bitterly, "and they'll pay a price they never calculated!"

A low roar; it was not a loud crowd; the noise was a throaty, deep one.

Robeson promised then that he would sing again at Peekskill.

"Yes, I will sing wherever the people want to hear me," he said, "I sing of peace and freedom and of life!"

When the meeting was over, finally, the people poured out of the hall. The crowd outside had increased, and now the whole joined throng flurried and swept the police away. It swept them away without violence, but swept them away, and then turned into the avenue and formed ranks, and suddenly there was a massive parade marching down Lenox Avenue. Now the horse cops had come up, the "great" ones on their chestnut colored steeds, but they would not stop this tonight and they too were swept out of the way and the huge concourse of people marched on down Lenox Avenue . . .*

That was Howard Fast's account of the mass meeting in Harlem, at which the people of that Negro city showed their

* Fast, *Peekskill, U.S.A.*, p. 65.

feelings toward Paul Robeson, even as the white community—the so-called responsible community—indicated its disapproval of the violence in Peekskill, but also its disapproval of Paul Robeson.

Paul was eager to challenge officialdom in this case, eager to sing at Peekskill, no matter how many or how great the threats. He believed that the Ku Klux Klan was mixed up in the rioting and said as much, demanding an investigation of the Klan's role by Governor Thomas E. Dewey. By 1949, the Cold War had made white Americans very nervous and Paul had sharpened the fear of many whites that the blacks and reds were planning insurrection.

Now, when faced with a second attempt to hold a Robeson concert, the American Legion and its supporters reacted as might be expected: they were determined that the Robeson concert would not be held. Paul was the symbol to a growing segment of white Americans of all that was evil. He was a Negro and a successful one. He sympathized openly with the Soviet Union. His son had married a white girl that summer. These facts were inseparable, and they were jumbled together in the violent attitude of the good men and women of Peekskill who came out on this second attempt to hold a Robeson concert.

The concert was to be held on September 4, and this time even the sleepy State Police and the Westchester County Sheriff's office knew there was going to be trouble. Some twenty thousand left-wingers and Negroes and liberals thronged inside the concert area. Thousands of Legionnaires and others marched outside, singing and carrying flags. One of their songs, sung to the tune of "Roll Out the Barrel" was "Roll Out the Commies." And from the roadsides, as the concertgoers entered by bus and car, could be heard shouts: "We'll kill you!" accompanied by curses and epithets. It promised to be a lively evening.

Paul arrived at the concert grounds at around noon. Few of the concert-goers expected trouble, at least before they arrived, because so many of them had come to show their support for Paul Robeson, People's Artists, Negro rights, the Communist party, or just to hear a great singer. There was a security force in Howard Fast's organization this time, however; the organizers expected trouble. It was rumored that an attempt would be made to shoot Paul Robeson, and the sound truck was placed under a tree and he was surrounded by a protective cordon of men, blacks and whites, as he sang. He did sing, even though harried by a helicopter that kept swooping in over the grounds trying to drown out the sounds. He went out, protected by bodyguards, and he was involved in an incident that night—but nothing like the violence that the other concert-goers suffered. After the concert ended, the good folk of Peekskill on this September night lined the roads through which buses and cars must pass and beat at the occupants with stones and sticks and bricks. The windshield of Robeson's car was smashed by a stone, but it was only symbolic: he was unhurt. Others were seriously injured in that night of fighting, unprotected by American police because, truly, the crowd represented the views of the authorities, more or less—at least enough that no effort was made to protect the radicals who had come out to hear Paul Robeson sing.

Paul's friends had asked for an escort for the afternoon's performance, but the District Attorney's office did not provide it. The concert had begun at two o'clock in the afternoon. It was nightfall before many of the concert-goers left the grounds, and then they had to run the gamut of hate.

When it was all over, when the broken heads had been taken to hospitals to be bound up, and all that remained were the bitter memories of the concert-goers and the sharp hatred of the assailants, the United States was the loser. If he had not been convinced before that the United States was traveling the road to Fascism, Paul was now convinced. The New York state authorities tried to hush up the affair. Governor Dewey reported that the assemblage was made up of followers of the Communists—as if this made any difference to the breakdown of law and order in Peekskill.

Newsweek and other publications tried to play down the miserable showing of Americans in this hour of trial, indicating that the main issue at Peekskill was that "with the aid of anti-

Communist hotheads, the Communists had won a smashing propaganda triumph."

But there was more to it than that, and *The Nation* caught the implications better than any other publication, from the moment that the authorities refused to grant the pleas of the left-wingers for protection, before the concert day came.

It was against this background of official irresponsibility that the lawlessness broke out after the concert. In this second Battle of Peekskill at least 140 persons were injured, some seriously; hundreds were bruised; innumerable cars were wrecked; violence raged over a ten mile area; and for hours no car was safe from volleys of flying rocks. Radio commentators, broadcasting from the scene, asked in horrified tones whether this could be the United States in the year 1949.

Continued *The Nation:*

In an immediate sense Governor Dewey is now on trial. His first move was to demand an inquiry by the sheriff, the district attorney, and state police—all of them reasonably charged with negligence on the occasion when the concert was first scheduled. Unless this action is made to serve merely as a preliminary report, to be followed by a vigorous and impartial investigation, the Governor will not and cannot be acquitted. But far beneath the level of official culpability lies the sinister layer of hate and hysteria which converted an anti-communist demonstration into a witch's holiday. Paul Robeson's recent statements have been stupid and uncalled for, if not deliberately inflammatory, but the explosion at Peekskill was not merely anti-communist. It was anti-Negro and anti-Semitic as well, charged with indiscriminate hatred. What was more horrifying than the ignorance of the veterans, who have done a fine week's work for Josef Stalin, was the revelation of Nazi-like violence in the teen-agers, who carried out most of the terror. That is something that should haunt school officials, the parents, indeed all the citizens of Westchester County long after the Robeson nightmare is forgotten.*

Nightmare was the word. The affair was not forgotten. It was turned into a *cause célèbre* in the world beyond the

* *The Nation,* September 10, 1949.

American frontiers, and many people in foreign lands began to believe that the United States was giving way to terrorism. In time the American Civil Liberties Union would come forth with a report placing blame where it belonged—on the failures of public officialdom and the excesses of the West-chester County press. Yet more significant to those like Paul who lived through that day and that night were the epithets and the raging of a crowd that had all the earmarks of a southern lynch crowd. A southern lynch mob in Peekskill, New York? From the Negro's point of view, and particularly from Paul's point of view, another hope had been found to be an illusion. How much real difference was there between North and South in the attitude toward the Negro? The question was raised at Peekskill as it had not been raised for many years.

How much loyalty can a nation demand of an individual citizen? This question became germane in Paul Robeson's affairs in the year 1949. It was an ineluctable fact that Paul's political opinions were detested by the vast majority of white Americans, and his apology for Communism became the most important aspect of his relationship with white America. This was not so with Negro America. At his homecoming in Harlem he was greeted by a crowd of thousands that summer—months after his first "The Negroes will not fight the U.S.S.R." statement. After Peekskill, Paul's personal following did not diminish among Negroes, even though many might disagree with his political views. The Negroes of America knew what Paul was fighting for, and that was what every one of them wanted and what they hoped so desperately to achieve in their lifetimes: total citizenship in the United States of America. Paul's entire political life, since 1938, had been dedicated to this cause, and the Negroes of America knew it.

Not so the whites—or, to put it another way: Paul's underlying motivations made no difference to the whites. They judged his actions as they saw them. Nowhere could there be a better illustration of the gap that separated white and black America than in the attitudes of white and black America toward Paul Robeson.

In a profile of Paul in 1928, *The New Yorker* magazine had used such extravagant praise to describe Paul as "the promise of his race," "king of Harlem," and "idol of his people."

"Everywhere Paul went in Harlem everyone spoke to him," wrote Mildred Gilman in her profile. " 'There goes Paul Robeson' they say to one another. Managers won't let him pay for tickets. Waiters lead him proudly to their best tables. Negroes say that his influence is greater than that of a dozen agitators because he sings their songs the way they want them sung. They hear their own voices in his spirituals. . . ."

Twenty-one years later *The New Yorker* magazine had grown far more sophisticated and had adopted a lively interest in the white American attitude toward Paul Robeson. In 1928, *The New Yorker* had attempted to examine Paul from the inside out. In 1949, the same magazine, in the Talk of the Town editorial section, passed a few judgments on Paul from the white American point of view. Robeson had said he was going to sing where ever he wanted to sing. What *The New Yorker* objected to was his mixture of singing and politics. While defending his right to make pronoucements that were unpopular, the magazine claimed that by doing so Robeson was putting civil rights under great strain.

What was Paul's attitude toward America and the whole of the American people at this time? For the answer, one can hardly go to his public pronouncements. They had begun to assume the regular rhythm of the Communist party line. Rather, a statement made by Essie in an angry letter to the editor of the Springfield, Massachusetts, *Union* tells much of the Robeson view; Essie was always ahead of Paul in political matters.

Essie said that she felt no loyalty to fellow citizens who wished her evil.

"I found," she wrote, "that my loyalty is given to the laws of my country as set down in our beautiful Constitution and our Bill of Rights, to those communities which obey the laws, to my fellow citizens, fellow progressives, and friends here in my country and all over the world who think, feel, and work for the equality of man."

Here is insight into the Robeson credo of the summer and fall of 1949. It was basically the same as ever. Paul was interested primarily in the welfare of the Negro race; Essie was perhaps even more interested than he.

Paul stated it a bit differently at a rally in Harlem that summer, the welcome-home rally that was staged before what *The New Yorker* called the "mechanical" words began to come out.

". . . I'm looking for freedom, full freedom, not an inferior brand," he said. "That explains my attitude to different people, to Africa, the continent from which we came. . . . This explains my feeling toward the Soviet Union, where, in 1934, I for the first time walked this earth in complete human dignity, a dignity denied me at the Columbia University of Medina [Judge Medina of the Communist trial], denied me everywhere in my native land."

He answered what had been a friendly New York *Times* call upon him to become his old self again. ". . . personal success can be no answer. It can no longer be a question of an Anderson, a Carver, a Robinson, a Jackson, or a Robeson. It must be a question of the well-being and opportunities not of a few but for *all* of this great Negro people of which I am a part."

A decade and a half later, editor James Hicks of the Amsterdam *News* would go back through his files and he would note that in these years Paul Robeson was saying what the Negroes as a group would not begin saying for another five years, not saying loudly for another decade. Here was the militant Robeson, sounding the Negro cry.

Speaking of the majority of whites, at least the whites who held power in America, Paul said: "They can't imagine that our people, the Negro people—forty millions in the Caribbean and Latin America, one hundred and fifty millions in Africa, and fourteen million here, today, up and down this America of ours—are also determined to stop being industrial and agricultural serfs. They do not understand that a new reconstruction is here, and that this time we will not be betrayed by any coalition of Northern big finance barons and Southern bourbon plantation owners. They do not realize that the Negro people, with their allies, other oppressed groups, the progressive sections of labor, millions of the Jewish and foreign born of former white indentured labor, north, south, east and west, in this day and time of ours are determined to see some basic change."

Paul was ahead of his time. He was also a little off center, for the Negro would learn that his battle had to be fought by the Negro for the Negro, and Paul's hopes that the "working class" could be brought into the fight would prove groundless.

Except for the extreme left, the attitude of the white community toward Paul was a compendium of fear and hatred, exaggerated now almost beyond belief. Columnist Westbrook Pegler referred to Paul as one "spoiled by years of flattery and social toleration by white debauchers addicted to the 'arts' as a pretext of abandoned conduct." In a way Pegler might be called the Puritan conscience of America, for his morality was a Puritan morality, unyielding and stern. George Sokolsky, a more erudite and more politically-minded writer, wondered why Paul chose to live in the United States, rather than go to Soviet Russia, which he said he would prefer. Others asked Paul this same question, and he brought up his mother's relatives, who claimed to have baked bread for George Washington as free Negroes, helping in their way to fight the American Revolution. Paul was not going to be driven from his native land, he said.

There is no doubt but what he was sometimes wistful for the personal love and freedom he found in Soviet Russia, and that life would have been far easier for Paul had he gone to Russia to bask in the glory he had attained there, rather than face contumely and restriction in his own country. But Paul felt that he had a battle to fight in behalf of his race, and the downtrodden workers of the world with whom he had been persuaded to ally himself, even if the vast majority of the Negroes of America could not go so far.

It was too bad, in a way, that more whites did not know more Negroes, in the manner that columnist Ed Olly of the New Brunswick Sunday *Times* knew Paul. They had gone to

college together, these two, and, in September, at the height of
the frothing hysteria about Paul and his behavior, columnist
Olly devoted his column in the Sunday *Times* to Paul. "Somehow, I can't take Paul Robeson seriously," said columnist Olly.
The Paul he knew was the Paul with whom he had played
football so many years earlier. Olly recalled the old days when
the home folks used to brag about knowing Paul. Olly said,

> Then came evil days. The Robeson legend curdled as Paul
> went pink and began to plump for communism. Now veterans
> gather around his concert halls and picket them to prevent
> his appearance. The rocket which rose so high has fallen to
> the ground.
> Others may rant about Paul Robeson but I cannot join the
> chorus. To me he is just a big man—by race a Negro, which
> has no particular bearing on the matter. He is not a spokes-
> man for his race and to say so is just silly. The Negroes have
> no spokesman any more than the white people have a spokes-
> man.*

Columnist Olly spoke truth, or part of the truth, but aside
from that, his calm about Paul was based on a certain knowledge of a young Negro football player. He had the background
to appreciate Paul Robeson as a human being, which very few
Americans did.

After Peekskill, after the abortive attempt to testify in the
Communist leaders' trial, Paul went on concert tour again, this
time sponsored by the Council on African Affairs, since he was
no longer singing on the formal concert stage.

The concert tour was a miserable failure as an artistic effort.
The American Legion set out to try to stop Paul from singing
or presenting his views anywhere. Why the Legion should
constitute itself the defender of public morality was more than
could be understood; this attempt to undermine a single man
represented as dark a period as the Legion has ever under-
gone, and it was a tribute to Paul that he should have so much
attention from so many.

* The Sunday *Times* (New Brunswick, N.J.), September 4, 1959.

On this tour Paul's appearances were sponsored locally in cities by Negro churches, Negro newspapers, and civil rights groups. Nearly everywhere, in the past, Paul had been good newspaper copy and had been interviewed as he traveled across country. Now he had become a pariah in white America. Biographer Marie Seton, who shared many of Paul's political views, said that, on his visit to Chicago, where before Paul had been subject of newspaper stories and editorials on nearly every visit, in this autumn of 1949 a "blackout" was imposed by the white press, and virtually no mention was made of Paul's visit although he made many public appearances.

When Paul went to Los Angeles, right-wingers publicized his concert scheduled for Wrigley Field under the auspices of a Negro newspaper, by advertising in the white press for citizens to stay away from the Robeson presentation. Although many efforts were made to stop the concert, some 16,000 persons attended.

Obviously, Paul was not a pariah everywhere in his own country, although he had gone a long way down the road to Moscow.

Chapter 15

THE BATTLE

The year 1949 marked the end of Paul Robeson as singer in America, as *The New Yorker* had indicated. After Los Angeles he went to other cities, to Detroit and to Cleveland, where there were large Negro populations. He turned more to the Negroes in this hour of crisis and less to his left-wing friends who were centered on the East and West coasts.

Paul was not uniformly accepted by American Negroes. The wealthy Negroes, who had acquired property and even position in Negro society, wanted no part of so controversial a figure. He threatened their economic welfare, they believed. Then, and later, Negro industrialists took stance against Paul and his radicalism. Bankers, manufacturers, and others behaved remarkably like their white contemporaries. They had arrived—had achieved something of what they wanted in a white America.

But for the majority of Negroes, Paul represented something special in life. Every Negro knew that Paul had no need to remain in America, and that his popularity was international. Now, in 1949, he had every reason not to remain in America, for this was the one nation of the world in which the ruling group had set its hand against him. He toured until January, often at considerable risk to himself. Friends said that he aged visibly in the four months of tour, but he made himself known favorably to millions of American Negroes who had previously worshiped him or admired him only from afar. Paul was not

198

ever very important in white America, except as a symbol of
opportunity and later as a symbol of evil. In Negro America
Paul's reputation grew immeasurably in 1949, because he
showed himself willing to struggle against the whites. Politics
was the least of it in Negro eyes. The struggle Paul waged was
the important part, and when he struggled in their behalf the
Negroes of America could forgive him anything.

The year 1949 marked the beginning of the end of Paul's
career as a recording artist in America. His records were with-
drawn from many music stores in America. Biographer Seton
tries to make a case, stating that at about this period any
reporter, columnist, or radio commentator who mentioned
Paul's name except to abuse it would be immediately fired
from his job. This is arrant nonsense, of course. The American
press has never worked that way in spite of the tight control
that the left-wingers have imagined. But the fact was that Paul
represented a philosophy that most segments of the American
press detested, and most reporters, columnists, and radio commentators had no desire to say anything friendly about Paul.
Very, very few white Americans realized Paul's true position in
the Negro world.

Perhaps fewer realized what he was trying to do almost
single-handed: he was trying to bring the Negro into the left-
wing movement operated by the Communists, not for the
purposes of the Communists, however, but for the purposes of
the American Negro.

Paul outlined this position in a statement made to Dan
Burley, managing editor of the Negro newspaper, New York
Age, just after Peekskill. Many of Paul's statements sound as
though they were written in a dank room in the basement of
the *Daily Worker* building, and there are parts of the statement to Burley, as reconstructed by Burley, that so ring also.
But there are other parts that are pure Robeson.

Note the differences.

Paul and what was then the Communist party line:

"To be completely free from the chains that bind him, the
Negro must be part of the progressive forces which are fighting the overall battle of the little guy—the sharecropper, the

drugstore clerk, the auto mechanic, the porter and the maid, the owner of the corner diner, the truck driver, the garment, mill and steel worker.

"I am well equipped now, although I have not always been so, to make the supreme fight for my people and all the other underprivileged masses wherever they may be. Here, I speak of those bereft of uncompromising, courageous leadership that cannot be intimidated, and cannot be swerved from its purpose of bringing true freedom to those who follow it."

Paul, speaking out as Paul:

"This thing burns in me and it is not my nature nor inclination to be scared off.

"They revile me, they scandalize me, and try to holler me down on all sides. That's all right. It's okay. Let them continue."

By 1950, Paul had become a professional Negro as well as a professional politician. That year, when Paul went to Chicago in February for a meeting of the Progressive party leadership, he failed to stay at a downtown hotel in white Chicago, as he had always done before, and moved into a Negro hotel on the south side. His reason, he said, was that he would not stay in a hotel where his Negro friends could not stay.

Paul's orientation to Communism was now complete. Peekskill had done that to him, if a final seal was needed by 1949. The Soviet government did him high honor and named a mountain for him, placing a bust of him on its peak.

Early in 1950 was published the text of Paul's address given late in 1949 to the banquet of the National Council of American Soviet Friendship at the Waldorf Astoria Hotel. The occasion was the celebration of the thirty-second birthday of the founding of the Russian revolutionary government. Paul again showed his orientation to the Russian bloc, and his willingness to use his voice in behalf of the U.S.S.R. against the United States government.

"I am deeply grateful," he said, "for this opportunity to join more than one half the people of the world in celebration of a great anniversary. Yes, with fully one half of humanity—and even this is an underestimation. For it would be a mistake to assume that this thirty-second anniversary of the Union of

Soviet Socialist Republics is an occasion of joy and pride and thanksgiving only for the 800,000,000 who live in the Soviet Union and the Progressive Democracies of Eastern Europe and China. . . .

"I traveled recently to Western Europe and Scandinavia and I know from what I saw and heard in those countries that there, too, the peoples are able to struggle against the total colonization of their countries by Wall Street principally because of this new balance of power. And if the Viet Namese and the Indonesians, if the Burmese and the Malay people, indeed, if the people of long-suffering India have advanced to a higher stage of struggle for their independence, it is because of this sum-total of factors and the decisive influence of the Soviet Union."

There is no question that Paul really believed this statement.

In March, in his role as co-chairman of the Progressive party, Paul was asked in behalf of Mrs. Eleanor Roosevelt to appear as one of three Negro speakers in a discussion program she would lead on the National Broadcasting Company television network, dealing with the Negro in American politics. Congressman Adam Clayton Powell, Jr., and Perry Howard, a Mississippi Negro, were also to appear. Protests began to flow into the NBC offices, and NBC dropped the idea immediately. A spokesman said that some two or three hundred protests had been received. Mrs. Roosevelt indicated that her invitation to Paul had been "misunderstood." Mrs. Roosevelt's son Elliott, co-producer of the planned program, said Paul might "confuse the issue." Charles R. Denny, executive vice-president of NBC, said, "no good purpose would be served in having him speak on the issue of Negroes in politics." Another NBC man said, "we are doubtful that Robeson will ever appear on the NBC except under circumstances beyond our control."

Paul, naturally enough, took the position that an attempt was being made to muzzle him, and he grew unrestrained in his criticisms of his government, the American business community, and American foreign policy.

In 1950, if not before, Paul came under the surveillance of the Federal Bureau of Investigation. The only conceivable reason for this surveillance was that the federal authorities must have suspected him of either espionage or participation in some conspiracy against the government. The government did not choose to believe, it seemed, his statement that he was not and had never been a member of the Communist party, or perhaps government officials believed he had joined the party since 1946 when he made that statement. Agents staked out his house and followed him. He said his telephone was tapped. Those who spoke to him may have found the records of those conversations put down in dossiers of their own, for which they might some day have to account.

It was a tribute to Paul, although not the tribute of a very healthy or stable political body, that the United States government was enough afraid of him and his ideas to single him out for surveillance, and later for administrative punishment.

Apparently, the government investigators "discovered" that Paul had a number of Communist associates and friends, and that he was most outspoken in his defense of the Soviet Union and the other Communist countries of the world, and also outspoken in his attacks on the United States government and the general conduct of American society—white society.

A tide of protest arose against Paul, fomented from several sources. The House Un-American Activities Committee was extremely fond of using his name. Various right-wing organizations found it useful to condemn Paul in prefatory remarks about Communism. At Rutgers University, Paul's alma mater, some of the alumni of his class suggested that history be rewritten by striking Paul's name from the rolls of the college and rescinding his academic degree and the honorary degree Rutgers had given him. Dr. Benjamin Mays of Atlanta's Morehouse University, the Negro college that had given Paul an honorary degree, indicated that Paul would not have received the degree had the college known his opinions.

Times had changed, and in relationship to Communism, there was very little room for common sense in the United States in the early 1950s. One such note was spoken in that spring of 1950 by Earl Schenck Miers, the Rutgers official who had written the biographical novel, *Big Ben,* and knew more about Paul than most white men.

All around the country, the columnists were speculating on what had gone wrong with Paul. Some thought it was the machinations of Josef Stalin's minions, who had set out to entice Paul to Communism. Some thought it was the spoiling of Paul by his easy successes.

Not so, said Earl Schenck Miers, and, in an article in *The Nation* that spring of 1950,* Miers had some cogent remarks to make about Paul Robeson and America.

> Apparently it has never occurred to Robeson's classmates that if he is a communist he may be largely an American-made product for which they are partly responsible, that his political revolt, now so violently condemned as an attack upon the American form of government, is essentially a revolt against the complacency of a generation that has failed to understand much of the world around it.
>
> . . . the emotional Robeson, the man living within his heart, is not really different from other Americans who have sprung from a similar environment and experienced similar frustrations, and whose spirits show the results of day-by-day chafing in the scar tissue of lasting resentment.
>
> As a product of his times Robeson today is perhaps more all-American than he was as a member of his college football team.

Miers suggested that Paul's tragedy was the tragedy of his generation. Miers pointed to the situation of Bucky Hatchett, a Negro football star at Rutgers in 1950 who was the overwhelming choice of his fellows for senior class president, and who attended college dances without an eyebrow being raised. Miers suggested that the differences between Paul and Jackie Robinson were the differences of generations and not differences of ideologies.

But there was a basic difference. Jackie Robinson had already begun to identify himself with the business community. He would go on to become a businessman, and later a wealthy banker. Paul identified himself with the intellectual and artistic communities. And, as events of a few years later would show, the difference was not solely that of generations at all, but of

* May 27, 1950 issue.

philosophies—including the question of how much and how fast for the American Negroes. Paul would never accept as a definitive answer the story of Bucky Hatchett, any more than he ever accepted the story of his own success as any proof that the Negro in American society was receiving the treatment he deserved.

Miers made one clear, ringing call for sanity, however, in spite of his shortsightedness on the racial problems of the Negro.

"America's security can be little endangered by Robeson," he said, "no matter how violent his statements."

At about the time of the publication of this article in *The Nation*, Paul went to Europe to attend one of the innumerable "peace" meetings of the various committees to which he belonged. He returned to go to Chicago in June and speak before the National Labor Conference for Negro Rights.

At Chicago, Paul made a standard, Communist party-line, anti-war speech, talking about A-bombs, hydrogen bombs, and bacteriological warfare with the implication that the Western world might use these against the Communist world but that the Communist world would never threaten anyone.

Paul's remarks were tiresome. They were fitted to the Communist position. He was now more than a philosophical Marxist who happened to travel the same road as the Soviet-inspired Communists, he was an out-and-out Soviet Communist apologist. This change became clear that summer of 1950, when the liberal publicist and lawyer O. John Rogge suggested that if the World Peace Committee was truly sincere, it ought to reinstate peace-loving Yugoslavia into its ranks. But peace-loving Yugoslavia was deep in a quarrel with the Kremlin. Paul was one of the loudest to shout no—that the Yugoslavs were warmongers and traitors to Socialism.

What this matter had to do with Negro rights is a good question, and one that could be answered only by the convoluted process of saying that the Negro must support the workers who must support the U.S.S.R., and thus the question of Yugoslavia's struggle with the Kremlin over ideological independence was germane.

Tiresome as Paul's ideological maneuverings had become, they were not treason or criminal. Wrong-headed, and pig-headed, and foolish, yes, but illegal, no. But, in the summer of 1950, when the North Korean armies marched swiftly and steadily down toward the tip of the Korean peninsula, and no one knew what would happen, American officialdom became very nervous about Paul Robeson's speeches and public statements. War came in Korea. President Truman brought the United States into the war, and the United Nations came into the war, in the absence of a Soviet delegate who was then boycotting the Security Council and could not veto the action.

For reasons directly connected with the American hysteria of the late 1940s and the early 1950s, the federal government of the United States decided that Paul Robeson must not be allowed to travel abroad and speak out as a Negro American. There was not yet a way that it could prevent him from speaking out, but the government could prevent him from traveling, by refusing to grant him passport privileges. The principle followed here was that the American citizen does not have a right to travel abroad; travel is a privilege, granted at the convenience of the government. In the summer of 1950, the government decided that it would be inconvenient to have Paul Robeson go abroad again.

Paul was planning a trip to Eastern and Western Europe to fulfil some concert engagements. It was to be expected that he would attend a handful of pro-Communist meetings and make pro-Communist speeches, but why this standard procedure should worry Secretary Dean Acheson or the State Department so much was difficult to understand. Nonetheless, the idea did worry the State Department, and officials tracked Paul down in Harlem and demanded that he yield his passport. He refused, whereupon the State Department canceled the passport.

It is small honor to the press of the nation that few newspapers took much interest in the case, and those that did take an interest mostly approved of the State Department action, as did the New York *Herald Tribune*. That newspaper approved because Paul was an agitator, and thus his travel abroad was not "in the best national interest." Many other passports were canceled, too, and there was very little public outcry against this abridgement of a basic freedom.

Paul began agitating for the return of his passport. He was offered a chance to get it back—if he would submit to extortion. He only need sign a statement that he would not make any speeches when he was abroad, the State Department told him, and he could have his passport.

This offer was made at the end of August 1950, when Paul visited the State Department with a demand that he be allowed to see Secretary of State Dean Acheson and secure an explanation of the government's conduct.

So it was not really a question of Paul's travel being in the interest of the government, as the *Herald Tribune* had so quickly said it was—it was a simple attempt to coerce an American citizen into refraining from stating his political views because they did not agree with the government in power.

Whatever this was, it was not an exercise in freedom, and from Paul's point of view it could scarcely have endeared to him the "American way."

Soon, Essie Robeson's passport was revoked, and so was Pauli's. Essie's case is understandable, because she was Marxist when Paul was a concert singer without a political thought in his head. Pauli's case was less easy to understand, for as far as was known he had never been on record with any political statements whatsoever. But, in 1950, the fact that Pauli was Paul Robeson's son was enough. The young man had gone to school in Soviet Russia—and with Stalin's daughter!

The passports lost, in 1950 began a dismal charade in which the powers of an American federal government and an American business community tried to destroy a man because of his political views. Paul was, as his friends put it, "a prisoner" in America. This was true in more ways than one. Had he been able to leave the country, he could have earned money in concert tours abroad. At home he could earn only by singing for leftist organizations, for the concert stage; the white-tie-and-tails set and the Sunday afternoon musical societies were closed off to him.

Paul even found it difficult to hire a hall, or some halls, in which to stage meetings to protest publicly his passport revocation: Madison Square Garden barred his Council on African Affairs when it wanted to hold a Robeson passport rally there in the summer of 1950.

The long process of bringing suit against an unwilling federal government began. This procedure was still possible; the judiciary never did succumb totally to the hysteria of the times—no matter what Paul said about the conviction of the Communist leaders under the Smith Act. The judiciary's tread was measured, and the wheels of justice ground very slowly, but they did grind.

Paul had friends, and not all of them were left-wingers. The Harlem Trade Union Council came to his side. But so did the government of Lvov, Poland, which named a street in his honor. Paul received the World Peace Congress peace award, which was another Soviet-oriented gesture, and which did not help affairs at home.

In 1951, Paul's passport suit against the Secretary of State was dismissed by the federal district court. The dismissal came in April. It was not until August 16 that it could be appealed, for there was no tendency on the part of the government to speed this matter. That summer Pauli applied for a passport. His application was denied.

The next year, Paul tried to travel to Canada, but he was refused permission by his government. Travel to Canada also was a privilege, not a right, said the United States government. Paul had accepted an invitation to visit Vancouver, and he was stopped at the border and handed a paper that told him that he would be subjected to a $5,000 fine and up to five years imprisonment if he crossed. Of course, Paul could have crossed the border and not come back. The Canadians would have given him asylum. But he did not choose to run away from this fight—no matter what it did to his bank account or his soul. The ugliness of his government only renewed Paul's determination to fight.

One need not have agreed with Paul or with anything he stood for to sympathize with this strong man in an hour of trial. The United States of America had always prided itself on its respect for individual freedom. Here was a signal case of a man who was hounded and destroyed in his profession by a combination of government and public unpopularity. The public unpopularity was his own doing—and any man must be prepared to live with that. But the government harassment of Paul Robeson was unforgivable in a society that proclaimed itself a defender of freedom. It made no difference what Paul Robeson said or advocated, if he was an American citizen he had the right to say or advocate what he wanted within the bounds of the laws. Paul had not broken any laws; that must be remembered. He had simply spoken out more strongly than any other popular American figure for an unpopular cause. Administrative punishment, violation of the spirit of the American Constitution by the duly constituted authorities: that was the only way to describe what was happening to Paul Robeson in the 1950s.

It would be boring to a reader to try to trace Paul's activities during the next few years. He was in constant struggle over the same grounds. The struggle followed the pattern of one at Hartford, Connecticut, in the autumn of 1952, when Paul was scheduled to give a recital as part of the People's party presentation at a public school. Several civic and patriotic groups protested the use of the public school by this unpopular man. The city council of Hartford voted to ask the board of education not to let Paul sing at the school. The Board of Education had more common sense than the Hartford City Council, and the board refused to cancel permission of the group to hold its meeting and hear Paul.

Such incidents occurred time and again, to the disgrace of America.

Just before Christmas 1952 came a bolt from the blue, a shock to Americans that brought anti-Robeson feeling to a new high. Paul was awarded the Stalin Peace Prize by the government of the Soviet Union.

Now had the government of the United States been truly concerned with its own self-interest and with the reactions of the millions of colored peoples in the world, the government would have won a propaganda victory by congratulating Paul Robeson, American, on winning the Stalin Peace Prize. But the government was so steeped in the juices of fear that no responsible official dared make so obvious a suggestion, and had he made it, no other would have dared carry it out. Not only was this opportunity lost, but the American government was made to look small and venal because Paul was denied permission to travel to Moscow to receive the prize, and it had to be presented to him in New York City by Soviet officials there.

To add injury and insult, Essie, who had gone into local Connecticut politics on her own, was barred from the state ballot this year by the Connecticut Secretary of State.

If ever a man was given cause to hate his own government, it was Paul—there was no question about that. He was shadowed and harried, and most important of all, his right to make a living was impaired by his government. One might think that average Americans would consider the plight of this prominent citizen and would begin to wonder if this same problem might not come to them some time under some government they might not like. Average Americans were not thinking in so theoretical a fashion in the year 1952. They were thinking about a presidential election in which the charge of treason was still being levied against *Democrats* for the loss of China to the Communists, about the depredations of Senator McCarthy, who was paralyzing and destroying the career staff of the State Department, of the abortive Korean war, which everyone in America wanted to end as quickly as possible—the only difference being that some insisted on victory and some would settle for stalemate.

The American treatment of Paul Robeson in the 1950s continued to be ridiculous. Here was the most prominent single member of the Negro community—loved or hated—and his name did not appear in *Who's Who in America*. It appeared in the British *Who's Who*, but not in the American. Some idiot even went so far as to take Paul's name out of the *American Sports Annual*. For the years 1917 and 1918, when Paul had been designated football's all-American end by Walter Camp, history was rewritten, the long dead Mr. Camp was overruled, and Paul's name was removed from the list.

Such useless and stupid insult made propaganda for America's enemies. It showed to the colored peoples of the world an America that was petty, venal, evil. A million dollars, a billion dollars in propaganda about the good works of the Americans could not undo a single tale such as this. Small wonder that the Russians had so much success in convincing colored peoples of the essential enmity and colonial tendency of the Americans.

In 1953, the Robesons sold their house in Enfield, Connecticut, no longer content to live among the people of that state, and perhaps pressed a little for funds now, too, because Paul found it difficult to earn the large sums that he had once earned. To be sure, no new venality had been exercised against him abroad; he still received royalties from British, French, and other foreign recordings, but his major sources of livelihood, the concert stage, the cinema, the theater—these were cut off.

The punitive actions continued, not only by the government but also by certain white groups and individuals. When Paul was invited to Chicago in 1952 to give a concert, some Negroes who held federal jobs were told that if they attended the concert they would be fired. Such discharge was impossible— unless the government wanted to try to say that listening to Paul Robeson sing was subversive activity, but such were the times that federal job holders were easily intimidated. The concert was not held because, a few days before its scheduled date, the mortgage holders on the church threatened that if Paul sang there they would demand immediate payment or foreclose.

The deprivation of his rights to travel and be heard did not silence Paul, if that was what the State Department had wanted, and there could be no doubt about the State Department's wishes after the memorandum they asked him to sign. In 1953, Paul wrote a foreword to the book *Born of the People*, by Louis Taruc, the leader of the Hukbalahap revolutionaries of the Philippines. The book was published by the People's Publishing House of Bombay. Now, had Paul been allowed to travel, and had he gone to the Philippines to see that republic in action, a colored government run for and by colored peoples, without American or any other interference, Paul might have become convinced that there was a road to colored freedom other than the Communist road. He was scheduled to go to Australia and the Far East and he had very much wanted to make the trip. But the State Department was adamant. Paul applied for a passport again in 1953 and was again rejected. The slow process of suing for his rights continued.

In 1954, Paul was denied a passport again when he applied in order to attend a Soviet Writer's Conference in Moscow, to which he had been invited as an honored guest. The All-India Peace Council that year circulated in India and in America a plea for the return of the Robeson passport so he could visit India. The State Department turned deaf ears.

Throughout the world of colored peoples, as well as the Communist world, the United States government became infamous. "A prisoner in his own country," they called Paul in these countries. What could any American in those countries say? It was not enough to say that Paul was irresponsible, by the government's standards. The questioners would ask who set those standards. It was not enough to say that Paul did not represent Negro opinion in America. Why were the American officials afraid to let him speak, then? asked the questioners.

Paul kept asking for the return of his passport. In 1955, he asked for a limited passport, to visit various countries in the Western Hemisphere to which he had been invited. It was again denied, but he was given permission to travel in Canada. He arranged a concert series in Canada, at least partially to replenish his badly-depleted finances, but when the concert tour was arranged, the Canadian government succumbed to pressures and refused to allow him entrance into Canada.

Again in 1955, Paul filed suit against the government to try to force issuance of a free passport, but again the courts held that the State Department had the right to restrict the travel of any American citizen in the national interest. The problem was made very clear this year: the federal judges indicated that Paul must file a non-Communist affidavit if he wanted a State Department hearing on his application for a passport. Paul refused, on principle, to file the affidavit. The passport was denied.

In 1956, the argument was waged again. It became the central factor in Paul's life, this struggle for a passport so that he might visit his friends and earn a living. All over the world the cost of Paul's forcible incarceration in America was very high, in terms of loss of American prestige. From Delhi to Moscow came pleas that the United States government free this man. Trade union groups, peace groups, revolutionary groups all harped on the subject. Quite possibly, the detention of Paul Robeson within the national limits of the United States during these years was the single most costly act America might have taken in terms of propaganda to the colored peoples of the world.

Constantly Paul was receiving invitations and messages of condolence and support. Very little of this appeared in the American press, at least not in the white American press. Much more was apparent in the Negro press, which continued to follow Paul's affairs after he became only a symbol of radicalism and defiance to the white rulers of the nation.

In Britain in 1956, many of Paul's friends banded together to put pressure on the American government to free him for travel. Some sixteen members of Parliament led a movement to bring Paul to England to sing. They were joined by trade unionists, university professors, and church leaders. Paul could not attend, but he could tape-record a speech and songs, and he did so. These were played at a conference in Manchester.

Meanwhile, Paul appealed to the United States Supreme Court for his passport, and the Supreme Court turned him down, too.

In 1957, the international agitation for Paul's freedom became even more intense, and equally intense was the embarrassment of the United States government because of the bad press the United States was receiving throughout the world.

Passport, or not, Paul was not silenced now. He appeared before the House of Representatives Un-American Activities Committee again. He was asked how he felt about Russia. He loved Russia, he said, because there, for the first time "I felt myself a man who is valued equally."

There it was, the old Robeson principle, the attitude that personal success of the exception was not enough, that man must have his equal rights no matter his color. How many times had he repeated this in America in the past fifteen years? How many people had heard, and how many had listened? Again this June, as he spoke, very few Americans seemed to be listening.

There was a change in America, but its full import was not yet known. In 1954 the American Communist party was outlawed, but that same year the leader of the extremists on the other side, Senator Joseph McCarthy of Wisconsin, was censured by the Senate, and his power was broken. The following year, 1955, twenty-nine Asian and African countries met at Bandung in Indonesia, and condemned so many American policies so roundly that the United States government suddenly began to realize how inept it had been in its relationships with the colored peoples of the world. The United States Supreme Court that year stated that public education in America must be free and equal, and without discrimination; here was the first major victory the Negroes of America could claim in the days since Reconstruction. There must be no more segregation of races in America, was the effect of this statement.

In 1957, the pressures on the State Department continued and increased. Paul sang by transatlantic telephone to a group assembled to hear him in England. He ended his program with his radical bowdlerization of "Ol' Man River," in which he had changed the last words from "I'm tired ob livin' and skeered of dyin'," to "I must keep fightin' until I'm dyin'."

Paul was continuing the struggle for Negro rights, but now that he was no longer alone, and the other Negroes began to see some results of the struggling, Paul was not among the front ranks of the fighters.

The trouble that Paul now faced was spelled out by some of the new leaders, the NAACP leaders who proposed to carry on the battle of the Negro with demonstrations, sit-ins, legal actions, and marches. The trouble with Paul, they said, was that he had frightened away the fighters for Negro freedom by linking the Negro revolution in America with the international revolution of the Soviets.

Thus, in 1956, when suddenly the lights began to brighten and some in the colored world could see hope for the American Negro's achievement of full citizenship in the foreseeable future, Paul was out of the leadership, disgraced, his name a currency of no value because it brought fear and loathing into the hearts of the white community. This was the progression of Paul's Shakespearean tragedy.

Chapter 16

VICTORY AND
DEFEAT

In the spring of 1957, when Paul sang to England over the new coaxial cable that had been laid across the Atlantic Ocean, the State Department was beginning to feel the stings of gibes from far and near. At that concert in May, with great ostentation the leaders of the meeting called on the American embassy in London to send a representative to the conference to explain why Paul Robeson could not appear in person. The embassy did nothing of the kind, but this fact was duly reported to the press, and even such pro-American newspapers as the Manchester *Guardian* took a few digs at the American government's position regarding Paul's travel.

The issue was focused on Paul Robeson, but he was not the only person involved. The issue really came down to the question of the American government's right to restrict travel of persons it thought would make bad "unofficial ambassadors" when they were abroad.

Paul was as intransigent as ever. He made many inflammatory statements, to Americans and to people abroad, speaking of "forces of evil" in control in the United States which still tried to kneel on the necks of the Negro people. He still made it a point to send messages of congratulation to the Communist world, as when, on October 20, he praised the Soviet Union on the anniversary of the 1917 Revolution.

There were more concerts by telephone, including one sung for the miners of Wales, where Paul had secured so much sympathy and understanding twenty years earlier. Paul and Pauli, who had become an electrical engineer, established a firm called Othello Recordings, and made a number of records, including one of a new song about six mighty rivers which Paul sang for inclusion in the sound track of a Dutch film.

In 1958, Paul sued again for the right to travel, and, in 1958, the political climate in America had so changed that the State Department was no longer granted this power of restraint over American citizens. The United States Supreme Court had ruled that citizens could not thus arbitrarily be deprived of passports.

By 1958, the pressures had become enormous. From India, Prime Minister Nehru and other leaders planned to honor Paul by a special celebration, on his sixtieth birthday. That birthday was marked in Moscow by the Soviet Union that April, and by Communist China in Peking. It was also welcomed and celebrated in England and in African nations—not just the Communists honored Paul, his special honors came equally from the colored countries of the world.

Yes, times had changed in May 1958; Paul gave his first New York recital in eleven years, at Carnegie Hall. In June, Paul received his passport; in July, he left the United States for Europe.

In his own way he was still fighting for the rights of the American Negro, yet he chose to go abroad at a time when every strong Negro hand was needed to carry that fight. There was a good enough reason for Paul's decision. He was not wanted by the leaders of the Negro community. As John Lewis of the Student Non-Violent Coordinating Committee said of Paul, he had "scared away the so-called responsible" Negro leadership. So he had. Paul's rash statements, his wedding to the Communist cause, made him persona non grata in the fight for full freedoms. Abroad, Paul might be able to serve the total Negro cause—the cause of colored peoples everywhere. At home he was nothing but a liability to his own people in their struggle for equality, for, although the political climate had changed, it had not reversed itself, and Paul's transgressions against the American government were not forgotten.

The Negro weekly newspaper, *Informer*, of Houston, Texas, stated the Negro case against Paul, and this was published in the white magazine *America*. *Informer* accused Paul of deserting the Negro cause.

Deserting?

Yes. "If he had stayed out of the ideology fight," said *Informer*, "he could have been of great service to his race. We think of Marian Anderson, Jackie Robinson, Louis Armstrong, a host of others who have been loyal to their government, and thus have secured the right to speak out with authority against injustices to their people.

"Truth is Robeson chose the wrong horse. He took his family to Moscow, put his boy in school for two years, vilified America, and praised Russia. He slandered the American Negro by saying the Negro would not fight Russia."[*]

That was a part of Negro opinion in the nation in 1958. The *Informer* certainly did not represent all American Negroes. It did not represent Harlem and many other Negro communities in the North. The Negro press, by and large, was most sympathetic to Paul as a Negro and as one who spoke out on the race question. This was always Paul's primary interest. He was praised when he spoke out against segregation, praised by the Baltimore *Afro-American*, the San Francisco *Sun-Reporter*, the Pittsburgh *Courier*, and other Negro newspapers. The California *Voice* said this, summing up what the majority of American Negroes thought about Paul:

> Robeson embodies the unrestrained and righteous rage that has broken bonds. His is the furious spirit wearied with tedious checker-playing that stretches through nearly a hundred years in order to gain the rights guaranteed a hundred years ago.
>
> Robeson's cry is for justice, happiness, and freedom here and now. . . .
>
> A sensitive tormented soul, he is that Other Self, the Alter

[*] *America*, November 2, 1957.

Ego that a million Negroes try in self defense to disown. His protest is the authentic Protest of the Negro. . . .*

It was as it had always been, since that moment in 1933 when Paul had been challenged by white friends, radicals, who convinced him that as long as any in the world were downtrodden, he would never be allowed to forget that he was a Negro.

The removal of Paul's travel restrictions was greeted with considerable relief by many in white America. It had become apparent to Americans of good-will that the pendulum had swung too far to the right in the last few years and that, under the excuse of anti-Communism, the immoderates were impinging on the freedom of the whole American people.

The *Wall Street Journal,* hardly a left-wing publication, editorialized in favor of Paul's new freedom, and against a move made by President Eisenhower in 1958 to seek laws that would let the State Department deny passports to those whom it disliked. Eight years after the fact the *Journal* found it easy to say what Paul had been saying all along:

> . . . we can see no reason why a man free to travel in any one of the 48 states should be barred from traveling overseas. If a man is a danger to the country, then the man should be tried and put in jail. A great many have. But if a man is not a danger within the country, we can't see how he can suddenly endanger the country once outside its borders.†

The *Journal's* position should have convinced Paul that sanity and regard for freedom had been restored to his country, for the *Journal* (and this position was echoed by others) took his side in a manner that soon caused the administration's defeat in its attempts to pass restrictive legislation on American travel for political reasons. The *Journal* went further:

> Paul Robeson is a man with whose opinions about this country we completely disagree. But can a radical baritone's voice drown out Mr. Dulles? Can his view threaten N.A.T.O.

* *Ibid.*
† The *Wall Street Journal,* July 14, 1958.

or nullify all the billions of dollars we've spent on foreign aid to make friends and influence other nations? If so, we have built a foreign policy that is insecure indeed; and we might be the better off for knowing about it.

The fact is that Paul Robeson can't possibly do those things. He will be acclaimed in London, perhaps, for his artistry, and acclaimed in Moscow for his political views. But what off-key remarks can Robeson make overseas that he hasn't said right here at home? And what has he said here that hasn't got overseas?*

Paul did not comment on this return to sanity in 1958. He had commented on the positions stated by the Baltimore *Afro-American* two years earlier, when the Baltimore paper said it did not approve of some of the activities and statements attributed to him, but he said that was fair enough.

The ice had broken slowly that spring and summer, but it had melted in the country before it melted in Washington. Paul had made a highly successful concert tour of the West Coast in the spring of 1958, and in April he had been invited by Vanguard Records to make a new album of recordings. The songs he sang for this album were nonpolitical: "Loch Lomond," "The House I Live In," "Drink To Me Only With Thine Eyes," and "Sometimes I Feel Like a Motherless Child."

In his concerts and in his album, Paul was praised for having come to a peak in his singing. Here is music critic Nat Hentoff's opinion, as expressed in *The Reporter* that spring:†

> There are those who feel that Paul Robeson at sixty is singing better than at any previous time in his career. The commanding depth and vigor of his voice seem not to have become frayed, and he interprets with more control and flexibility than he manifested during his years of greatest popularity, when there was often a wooden stolidity in his otherwise powerful performances.

Now, the San Francisco *Chronicle* called Paul's "the greatest natural basso voice of the present generation" and said it could be felt "as a physical force."

* *Ibid.*
† April 17, 1958 issue.

Just as in the old, pre-political days, it seemed, Paul would again become the darling of American concert-goers. White America was extending the olive branch. But Paul was not ready to take it. He had spent nearly eight years in virtual exile within his own country. "Enforced professional immobilization," he called it. He was not ready now to embrace those who had made him suffer. He was eager to get abroad into fresher air than that of America.

Under the new regulations, applicants for passports must sign affidavits stating that they did not belong to illegal organizations (such as the Communist party). The information was not made public by the State Department. In a way, Paul's signing of his passport application was a victory for him. In another way, it was a defeat. But, in 1958, the issue no longer seemed so important as it had in 1950.

So, on June 27, Paul had his new passport and, on July 12, he was in London, where indeed the English did hail him for his singing. On August 16, he was in Moscow, where the Russians did hail him for his political views as the *Wall Street Journal* had suggested they would.

And what now were those political views? Paul had set them down during the years of enforced idleness, between his studies of Chinese, and African, and other languages.

Paul's political views had matured considerably in those eight years between 1950 and 1958, as he indicated in his book *Here I Stand,* published by Dennis Dobson, London, in 1958.

Here I Stand was addressed to the American Negro people, and it was as clear a credo as Paul had ever presented. He had the presence to avoid the issue that had dogged him for so long, the linking of the affairs of the American Negro with those of the Soviet Union. He had learned that American Negroes were not willing to listen to discussions of Russia, and he addressed himself to the matter at hand: the Negro revolution.

The advice Paul gave, now shorn of its pro-Soviet trappings, was the advice he had been giving for years, strengthened here and there. It was his old position, representing his long concern, for the freedom of the Negro people, individually and in the mass. How much of this was Essie's and how much was Paul's is debatable; Paul was never much of a writer, it was difficult to get him even to write a letter, and Essie wrote a great deal. No matter how the book came to be created, the ideas were those that Paul had enunciated over the years.

He called for "new vigor, boldness and determination in planning our program of action and new militancy in winning its goals."

Negro leadership must bring about the freedom and full citizenship of the Negro, he said. There existed a vast reservoir of general good-will by the majority of the white Americans, but the Negroes still must lead themselves out of second class citizenship. Nor should the Negro settle for first-class citizenship alone. "Oppression has kept us on the bottom rungs of the ladder, and even with the removal of all barriers we will still have a long way to climb in order to catch up with the general standard of living." First must come equal rights, then. Second, must come special concessions to the Negro. Paul did not say this last directly; it was inherent in his remarks.

As to the power of the Negro, Paul carefully did not come out for meeting force with force as such, and yet, this was the implication of his remarks. He pointed to a picture of a Negro family that had moved into a white neighborhood, and had been set upon by racists. Where were the other Negroes? he asked. The point he made was that the Negroes must stand up for each other against mobs, must be willing to fight for their freedom.

". . . as I see it, nothing is more important than to establish the fact that we will no longer suffer the use of mobs against us. Let the Negro people of but a single city respond in an all-out manner at the first sign of a mob—in mass demonstrations, by going on strike, by organizing boycotts—and the lesson will be taught in one bold stroke to people everywhere."

He called for a single huge, mass Negro organization, with a single defense fund. Carl T. Rowan, later director of the United States Information Agency, had interviewed Paul and had come away with the opinion that Paul thought the Negro ought to speak with one voice and that the voice ought to be close to Paul's voice.

"Actually," Paul said, "that is *not* how I feel, and I would not want Mr. Rowan or anyone else to misunderstand my view of this matter. The one voice in which we should speak must be the expression of our entire people on the central issue which is all-important to every Negro—our right to be free and equal. On many other issues there are great differences among us, and here it is not possible for any one person, or any group of people, to presume to speak for us all."

Paul's Council on African Affairs had been suppressed in 1955—disbanded after it was termed a Communist-front organization. Paul lamented its going, for he had led the organization for eighteen years and had dedicated it to the unity of the people of African heritage. Now, three years later, he warned lest the Negroes allow the NAACP to be torn asunder on the grounds, claimed by some red-hunters and racists, that it was Communist-dominated. But here was Paul with his blinders back on—there was no similarity between the NAACP and the Council on African Affairs. The latter had slavishly adulated the Soviet Union in its heyday, following Paul's own personal political bent. Rightly or wrongly, that is the way it was. The NAACP was quite a different matter; in none but the broadest sense could it be called a political organization at all, and it was an organization dedicated to the principle of American Negro action.

With his personal blinders on, Paul went to the Soviet Union again. He had been so much the lion there for so long, and he still was, he was happy to learn. He appeared on Soviet television. He sang at the Moscow Sports Palace. He was invited to visit Nikita Khrushchev, then the Soviet premier, at his *dacha* near Yalta. He enjoyed the confidence of the leaders of the country—the only tragedy being that it was not his country.

In Russia, Paul was beloved by the people for himself and beloved by the leaders for his political opinions. He had been written about interminably in the Soviet press in the last few years. He was a Soviet folk hero. A motion picture had been made about his life. A Soviet biography would be written. No matter where he went, he was a celebrity and an honored citizen. It was apparent that he could spend the remainder of his life in the Union of Soviet Socialist Republics and never worry about his personal freedom or a single slight because he was a black man.

Paul had no intention of returning to the United States; he and Essie were embittered. He had been rejected by the white leadership of America during the worst years of the fear of Communism, but more important, he had been rejected by the Negro leadership in the years since 1954, when the Negro leaders of the NAACP and the nonviolent movements in the South were beginning to act for freedom. He had thrown away his American prestige by adopting the Soviet line, and so much must have been apparent to him in 1958. In London, when he was interviewed by friendly reporters, they asked him to comment on international affairs and particular positions of the Soviet Union—and Paul refused. The events of the last few years had affected him very deeply. The de-Stalinization of the U.S.S.R. had affected him—what man would not be affected suddenly, to discover that all that he had believed in was suddenly in jeopardy? De-Stalinization and discovery that the U.S.S.R. had followed a planned policy of anti-Semitism so affected Howard Fast that he broke with the American Communist party. Paul's position was not quite the same, but the experience was sobering none the less. The perfect nation had turned out to be less than perfect.

Chapter 17

THE AMERICAN OTHELLO

Once Paul had expressed the hope that at some time during his life he would be able to spend a few years in Russia, particularly in the Russia east of the Urals, among the so called "primitive" peoples who had been brought out of backwardness in a single generation by the government of the Soviet Union. Now, in 1958 and 1959, he was in Russia, but the chance was gone. In January, Paul fell ill and was confined to a Moscow hospital. In the next four years he was to be in and out of hospitals many times, for it developed that he had a deteriorating disease of the circulatory system.

There were moments of splendor, as in January, when Paul went to the Kremlin to attend a great ball with Essie, and when he was praised by Khrushchev and by Deputy Premier Anastas Mikoyan for his fight for the freedom of the colored peoples of the world. The biographical film was made that year—1959—and many other honors were heaped upon him in the U.S.S.R.

In the spring of 1959, Paul and Essie went to London again, for Paul was to appear in a new *Othello*. He did so, but this was a dismal performance; the old Paul was gone, and only the shadow of him remained. Friends, such as Rebecca West, indicated their sorrow that the years had dealt so harshly with him, but there was no mistaking the facts. The "presence" had disappeared. The voice was shaky. The career was over.

There were honors again. Paul was elected vice-president of the British-Soviet Friendship Society. He continued to be listed in *Who's Who*—an honor he never did achieve in the United States. There were flashes of the old militant, defiant Paul. Despite bans by the State Department on travel of American citizens to Red China and Hungary, Paul insisted that he would make trips there. It was still one of his cherished ambitions to go to China.

But it was not to be. His health would not permit such a trip.

Paul shuttled back and forth between Western and Eastern Europe—one of the few citizens of the world who was equally at home in both environments, and the only American in the world who could claim that distinction. Paul was now honored everywhere except in his own country. His name appeared less and less frequently in the press. There was little reason for it to appear after 1960, for he was virtually retired. He went to Moscow early that year, and he made some appearances at factories and at social gatherings. Sometimes he sang. Sometimes he spoke on the future of the colored peoples of the world.

In 1960, he was ill a great deal. In 1961, he was back in the hospital in Moscow. The next year Paul was offered a post as lecturer at the University of Ghana by his old acquaintance, Kwame Nkrumah, who had become president and was making himself dictator of that land. The newspapers said Paul considered accepting, but it is difficult to believe: how could Paul consider such a post seriously?

Paul spent much of 1962 in Russia and in Eastern Germany and in London, and all too many of those days were in hospitals and nursing homes. His health had deteriorated to the point where the idea of resuming his career was gone.

In 1963, there arose a strange phenomenon regarding Paul. From time to time in the press of the United States and of Great Britain appeared speculative articles which indicated that Paul had become disenchanted with Communism. There was no truth in the statements, and Essie and Pauli tried to establish the facts, but the rumors persisted. It would have been the proper ending—from the Western European and American point of view—had the prodigal son come home, admitting that he had been wrong all these years.

In December 1963, just before Christmas, Paul Robeson and Essie did come home to the United States. They came on a British Overseas Airways jet airplane, and when the plane arrived at Idlewild Airport Paul walked slowly down the ramp, wearing a heavy overcoat, an old, tired man whose face was lined and thin. He had nothing to say about politics or anything else, except when he was asked if he would take part in the civil rights program. Only then was there a brief spark:

"Yes," Paul said. "I've been part of it all my life."

Essie fielded the questions. No, Paul was not disillusioned with Communism, she said. She had to answer that question three times before the reporters would let her go.

They were met by Pauli and Marilyn, and by their two grandchildren, David and Suzy, who were now quite grown up—in their teens. There was no trouble with customs or any other incident. The only remarkable point about the return of this tired, old man and his wife was the number of strangers who came quietly up to him and insisted on shaking his hand. A policeman and a half dozen passersby stopped to speak a few words of friendly greeting to this most controversial American of his time.

And then the Robesons were gone, home, hidden, inside the quiet of Pauli's apartment on Old Broadway in New York City. Paul and Essie stayed with the children for a few days, then they took a house on the edge of Harlem on a very quiet street that was just a block long. A telephone was installed, but the number was unlisted. They were known to the mailman, but most mail went unanswered. This way had always been Paul's way; he seldom answered letters and he disconnected the telephone whenever he wanted to concentrate. But now the Robesons were basically alienated from the society around them. They were home but they were not at home.

Essie continued to be spokesman for the family. Paul had virtually nothing to say, and he saw very few people. One old friend, Hope Stevens, a prominent Harlem attorney, made a quiet attempt to be in touch, but was more or less rebuffed. He told Essie that he did not wish to interfere but he did want her to know of his good-will and that he often thought about the Robesons.

For Paul, it was virtually the end. Career gone, voice gone, strength ebbing, he lived a quiet life, avoiding the honor that Harlem and millions of Americans, black and white, would give him. The friends of Paul Robeson tried to show him something of this one night in the spring of 1965, when they staged a Salute to Paul Robeson. There were some in the Negro community who still called Paul "commie" and sneered at his name. There were far more, like James Hicks of the *Amsterdam News*, who realized that Paul had been saying to the Negro "stand up and fight for those rights you want" for twenty years—and that only in the 1960s was the Negro standing up to fight.

The greatest of all tragedies came into Paul's life. Alone except for family and a handful of close friends, he discovered that Essie was seriously ill, Essie, the companion of his joys and sorrows, his political mentor and his constant intellectual support. Paul's own illness was serious enough: one day in October he went for a walk and was later found, collapsed, in a vacant lot—semi-conscious from the effects of his disease. Two months later Essie Robeson died, and then, except for Pauli, Marilyn and the grandchildren, Paul was alone in New York.

He kept the house after Essie's death, but he went to spend much of his time with his sister, wife of a physician in Philadelphia. He did not answer telephone calls. He did not answer letters.

Occasionally in these latter years he would come forth, as at the death of Lorraine Hansbury, author of *A Raisin in the Sun*, who had fought so strongly for civil rights. Paul made one of his infrequent public appearances to honor her memory in the last days of 1965. But, except for this, he sought oblivion in America, this man who had come home because America was his home, although he might have remained in Soviet Russia, honored by premiers and loved by the people of all the land.

That was his tragedy, the tragedy of loving not wisely but too well. There might have been a time when Paul wished he had abandoned or never entered politics, when he could have stepped off into the eastern Soviet with a clear conscience, and lived a quiet life as a teacher, free, a man among equals.

But that life was never for Paul. His life, he found in later years, was bound up with the civil rights movement in America. No matter what anyone said about Paul's alienation from his people, his taking of the wrong road and trying to lead them down it; these were small matters in the life of Paul Robeson. He was and would be a Negro hero forever, because no man had suffered more than Paul, none had ever called the plight of the Negro more firmly to the attention of white America. Paul's personal tragedy, his sacrifice of the trust and confidence of the white leadership of America, and his sacrifice of wealth and position in his own country were personal matters. When the importance of riches or poverty and position and the question of black or white had withered with time, there would remain the name of Paul Robeson. To the honor of all Americans in the last half of the twentieth century, it was apparent that it would always be a martyred name. No matter how unwisely he had loved or how wrong he might have been, Paul Robeson was a man.